The Pressure Zone

(The story of a pioneer Saturation Diver)

mike cooke

Copyright © 2023 Mike Cooke

ISBN: 978-1-923078-08-6
Published by Vivid Publishing
A division of Fontaine Publishing Group
P.O. Box 948, Fremantle
Western Australia 6959
www.vividpublishing.com.au

 A catalogue record for this book is available from the National Library of Australia

All rights reserved. No part of this publication may be reproduced, stored in a retrieval system or transmitted in any form or by any means, electronic, mechanical, photocopying, recording or otherwise, without the prior written permission of the copyright holder.

Dedicated to my son, Michael
With lotsa love

And a very special thank you to my awesome proofreader, Chrissie, for her understanding, patience, perseverance and encouragement, without which I'd still be trying to finish this endeavour.

I love you, my lady.

Thank you so very much.

Contents

Preface	VIII
Acknowledgements	IX
Chapter One – 1948-59 (A kid from the Home)	1
Chapter Two – 1959-64 (The Navy Years)	17
Chapter Three – 1964-69 (Commercial Diver – Surface Air & Mixed Gas)	48
Chapter Four – 1969-78 (Saturation Diver) including my original story	92
Chapter Five – 1979-85 (Commercial Diving Management)	226
Chapter Six – 1985-2003 (Post Taylor)	232
Chapter Seven – My Hockey Years	233
Chapter Eight – 2003 - present (Back to basics – full circle)	237
Appendices	265
1. Acronyms	266
2. The Evolution of Diving – Diving History 101	267
3. The Challenge of Deep-Sea Diving – A paper presented by me at American Welding Society Conference November 1980, New Orleans, Louisiana	276
4. A Very Short History of Saturation Diving – by James Vorosmarti, Jr, MD	284
5. My 1200 ft. home – General Description of Operation and Purposes of Manned Hyperbaric Research Facility – A paper by George Morrissey, VP Taylor	294
6. Rescue and Recovery of Disabled Bell (SDC) Diver – A paper presented by me to the International Diving Symposium February 1980, New Orleans, Louisiana	301
7. Taylor Diving Hyperbaric Welding – Brochure	315
8. Taylor Diving Special Edition 'Diver' Magazine 1978	330
Sources	342
Recommended Reading	344

Preface

The original draft of this story was written during my many saturation dives between 1969 and 1978. It started out as a fictional story about a saturation diver. But in the end, it has become an autobiography focused primarily on that period of time in offshore development. It is a recollection of my experiences - the people and places are how I remember them.

It is the story of a kid who came out of the Montreal welfare system (three juvenile homes from age 6-16), pulled out of high school and sent to work at sixteen. Joined the Royal Canadian Navy at seventeen. Five years later, he was honourably discharged. The youngest Clearance Diver (CD) to be trained at that time. He would be the first person to walk on the bottom of the Gulf of Mexico at a depth greater than 1,000 feet. And the first person to work on the bottom of the North Sea at 1,065 feet.

It was an exciting time for an aspiring young diver. Offshore saturation diving was new, and we were the pioneers.[1]

This is my story.

---

[1] ***The firstcomers*** *'Pioneer diver' is a term which has been applied to all those who worked under water from the late 1960s until well into the 1980s, when diving became more regulated.*

[The pioneer divers in the North Sea - Report from the Commission of Inquiry to investigate all circumstances relating to diving in the North Sea in the pioneer period - NOU 2003:5
  Source: On the Edge, Under Water Offshore Diving in Norway, page 80-81.]

Acknowledgements

I was lucky enough to work with some great guys that I need to acknowledge, for without their association, friendship and guidance, this wouldn't be my story.

- Dan McLeod - my first Navy dive buddy, Clearance Diver (Ships) (CD(S)) HMCS Gatineau, assistant course instructor HMCS Granby - Operational Diving Unit. Taught me not only how but also what it was to be a diver. Lesson 1 – "Get that fucking chip off your shoulder". My first mentor.

- Linden Leask - my closest friend, shipmate, clearance diving course buddy, commercial diver, saturation diver and best man - was there from the start and still is.

- Mitch Cancienne - the go to guy at Taylor Diving & Salvage (Taylor) - he knew where all the skeletons were hidden, but first and foremost my friend and mentor. We had a lot of laughs and good times together. "Why do it if you can't laugh about it".

- Tom Duncan - my 'Life Coach'. Helped me see and experience life as it should be. One of his favourite sayings was "If you ain't got class, then you ain't got shit". So do it in style. Friend and mentor.

- Ken Wallace - retired USN Master Chief Diver, President TDS, friend, boss and mentor.

There are many other great people with whom I had the privilege of working, living and experiencing life. The list is extensive and some 30 years later I've forgotten the names of quite a few, but I still remember:

Alan 'Doc' Helvey, Alan 'Sweet Al' Voves, Alan, Peter & Jeannie Bradley, Allan 'Crazy Al' Anderson, Andy 'Lil' Muff' Waysham, Archie Weiss, Art Herman, Bill Lukeman, Bert Blouin, Bob McArdle, Boyd Vassey, Buddy Eglin, Buddy Mayfield, Buddy Saffron, Carl Goring, Charlie Coggeshall, Charlie Duff, Chris Daldrey, Chuck Peel, Danny Ellis, Dennis Webb, Dick Murphy, Dick Ransom, Ed Russell, Eddie & Melvin Arroyo, Eddie Volmer, Enola, Fred (Mitch's driver), Frank Brock, Fred Collins, Fred Miller, Frenchie Collins, George Cundiff, George Layton, George Morrissey, Harry Rude, Jay Jones, Jean Valz, Jeff Sherry, Jensen Serpas, Jerry Mehl, Jessie Robie, Jim Pickle Nicholson, Joe Cascante, Joe Lazisky, Joe Schouest, John Harter, John Luck, John Propeck, John VanBerschot, Ken Tatam, Larry Huff, Lee J Carroll, Lee Gates, Len Andrews, Louie Giacona, Lyle Stockdale, Mark Banjavich, O'Neil (Neil) Landry, Paddy Mansfield, Pete Weichert, Red & Whitey Patterson, Rick Higgins, Rick Webster, Robbie Robinson, Roger Holdsworth, Ron Schwary, Ted Oppershal, Terry Wilson, Vernon Dillinger, Vic Becker and Dr Workman.

Thanks also to Paul Kalman who arranged some artwork for my original story.

The origins of diving are firmly rooted in the needs and desires of men to conduct military or salvage operations, to engage in underwater commerce, and to expand the frontiers of knowledge through exploration and research.

US Navy Diving Manual

'The sea is everything. It covers seven-tenths of the terrestrial globe. It is pure and healthy. It is an immense desert, where man is never lonely, for he feels life stirring on all sides. The sea is only an embodiment of a supernatural and wonderful existence. Nature manifests herself in it by her three kingdoms, mineral, vegetable, and animal. The sea is the vast reservoir of nature.'

Jules Verne, Twenty Thousand Leagues Under the Sea

Conversation between Professor Aronnax and Ned Land – Twenty Thousand Leagues Under the Sea by Jules Verne, first published 1896:

'... it requires incalculable strengths to keep one's self in these strata and resist their pressure. Listen to me. Let us admit that the pressure of the atmosphere is represented by the weight of a column of water thirty-two feet high. In reality the column of water would be shorter, as we are speaking of seawater, the density of which is greater than that of fresh water. Very well, when you dive, Ned, as many times thirty-two feet of water as there are above you, so many times does your body bear a pressure equal to that of the atmosphere, that is to say, 15 lbs. for each square inch of its surface. It follows then, that at 320 feet this pressure = that of 10 atmospheres, of 100 atmospheres at 3200 feet, and of 1000 atmospheres at 32,000 feet, that is, about 6 miles; which is equivalent to saying that, if you could attain this depth in the ocean, each square 3/8 of an inch of the surface of your body would bear a pressure of 5600 lbs. Ah! My brave Ned, do you know how many square inches you carry on the surface of your body?'

'I have no idea, Mr Aronnax.'

'About 6500; and, as in reality the atmospheric pressure is about 15 lbs. to the square inch, your 6500 square inches bear at this moment a pressure of 97,500 lbs.'

'Without my perceiving it?'

'Without your perceiving it. And if you are not crushed by such a pressure, it is because the air penetrates the interior of your body with equal pressure. Hence perfect equilibrium between the interior and exterior pressure, which thus neutralize each other, and which allows you to bear it without inconvenience, but in the water it is another thing.'

'Yes, I understand,' replied Ned, becoming more attentive; 'because the water surrounds me, but does not penetrate.'

Precisely, Ned; so that at 32 feet beneath the surface of the sea you would undergo a pressure of 97,500 lbs.; at 320 feet, ten times that pressure; at 3200 feet, a hundred times that pressure; at 32,000 feet, a thousand times that pressure would be 97,500,000 lbs. – that is to say, you would be flattened as if you had been drawn from the plates of a hydraulic machine!'

The deeper the dive, the greater the pressure.

Welcome to the Pressure Zone…

The Pressure Zone – Mike Cooke

Chapter One 1948 – 1959
A kid from the Home

Daddy's flown across the ocean
Leaving just a memory
A snapshot in the family album
Daddy what else did you leave for me
Daddy what d'ya leave behind for me
All in all it was just a brick in the wall
All in all it was just bricks in the wall

Pink Floyd – The Wall

I don't have many memories before 1948. We lived at St Mary's Abbey Hotel in Bedford which my grandfather had bought in 1936. My mom managed it while my Dad worked as a mechanic. She sold it in 1947, after which we moved to Luton. It had a fascinating history.

St Mary's Abbey Hotel, Bedford - the family home in England.
Registered in the Doomsday Book, 1086 AD, it's age then was given as 102 years.

"Sunday Empire News" – Reporter (circa 1946/47)

Hooded ghost needs a house to haunt

The hooded monk from the thousand-year-old St. Mary's Abbey Inn at Bedford is doing a little home hunting. For some years, a matter of centuries in fact, he's had a cosy little blasted oak to live in just outside the inn, but last month it was struck by lightning, and to-day is not much of a home for anyone, least of all a ghost.

The Inn is for sale, and if the ghost had any tangible assets, he might buy it. For, from the spectre's point of view, it is a highly desirable residence with all modern haunting conveniences.

A tiny boxroom, sealed on the inside with hand-made bricks, which has been unopened for hundreds of years, a secret panel and an underground tunnel leading to the river Ouse – what more could a ghost ask?

Since the tree was struck the hooded phantom has vanished.

*Mrs CD Cooke (*my mom*) the present owner of the Inn says: "I saw him one night when I was on the staircase with my pet bull terrier. A phosphorescent light appeared, and at first I thought it was a guest smoking a cigarette, but the dog began to growl and the light disappeared. The dog would not go near the spot after that."*

A King's Treasure

Henry Wilson, general handyman at the Inn, showed me the cobwebbed entrance to the tunnel leading to the River Ouse. "In that's the way he went." He observed, "he won't have travelled far."

Twenty years later, when I was working in the North Sea, Pete Bradley was my first diving tender. Who would have thought, here's a guy that lived at 10 The Embankment almost directly across the River Ouse from the Abbey – which had by then become part of a girl's school – Dame Alice Harpur School.

1948 – 1958 The Beginning

My mom, sister and I departed Southampton on Tuesday 13 July 1948 and arrived in New York eight days later on Wednesday 21 July. We were on our way to join my father and start a new life in Montreal, Canada. I was six.

The trip across the ocean was onboard the SS Marine Falcon, a converted World War ll Liberty Ship. I don't remember that much about the trip except that my kid sister Nicolette (Nicky) who was four and I slept in bunks with a barf (seasick) bag attached to the side. Was it really going to be that rough? The most significant thing I remember was I got introduced to Wrigley's Chewing Gum - double mint and juicy fruit. Hey, it was an American ship and I was a kid born during the war. It was the greatest treat ever. And I still have the habit.

During the day, we would go out on deck and check out the other passengers sunning in the stripped down gun turrets. There was also table tennis and movies.

It was a beautiful sunny day when the ship came alongside in New York harbor. My sister and I were hugging the guardrail, our eyes and mouths open in amazement starring at the New York skyline. We'd never seen buildings so tall before. What a fantastic welcome to the new world.

From New York we caught the train to Canada. The beginning of a new life.

Skyscraper City – New York City Skyline – Circa 1948

Shortly after our arrival in Canada, my folks decided to go separate ways and leave my sister and I without a family. Over the next 11 years, we would be shunted from one children's home to another, three all up (*"All in all it was just bricks in the wall"*). In retrospect, I can say that this wasn't all a bad thing. Actually, we probably did a lot better than having to spend time in a broken family home.

Victoria School, on Maisonneuve Boulevard, was my first school in Canada.
I was there for Grade 1.

The Home Years

The first home we were placed in was the Friendly Home - a big brownstone house on Dorchester Street between Guy and Atwater Street. This was for a short period during the summer of '49. The most memorable thing about that time was we lived close to the Montreal Forum and got to see a real live circus for the first time - the Ringling Bros Barnum and Bailey 'Greatest Show on Earth'.

That was the first home.

During that summer we got placed in the second home. The Lachine Children's Home was on St Antoine Street across from Central Park. I was there from 1949-53. Lachine was a suburb of Montreal with a mixture of English and French areas. We always seemed to be getting into trouble with the French kids.

Lachine Children's Home – 1949-53

School classes started in September after the Labor Day Holiday. Although we lived at the 'home' we went to public schools. I entered Grade 2 at Central Park School. Usually at that age (seven), entering a new school, one of your parents would have taken you. In the home you were on your own. I followed the older kids to the school. There was no one to tell me where to go – no teacher, no principal, no parent. It was one of the loneliest, most frightening days of my life.

All the kids were lined up to go to pre-assigned classrooms. I went to the end of the longest line, trying not to be noticed. As luck would have it, it was for Grade 2. When I entered the classroom, the teacher asked who I was and what I was doing there. Luckily, there was another boy from the home who explained that I was a new kid – another kid from the home. I was educated in the public school system and in class was commonly referred to as 'a kid from the home'.

Kids doing homework

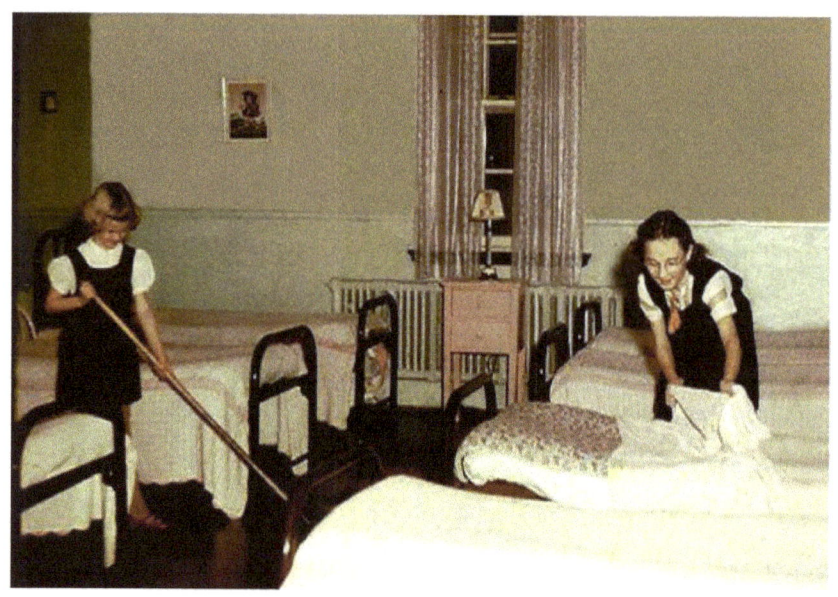

My sister Nicky (with the broom) and Luba

With the ladies in charge of the home.
Front: Nicky 3rd from left, Back: I am first on the right

Photos courtesy of Luba Pankiw

It was during my stay in the Children's Home that I got introduced to swimming in 1952. I learned to swim in Lac St Louis (St Lawrence River) at the YMCA camp on Ile Perot. I had no idea at that time that my first commercial diving job would be in that same river in the Montreal Harbor in 1964.

I was obviously destined for bigger and better things!

At the end of June 1953, my sister and I got separated. She stayed in the Children's Home and I got sent to my third home - Weredale House Boys Home. I was 11.

For the next five years I would learn what life can be really like and what happens when you step out of line. Here you got punished.

Getting the teacher's ruler across your hands was child's play. It was when you went to high school and were in the showers after gym class and the other guys wanted to know how you got those cuts and bruises on your butt that looked like razor strap marks you knew you'd been punished.

That was the bad side.

Weredale House, 6 Weredale Park, Westmount, Quebec

But there was a good side.

It had a gymnasium big enough to play floor hockey, a woodwork (manual arts) shop, a big library and best of all a swimming pool. An indoor swimming pool in Quebec – now that was luxury!

The Pressure Zone by Mike Cooke

In the summer, the backyard was big enough to play baseball and in the winter a hockey rink. Next to the backyard was the train tracks. After every snow fall, the rink needed to be scraped clean - making lots of snow and ice projectiles to be placed on shovel handles positioned on the ground facing the tracks. When a train came by, we'd jump on the shovel blade sending a frozen projectile over the 10 ft high hurricane fence - and with luck - landing on the train with a thunderous bang – scaring the piss outta a few passengers.

But even better than that it came with its own summer camp on Lac de l'Achigan, in the Laurentian Mountains, north of Montreal.

> *In 1934, the Rotary Club of Westmount bought 260 acres, with a mile of shoreline, on Lac de l'Achigan, 55 miles north of Montreal, and gave the property to Weredale House to establish Camp Weredale. It was to serve as a summer home for the boys and the staff of Weredale House.*
>
> *From school closing until late August, Camp Weredale provided the boys with a well-equipped, well-supervised summer lakeside home. At the time, there were some two dozen buildings, with a dining room, recreation hall, crafts shops, hospital, shower rooms, sleeping cabins, play area, outdoor chapel, Indian Council ring, rifle range, a tree house, staff accommodations, and campsites. On the water there are rowboats, canoes, sailboats and outboards.*
>
> *There were 10 cabins with room enough to accommodate 10 boys. Sports included water skiing, swimming (the Red Cross course is given), archery, paddling, fishing, baseball, deck tennis, ping pong, football, and shooting on the range. Among the crafts, a boy can work at photography, leatherwork, Indian lore, and making paddles. The boys also enjoyed television, radio and movies.*

[Source: www.batshawcebtrehistory.ca/camp_weredale]

Camp Weredale – Lac de l'Achigan

Me in a canoe at Camp Weredale

We had canoes, rowboats and sailboats and a power boat for water skiing.
The raft in the middle was a 10 foot high diving platform.

Kids at camp. My good friend Ross at left. We still keep in touch.

Across the lake for a day out – I'm in the center

This is where my water skills improved. As growing boys, we were always competing. Underwater swimming was a major accomplishment. Looking back, if I had lived in a broken home I wouldn't have had these opportunities.

Swim time at Camp Weredale

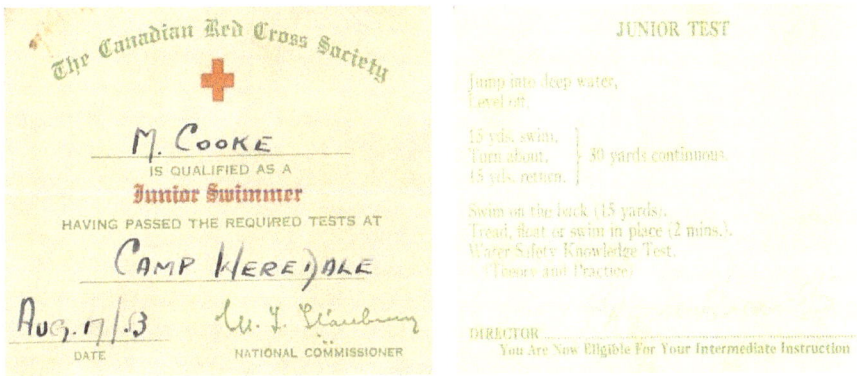

To see underwater was something special. For the meantime, a set of swim goggles would have to do.

In the home, we were allowed out between lunch and 8.30pm on weekends to visit family/friends, wander and sometimes get into trouble. We weren't supposed to get into trouble, but it wasn't hard.

For instance, jumping over the turnstile ticket barricade at the Forum to see a Buddy Holly concert on 15 September 1957. My first Rock & Roll show. If I'd been caught, I'd have been in serious trouble.

It was during one of these times when I was wanderin', wishin' and dreamin' in Eaton's department store where I came across a special gift for Christmas. With one of these I'd be able to explore the lake bottom at camp next summer in style.

It looked something like this – a swim mask with twin snorkels.

Well along came Christmas but no mask - just a pair of socks and a shirt. In the home that's what you got every Christmas – socks and a shirt.

Hey, one can dream.

Circa 1950 – Awesome

As kids, we were expected to write to our parents on a regular basis. Of course, we didn't know that once our letters had been passed in for inspection and mailing that they would be stamped with this on the back!

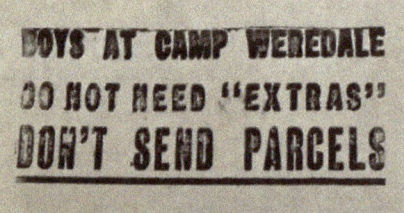

The cabins we stayed in at Camp Weredale were all named after Indian tribes. In alphabetical order - Algonquin, Blackfoot, Cayuga, Dakota, Erie and the like.

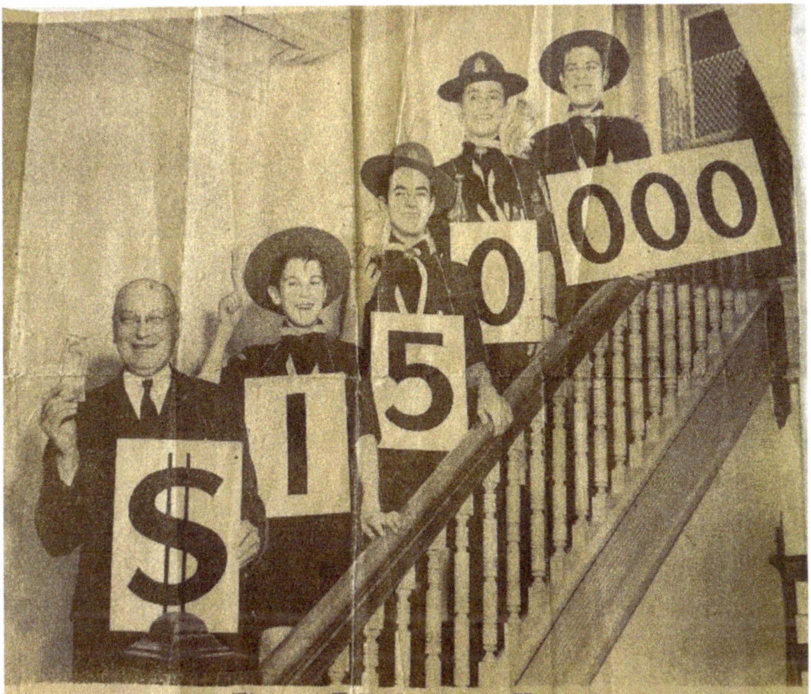

Figures Tell the Story Here

Campaign chairman and Boy Scouts give the signal for the $150,000 which is the objective of the Boy Scouts Association's 1957 financial appeal, to run from Feb. 4 to 23. Announcement of the objective and the acceptance of the chairmanship by R. C. Stevenson, OBE, was made today. Left to right are: Mr. Stevenson, Scout Walter Pankiw and Patrol Leaders Edward Eby, Michael Cooke and Ronald Duffy. The Scouts holding up a "cue" are regular members of the Weredale House Scout Troop.

I was in the Cubs at the Children's Home in Lachine and then the Scouts in Weredale, where I got the highest award of Queen's Scout.

Michael Cooke

As a Queen's Scout you have prepared yourself for service to God and your fellow men and have shown yourself a worthy member of the great Scout brotherhood.

May you continue, under God's guidance, to gain courage and strength to enable you fully to discharge your duty to your Country.

Chief Scout for Canada

Government House
Ottawa
Dated April 27th 1957

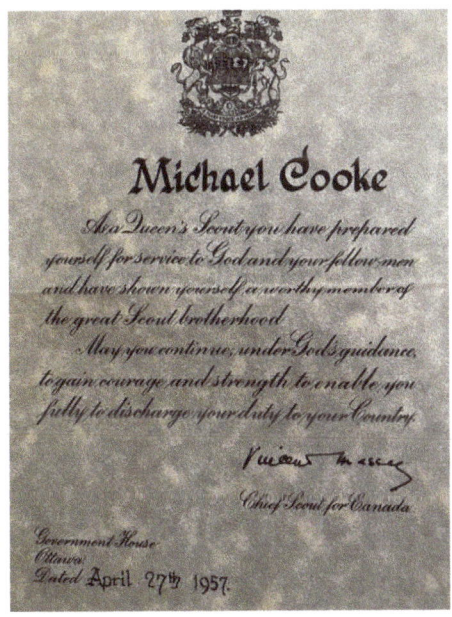

Christmas 1957

After Christmas lunch we were allowed to leave the home until 8:30 that evening.

My mom only lived a couple of blocks away, so I went to see her to give her a present. I'd been working helping a florist deliver flowers for the past two weeks for which he paid me $15. At least I could buy my mom a present.

While walking to her place through the snow-covered sidewalks, the wind blew up a $20 bill. Snatch.

Well, I had my mom's present and enough for Christmas dinner - Swiss Chalet BBQ chicken - that evening. I knew my mom wouldn't have any money.

There really is a Santa Claus.

1958

This would be a big year, my last in the home. I turned 16 on 3 February. Little did I know at the time just how significant this date, 3 February would be. A year later Buddy Holly would die in a plane crash and 20 years later I would make the first 1,000 ft saturation dive in the Norwegian sector of the North Sea.

On Monday 10 March 1958, one month and one week after my sixteenth birthday, I was taken out of high school. I came back to the home for lunch, which was the routine. We lived at the home but went outside to school. At the far end of the dining hall sitting on the central windowsill monitoring the kids entering, eating and leaving was THE MAN. As I approached to get in line for a meal, he called me aside to tell me they had arranged a job interview for me with a firm downtown. The next day I was employed as an office boy for Dominion Glass Company. I was paid $25 dollars a week, basically $100 dollars a month.

There were two major changes: 1) I would have to finish school at night and 2) instead of my father paying $30 dollars a month to the home, I had to pay my own subsistence. At least I'd have money in my pocket and wouldn't have to check milk bottles on doorsteps for some loose change on the way to school.

However, I did get to spend my two weeks' vacation at camp that summer and continue with my swimming and underwater explorations.

In September I left the home. I was more or less asked to leave because I was breaking the rules – coming and going to my own timetable and not theirs. A typical teenager – I didn't like being told what to do.

I was no longer 'a kid from the home'. It wasn't until many years later I discovered that my father had been a kid in the same home. He'd never said.

The Forum (circa 1949) Home of the 'Habs' – the Montreal Canadiens

* This is where my father worked at his drawing board. He was a chief draftsman for CD Howe Company.

On the ground floor level to the left looking at the picture is The Royal Bank of Canada and situated behind that on Atwater Avenue was the Forum Coffee Shop. This is where the 'Habs' players would meet for breakfast and lunch prior to or after practice. Sometimes, on my way to school, I'd meet my father there while he was having a meal in the hope of getting some allowance. But better than that I'd get to see my heroes sitting at the next table – Doug Harvey, Jean Beliveau, Jacques Plante and also 'the Man' Maurice 'The Rocket' Richard.

> *"Hockey in Quebec was bigger than the church.*
> *And Rocket Richard was bigger than the Pope."*
> [Source: Fire and Ice: The Rocket Richard Riot – 17 March 1955]

From my bed in the dorm at the Home (Weredale) I could hear the noise of the riot through the dormitory window.

Another big plus was my Mom not living too far away. She lived at 1111 Mountain Street for a while which is where I met Norman Brooks. His mother-in-law owned the building (rooming house).

First Quebec-born entertainer to sing in Las Vegas:

His Jolson-like voice 'a blessing and a curse'. When he sang, Norman Brooks sounded so much like Al Jolson, the rakish US blackface comedian and singer who died in 1950, that he was able to build an astonishingly successful career as a Jolson tribute singer.

Brooks portrayed Jolson in the 1956 movie The Best Things in Life are Free, and it was Brooks, not Jolson, who belted out I'm Sitting on Top of the World on the soundtrack of Woody Allen's 1983 movie Zelig.

Billed as The Voice That Lives Again, Brooks was also the first Quebec-born entertainer to play Las Vegas, selling out the Copa Room at The Sands Hotel and Casino for 44 weeks in 1959. He also appeared in the 1960 version of Ocean's Eleven, which was filmed in the hotel.

[Source: The Montreal Gazette, 15 Oct 2006]

Just up the street was CJAD Radio where DJ Mike Stevens hosted 'Club 800' on Saturdays. These shows were aimed at Teens and played the hit parade exclusively. I got to win my first ever record – 'Rock Island Line" by The Lonnie Donegan Skiffle Group and also see 'The Platters' live.

My last summer in da hood – 1958

Montreal was a unique place to live - at least until the French Separatist started blowing up mailboxes and maiming people. Hard to believe it was the largest city in Canada and the center of commerce, yet the milkman still delivered dairy products by horse and cart. Which in the winter, especially around Christmas, was a blessing for him. By the time he made it to 1111 Mountain Street he was in no condition to remember where he was – a merry Christmas here, a merry Christmas there.

My mom would take the milk and put it in the double window to keep it cold. Thank god for the horse which patiently waited in the freezing cold to take the milkman to the next stop and home.

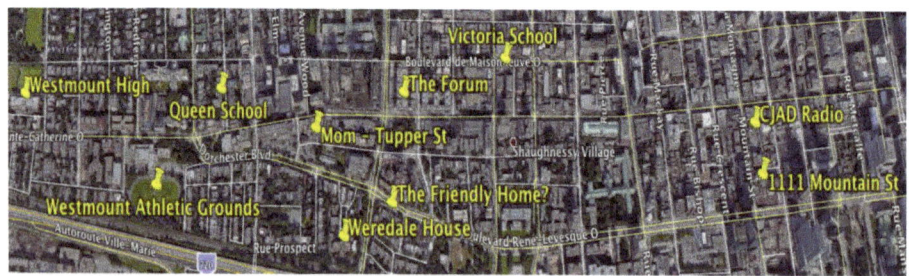

Da Hood
Westmount High – 0.7 miles from Weredale
0.9 miles from the Home to Mountain Street

The Pressure Zone by Mike Cooke

Chapter Two 1959 – 1964
The Navy Years

> *"It is noted that individuals who may demonstrate slightly neurotic characteristics in normal life might better adapt to a career of diving and underwater work than those who seem better balanced."*
>
> [Source: European Undersea Bio-Medical Society Stockholm, June 1973]

Humping overweight canvas mail bags up Beaver Hall Hill especially in the freezing ass cold of winter along with finishing school courses at night at Sir George Williams College was beginning to take its toll. Trying to combine weekdays with work, weeknights with school, Friday nights at the Esquire Show Bar, Saturday afternoons at Mike Stevens CJAD Club 800 Music & Dance Show, Saturday night and Sunday afternoon at Lucky Seven Dance Hall. It was seriously putting a lot of pressure on a 17-year old's free time.

I needed a change real bad. As fate would have it, the college was just down the street from the Royal Canadian Navy (RCN) recruiting station, HMCS Donnacona.

In the spring of '59, having acquired the requisite education, I signed on the dotted line. It was for five years, which was the minimum at that time. The recruiting Petty Officer said:

"If you wait a couple of months, you'll only have to sign up for two years."
My reply: "Can't I sign on for ten years?"
His response: "Take the five!"

It was some of the best advice I ever received.

I had a couple of weeks to say good-bye to friends and family before catching the train to HMCS Cornwallis, boot camp and basic training.

It was my first step in becoming a Matelot!

Boot camp was a breeze – it was like being back in the home again.

I was in a dorm with a bunch of guys – same as the home. Told when to get up and when to go to bed – same as the home. Do this, do that – same as the home. Big difference – the food was better.

I gained about 30 pounds – all muscle and bone, no fat. Life was good. I was on the division track team, swim team and soccer team.

Too young to go into the bar

What is a Matelot?

A Matelot is not born, he is made out of leftovers!

God built the world and the animals and then recycled the gash to create this dastardly weapon.

He took the leftover roar of the lion,, the clumsiness of the ox, the stubbornness of the mule, the slyness of the fox, the wildness of the bull and the pride of the peacock - then added the filthy evil mind of the devil to satisfy his weird sense of humour.

A Matelot evolved into a crude combination of John Dillinger, Errol Flynn, Beau Brummel and Valentino - a swashbuckling - beer - swilling - lovemaking - **LIAR**!

A Matelot likes girls, rum, beer, fights, uckers, runs ashore, pubs, jokes. long leaves, his mates and his ticket.

He hates officers, rounds, divisions, saluting middies, naval police, painting the side, jaunties, navy scran, his turn in the barrel and signing on!

A Matelot comes in four colours; white, off white, dirty and filthy - all looking alike under a tan and a uniform.

He is brave drinking beer, abusive playing crib, brutal defending his pride and passionate making love.

He can start a brawl, create a disaster, offend the law, desert his ship, make you lose your money, your temper and your mind!

He can take your sister, your mother, your aunt, and when he is caught get his captain to vouch for his integrity.

A Matelot is loved by all mothers, sisters, aunts and nieces; hated by all fathers, brothers, uncles and nephews.

He has a girl in every port and a port in every girl. He breaks more hearts, causes more fights and begets more bastards than any other man, yet when he is off to sea he is missed more than any other.

A Matelot is a man, hard drinking, fast running, mealy mouthed son-of-a-bitch, but when you are in strife he is a strong shoulder to lean on, a pillar of wisdom, and a defender of the faith and cause.

He fights for his mate, and dies for his country, without question or hesitation!

This is a Matelot!

LSEM Pierre Dubuc 35822-H

HMCS Cornwallis – Parade Ground during divisions on Saturday

After basic training I was sent to HMCS Stadacona navy shore base in Halifax, Nova Scotia to take a torpedo anti-submarine (TAS) course.

1960 – A Big Year

HMCS Gatineau

From there I joined my first ship - HMCS Gatineau - a destroyer escort, on 4 January 1960.

Winter had set in, one day snow, the next day rain. A good time for the fleet to be at sea doing exercises or cruising to foreign ports. My first cruise on the Gatineau was to Bermuda - the winter port for Canadian Navy (East Coast) - then on to San Juan, Puerto Rico.

This is where I got my introduction to navy diving. We'd been working over the ship's side and secured our tools for lunch. After lunch, we noticed the electrical cable for the angle grinder was dangling over the side in the water. On pulling it up, there was no grinder attached. Could it have fallen into the harbor?

Bring out the diver. Enter Dan McLeod, Clearance Diver Ships CD(S). He needed a diving tender. Enter yours truly – we were both messmates and TAS operators. Never did find the grinder. Then again, we were tied up alongside a dockyard jetty in San Juan where bright ($$$) things left unattended can mysteriously disappear.

Enter the buffer[2], Chief Petty Officer (CPO) George Broome. He was our immediate boss for ship's maintenance and not a happy chappy over the loss.

After sailing with him for the better part of a year, I managed to get a good report and recommendation for diving duty. I didn't know it at the time, but George had been in Weredale. His name is on the war memorial plaque in the auditorium. Heck, he was just another 'kid from the home'.

[2] *Buffer is the colloquial title for the senior seaman sailor; the formal title is chief boatswain's mate.*

The final port of call was Port of Spain, Trinidad. Nothing like spending a Canadian winter cruising the tropical warm sunny Caribbean. Prettiest water I'd ever seen. An awesome magnet - I needed to become a navy diver.

However, prior to that, there was another cruise to be made to Portugal to celebrate Prince Henry the Navigator. This wasn't just your average cruise - there were 32 ships from 14 nations.

It was also the closest I've come to being shot.

Picture from The Montreal Gazette - taken on the way to Portugal

HMCS Gatineau alongside

In Tribute – ships of 14 nations at anchor in front of the Monument of the Discoverers to honor Prince Henry

Monument of the Discoverers, led by Prince Henry the Navigator, which was unveiled on 9 August in Lisbon, during the naval review week which was the highlight of the 500th anniversary celebrations. Four destroyer escorts of the RCN were present.

The stunning and unusual sight of a line of ships under full sail passing between two columns of modern navy ships and the ear-splitting sound of a 21-gun salute by 32 ships was one heck of an experience for all hands on deck.

New and old ships of the sea pass during Portuguese International Review

But back to almost getting shot. Although there were several official functions, sail pasts, marches, etc we did have time to sightsee and check out the bars - one of the more notorious being the Texas Bar.

The Texas Bar, Lisbon

It had a bit of a reputation and was a hangout for many a matelot. The band played from a lifeboat and after a few too many beers someone always tried to 'let go the falls' – lower the boat.

This inevitably would end up in a bit of a scuffle which could get a little nasty. The night I was there with a few shipmates, things got out of hand with the locals and fists started flying. It was time to leave. However, the locals had been down this route before and were waiting for us outside the club. As you walked out the door some dickhead was waiting to hit you with a hunk of lumber.

And the band played...

I got it right across the back – he ended down on the ground with my boots doing a tango on his head. After what I'd done to the guy on the ground a large crowd was starting to gather - time to get outta there.

A group of us moved as fast as we could down the road to get away from the club – with the crowd of locals in hot pursuit. At the first corner, I took a left and headed towards the harbor as fast as I could.

Directly ahead was a row of bushes, a good place to get out of sight. On the other side of the bushes was a high chain link fence – damn. Had to find another way to escape. Cleared the bushes and ran into a gang of locals who formed a circle around me. I was turning around looking for an out when a gun was pulled and pointed directly at me. All stop. I thought I'd had it.

Then all of a sudden there was a Shore Patrol standing between me and the gun. It was Leading Seaman (LS) Malcolm Ashton, who was one of my messmates from the Gatineau. "Get your ass in the jeep" he hollered "while I sort this mess out". Talk about lucky, Malcolm just may have saved me from some serious damage.

I was escorted back to the ship and taken to sickbay. I had a temperature of 103 and a 12 inch gash draining blood down my back. So much for a fun night at the Texas Bar.

Things settled down the next day and a bunch of us took a sight-seeing bus trip. The first stop was The Shrine of Our Lady of Fatima, one of the holiest places in Portugal.

> *The story of a famous miracle in Fátima, Portugal, began in May 1917, when three children (ages 7, 9, and 10) claimed to have encountered the Virgin Mary on their way home from tending a flock of sheep.*

The oldest girl, Lucia, was the only one to speak to her, and Mary told the children that she would reappear to them on the thirteenth day of the next six months. She then vanished.

The controversial events at Fátima gained fame due partly to elements of the secrets, prophecy and eschatological revelations allegedly related to the Second World War and possibly more global wars in the future, particularly the Virgin's alleged request for the Consecration of Russia to the Immaculate Heart of Mary.

The published memoirs of Lúcia dos Santos in the 1930s revealed two secrets that she claimed came from the Virgin while the third secret was to be revealed by the Catholic Church in 1960.

[Source: Wikipedia]

Would it be revealed while we were there?

Behaving at Fatima - 1960

We were served lunch by the Sisters at the local convent. As an unexpected surprise they even provided wine in carafes which were placed on every table. Not wanting to be rude or impolite this was shared out evenly amongst us in the most gentlemanly fashion. Remember best behaviour!!

However, it was short lived. As soon as a carafe was emptied it was kindly replaced by a full one. The scene was set and just like that we became matelots again and hoped they wouldn't run out of wine.

Awesome lunch.

On to the next stop - Nazaré - famous for it's big wave surfing.

From there it was back to the ship. One heck of an enjoyable day and a fitting end to a memorable cruise to a beautiful country.

I made it back to Halifax ('Slackers' - for slack time) home port just in time to be selected for CD(S) course. I qualified CD(S) 14 October 1960 - one of my proudest moments and the first step to becoming a Clearance Diver.

I also got to wear another badge on my sleeve – crossed torpedoes (TAS) at the top and diving helmet CD(S) at the bottom – talk about good!

As a CD(S) we were trained to use US Divers type Aqua Lung, a self-regulated compressed air breathing apparatus (CABA)[3].

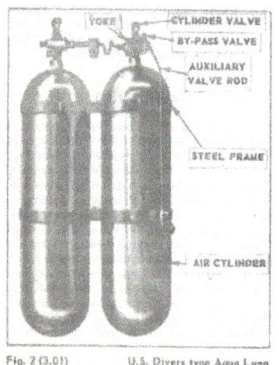 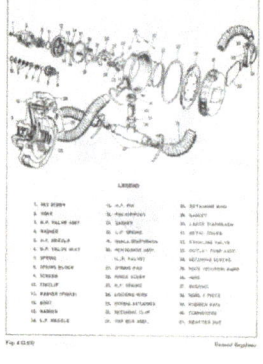 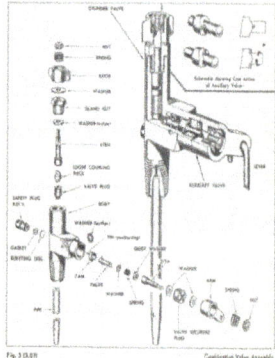

CABA – Air Cylinders/Twin Hose Regulator/Cylinder Valve J Type

Note: This was before the use of underwater pressure read out gauges (dive computers), in that the cylinder valve had a semi rotary type by-pass. The function of this is to maintain a reserve supply of air of approximately 300 psi (20.68 bar). When the pressure in the cylinders drops to this level, breathing gradually becomes more difficult, which is an indication that about only 1/8 of the air remains. Then you need to open the by-pass valve so you can use the reserve air and head for the surface. Now, with underwater pressure gauges, you know to head to the surface when you reach 50 bar.

[The above was adapted from my RCN Diving Manual.]

[3] *This was the Navy term which was used before SCUBA (Self Contained Underwater Breathing Apparatus) and before PADI, NAUI and other civilian and sport diving organizations.*

CD(S) Primary Functions:
- minor underwater ship's husbandry and maintenance;
- underwater ship's hull inspections;
- underwater search and recovery, and
- protection support to include locating and identifying clandestinely placed underwater anti-ship limpet mines and/or underwater sabotage devices and ultimately assist Clearance Divers (CD) with neutralizing these.

During the period I was a qualified CD(S), from 14 October 1960 to 10 November 1961, the most exciting diving I was involved in was to be temporarily assigned to the US Navy Base in Argentia, Newfoundland.

This was during February to March 1961 for cold weather/water trials on torpedoes. The torpedoes were even kept in a freezer on land, to be later dropped from a Lockheed P2V7 aircraft. I got to make a couple of retrieval dives and ride in the nose of the plane. Talk about getting religion on landing – there ain't much distance and/or protection between you and the ground.

Once the trials were completed, I went back onboard the Gatineau, which if memory serves me right, was in dry dock/refit.

My dive buddy and shipmate, Dan McLeod had been transferred to HMCS Granby, the Fleet Diving Unit (FDU) and training school to become a fully qualified Clearance Diver (CD).

It was during this period, on 27 July 1961, that Linden J Leask was drafted to the Gatineau. Linden was also a CD(S). He replaced Dan. Little did I know at the time that he and I would become the closest of friends, Navy dive buddies, commercial divers, saturation divers and he would be my best man. I'm also godfather to his two sons.

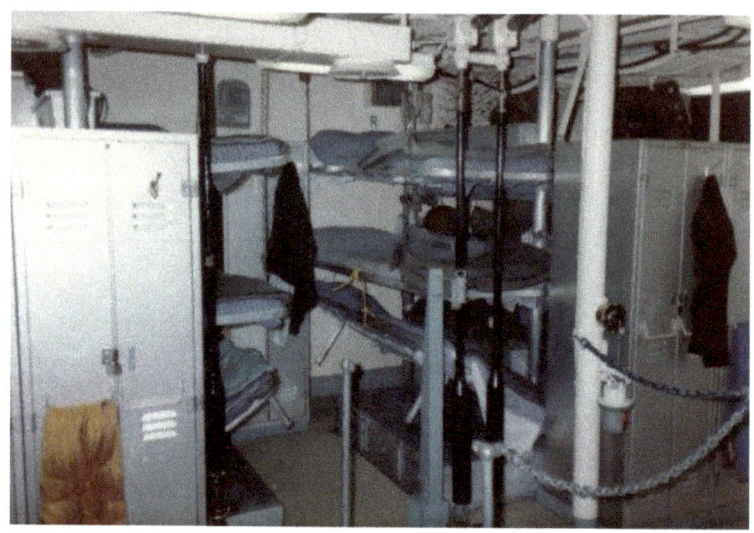

This was typical messing – where you lived onboard – you were assigned a bunk, a footlocker, and a locker.

Being the youngest and newest guess who won the top bunk?

But I was fortunate to have both Linden and Dan as messmates.

The Granby I remember

The Granby ship's crest

Alongside French Cable Wharf

The following is sourced from Canadian Naval Divers Association website:

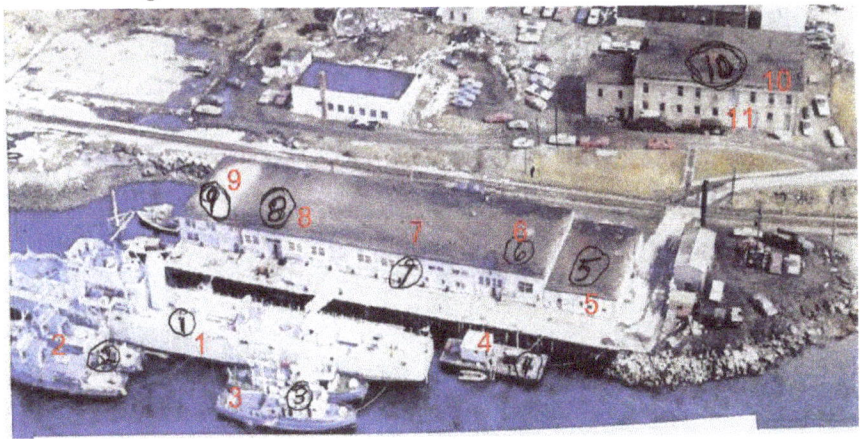

Fleet Diving Unit (Atlantic) - FDU(A)
Located at French Cable Wharf (FCW) Circa 1966

1. Vessel alongside is decommissioned HMCS Victoriaville which was re-commissioned HMCS Granby and replaced the original Granby in 1966. *(Photo was 2 years after I left the Unit, same Unit - different ship).*

2. A further addition to the Diver's capabilities was the introduction of Yard Maintenance Tenders (YMTs) 11 and 12 to the Tender fleet in 1962/1963. These YMTs (nicknamed "the Iron Clads"), were fully equipped with Mk 5 Standard gear and an onboard recompression chamber, which meant that diving operations could now be safely increased to 250 feet. The bottom of Bedford Basin was no longer inaccessible to us. Further, the improved living conditions onboard meant that diving operations could be scheduled further away, and the YMTs deployed for longer durations. These diving tenders had a steel hull with an aluminium frame, which at times acted like a sail in heavy winds and seas.

3. YMTs 6 & 8 were purpose-built MCM (Mine Counter Measure) Diving Tenders, in that they were built with non-magnetic materials, as far as possible, and equipped with degaussing coils. Wooden hulled, they were used for harbor work, attack swims and housed various working diver groups using CDBA – Clearance Diving Breathing Apparatus.

4. School's Diving Training Barge. Used by the diving training school for Ship's Diver CD(S), Clearance Diver and Diving Officers.

5. Administration Section

6. Workshop Area, storage area for stores and diving equipment

7. Diving School Training Section

8. Boats Engineering Section

9. Lower Deck ratings (Leading Seaman and below) Lounge and Locker Room

10. FCW building housed the Explosive Ordinance Demolition (EOD) Centre No.1 with a rifle, pistol and archery range, Underwater Weapons section - mines, torpedoes, rockets etc from various nations. On the first level was the recompression chamber.

11. Look closely at the photo and there are two vehicles parked in front which were used on mine exercises.

Glen Frauzel taught me how to drive for the first time on our way back from a dive trip to Shelburne, NS - and this was the truck. The roads back then were pretty bare and anyone coming the other way wasn't going to argue with this truck, so it was pretty safe driving.

The FCW has a lot of heritage. The present building, built in 1916, housed the undersea cable for the French Telegraph Cable Company (La Compagnie Française Des Câbles Télégraphiques).

Two of the original cable holding tanks were flooded, which we then used for diver training in underwater cutting, burning and welding, etc.

CNDA web site: I donated the artwork for RCN ODU badge (right)

Clearance Diver Training

On 10 November 1961, both Linden and I were selected for Clearance Diver training and transferred to FDU. Wouldn't you know it, the start of winter, the coldest fucking time of the year. I mean what other time would you hold an underwater diving course? There were 20 of us selected and all they needed was eight. If you couldn't hack it, you were gone - history.

One of the first things we had to undergo in our CD training was a chamber pressure test and oxygen (O^2) breathing. We were subjected to oxygen tolerance tests at depth and experienced first hand the hazards of oxygen poisoning and its associated conditions.

So we're in this strange environment, we're being put under pressure, the temperature starts to rise – it's getting warm in there. You have to wear an oral-nasal mask and start breathing oxygen under pressure. Unbeknown to us this can become debilitating, since you can only breath pure oxygen down to a certain depth. The next thing I knew, the guy sitting beside me has gone into convulsions. The Petty Officer in the Chamber with us tore off the guy's mask and instructs us to make sure we keep ours on – the test is not over. Well that took care of about four of the group – four out, eight to go.

The physical training and early morning swims in freezin' ass cold water (no gloves) took care of another four – eight out, four to go.

(FIG. 31) SLADEN LIGHT WEIGHT DIVING OUTFIT WITH CDBA (Weighted Belt not required).

The remaining four to go would be tested in the pool and in open water in the harbor. Our test dive in the pool was in the deep end. We were all familiar with CABA gear. It was all on the bottom of the pool – 12 ft down. The challenge, take a deep breath, hold it, get down to the bottom and get kitted up. If you didn't have your diving gear on when you reached the surface – you were out - two more gone – two to go.

The final two would drop out when we did the harbor dive in a Sladen suit – nicknamed 'clammy death'. One of the lads passed out on the dock before even getting in the water.

The ordeal of dressing and the discomfort of wearing it in the hot confines of a submarine, where sweat completely drenched the wearer prior to a cold exit earned it the nickname "clammy death."

Our initial training was extremely arduous with an emphasis on swimming, running and fitness. Those not up to both the physical and mental conditions were soon weeded out and returned to their original units.

Having survived the above, we were now a team of eight and went on to train as Clearance Divers using the Sladen suit and CDBA along with MK V Hard Hat and standard CABA.

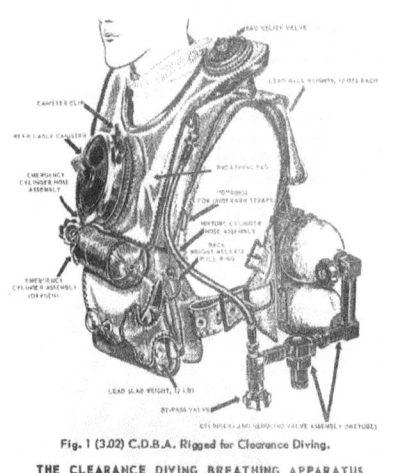

Fig. 1 (3.02) C.D.B.A. Rigged for Clearance Diving.
THE CLEARANCE DIVING BREATHING APPARATUS

(FIG. 41) UNDERWATER SWIM SUIT (CAN. MK. 3) RIGGED FOR CDBA

THE CLEARANCE DIVING BREATHING APPARATUS

The diving gear was non-magnetic, to assist in mine detection and removal. It could be used for either Clearance Diving (using oxygen-nitrogen mixtures to depths of 140 feet, Fig. 1) or Shallow Water Swimming and Diving (using pure oxygen to a maximum depth of 33 feet).

The Standard Diving Dress – MK V Hard Hat
Quote: "Hard hat divers wear *dresses*" – Bob Kirby

Although we would qualify in Standard Dress, I would do more recreational diving with it than I ever did as a CD. And at that time, hard hat diving was being replaced by the Desco Mask.

What better way to start the day than a long distance swim first thing in the morning in the middle of frigging winter. The swim, along with most CDBA diving, was done wearing a lightweight, waterproof suit, the primary purpose of which was to keep the swimmer dry and warm. All fine and well except for the hands being exposed.

Believe me after spending an hour at depth in freezing ass water your hands get so cold it brings tears to your eyes just fighting the pain. Enough. We need gloves.

Well, we finally got provided with gloves. White woollen gloves. Our hands were still exposed to the water – how was that gonna keep them warm and dry?

"It's not for that – it's to stop them from sticking to the ship's frozen ladder" our instructor advised.

We would spend a lot of time using the CDBA gear doing hull surveys and mine counter measures (MCM) – ie bomb disposal. One of our more exciting dives would be using CABA (air) diving gear to a depth of 150 ft plus in the Bedford Basin. Pitch dark on the bottom and the regulator kept freezing up.

How did I know?

Cause instead of air, I kept sucking in bits of ice.

The Granby
Frozen ladder, floating ice, friggin' white woollen gloves!

The Pressure Zone by Mike Cooke

As Clearance Divers, we learned precise skills about handling ordinance and defusing underwater mines. We also learned general seamanship skills, as well as diving physics and physiology, including:

- Search and inspection of the seabed;
- Underwater demolition;
- Mine counter measures;
- Explosives ordnance disposal;
- Salvage and rescue;
- Underwater ship repair and maintenance;
- Repair and Inspection of diving equipment
- Dive training; and
- Recompression chamber services.

But who said training couldn't be fun? Those high-speed pickups (diver retrieval) - now they gave you a real buzz.

Photos courtesy of British Pathe Film - Frogman Pickup 1959

The following is from www.navy.forces.gc.ca - Feature Article

Navy Divers – A league of their own, leagues under the sea

Training to be a diver is as rigorous as the job of being a diver. This is especially true of the program for Clearance Divers. "These are the Navy's elite professionals and for good reason, since they must carry out the riskiest assignments, often under difficult circumstances. A clearance diver has to possess extraordinary physical and mental ability to handle this kind of work. Neutralizing a mine can be tasking enough, but add about 100 metres of water over your head, and it adds a whole dimension of risk to the challenge."

Risk and adventure go hand in hand for navy divers. These professionals can be counted on to deliver nothing short of excellence every time. That's just the way things are done in Canada's Navy.

Couldn't have said it better myself!

Our Clearance Diver course would last six months, during which time Dan McLeod and Jim Onion would assist in instructions.

The Day – 19 April 1962

I qualified as a fully fledged navy clearance diver. Along with seven other divers - Linden Leask, Bill Lukeman, Moe Coulombe, Keith Jamieson, Mike Kettle, Gilles Lariviere, and Victor Vautor. (I think I qualified as the youngest CD in the navy – not even old enough to draw a 'Tot').

Got rid of other trade group designations (badges) TAS & CD(S) and proudly replaced them with the one and only 'Hard Hat'.

Our group would be broken up and sent to various diving tenders. Linden, Bill and I would be billeted on YMT 8 along with Dan McLeod.

Dan was on the Gatineau, on the clearance diving course, on YMT 8 and a major part of FDU the whole time I was there. In truth, he was my first diving mentor.

YMT 10 sister vessel to YMT 8

I was on YMT 8 from 11 May 1962 to 11 February 1963 during which time I got to do some interesting diving.

One was a mine exercise in Sydney, Nova Scotia. This was a combined forces operation with US Navy UDT (Underwater Demolition Team). As it would happen, one of the minesweepers got fouled by a tow cable wrapped around its screw. This was removed and salvaged by our dive team. Being made of copper wire it was worth a few bucks. A quick call to a salvage yard and we had enough money to cover our booze bill for the rest of the exercise.

Mine Exercise

Minesweeper tow Cable

The cruise from the Unit to Sydney and back took us through the scenic Bra d'or Lake and past the home of Alexander Graham Bell (see photo left).

Once we returned to the FDU, things got back to a normal routine for the dive boat.

Hull inspections and maintenance on fleet vessels and bottom surveys which could turn out to be rather rewarding.

On one such survey, I just happened to come across a 40 oz bottle half buried in the mud. Got it topside for a better inspection. The Chief of the boat, Chief Nick, took charge and said that it looked like a bottle of 'Pusser neat's – navy rum – which had found it's way over the side. But to be sure he would try a sample – one sip and it brought tears to his eyes – they were tears of joy – it was true Pusser neat's. So of course everyone onboard deserved a sample, a sip, a splash, a taste or a full 'tot'. In fact, there was enough for a few of the lads to 'splice the mainbrace'[3].

It was a happy crew that made it across the harbor and back to the unit that afternoon.

Navy (Pusser) Rum

30 Mar 1972 – Black Tot Day – Last issue of rum

If we weren't lucky enough to find some rum, then a lobster or two never went astray.

The jetty at the Naval Armament Dock (NAD) was made of wooden piles with rock fill behind them, which were ideal homes for lobsters. At the bottom of this one dock there was a huge rock which was home to a huge lobster. We had been trying for several weeks to catch this guy but as soon as you would come in from one side of the rock, he would scoot out the other side. On this particular dive, Dan McLeod stayed on one side on the rock and I went around to the other side to catch him as he came out. He never did come out, so I reached in to grab him. In fact, he ended up grabbing me and almost crushing my thumb. But I managed to hang on and brought him to the surface where Al Blanchard helped free my hand from the lobster's claw. The lobster must have been over 20 lbs because when we laid him out on deck, his claws spread out as far as four men standing side by side.

[3] *Splice the mainbrace is to issue and partake in an extra ration of alcoholic spirits, especially rum or grog, amongst members of crew aboard a sea vessel. (The mainbrace, is a brace attached to the main yard on sailing ships. 'Splicing the mainbrace' was the very difficult job of repairing this brace, one which earned the repairman an extra ration of spirits; eventually, this euphemistic secondary meaning became the primary one). As part of the celebrations for her Diamond Jubilee, the Queen gave the order to all in the Royal Navy to splice the mainbrace as a gesture of good cheer. The formation of the Royal Canadian Navy in 1910 carried over many of the Royal Navy traditions and the daily issue of a "TOT" being one that was continued until the 30th of March 1972. Canada was the last Commonwealth Navy to cease this tradition.* [More info can be found at ReadyAyeReady.com]

Food for thought, lobsters can grow to be four feet long, 40 pounds, and as much as 100 years old.

Every now and then the Unit would be contacted to do a body search for a drowning. Thank goodness I only had to do two of these. We also assisted the Royal Canadian Military Police (RCMP) in recovering drowning victims and investigated and dealt with mines and abandoned explosives.

If something of value went over the side, we'd be called upon to do a search and recovery (S&R). One of the more interesting S&R jobs was trying to locate a hydrofoil that had come off during a trial test run in the harbor by the Naval Research Establishment (NRE). At the time, Canada was a leading developer of hydrofoil vessels. The test run was highly classified. Details of the dive and search were therefore kept quiet, and in the end, we never did locate the hydrofoil.

Hydrofoil test run circa 1960s

Alexander G Bell Hydro foil circa 1918

Another interesting diving job we were involved in was the inspection, maintenance, and changing out of ships' sonar domes, which previously required dry docking. With divers now involved, this could be effected without the vessel dry docking which saved both time and money.

Ship's Sonar domes attached to hull

Sonar dome removed from hull

We also undertook deeper diving operations such as inspection of the deep degaussing ranges in Bedford Basin, demolition of underwater towers off Hartlen Point down to 140 feet, recovery of trial hydrostatic fuses down to 165 feet for NRE, etc.

On 11 February 1963, I was transferred to the diving support vessel 'Port St Louis'. This was the climax of my career as a navy Clearance Diver.

We spent that winter in Bermuda – definitely preferable to spending it up in Halifax. Over several weeks, we undertook propeller change out trials. The purpose of these was to evaluate different types of propellers with a varying number of blades and pitch. The Navy was assessing the best combination to reduce the acoustic value of the propeller underwater. In other words, make it more difficult for submarines' acoustic detection systems to pick up the sound of the propeller.

The process involved a lot of underwater rigging, explosives and timing. The destroyer escort would come alongside, moor and without completely shutting down the engines, the shaft still rotating ever so slowly, the propeller change would take place. The divers would rig come-alongs from the ship's hull down to eyepads on the ship's propeller, while it was still rotating. Prior to hooking up the come-alongs, we would get explosive cable (coretex) from topside which we wrapped around the propeller, making sure the loose end was taken topside to be hooked up to the detonator. Once this was done, we would wait till the propeller was in a suitable position to where the explosive could be ignited (and we were out of the water), so the explosive would loosen the propeller on the shaft. After the explosion, we would return to the water and remove the propeller from the shaft and secure the replacement propeller in position.

Typical twin propeller layout   Diver working on propeller removal

New propeller rigged and ready to be placed over the side for divers to install on the propeller shaft.

Twin propellers changed, ready to sail.

What we accomplished with this method had a major impact on vessel maintenance, thereby foregoing the need for a costly dry docking. This technique was also adopted by the US Navy.

It was a great way to end my tour of duty and what better place than the Royal Navy Dockyard, Ireland Island, Bermuda.

Warm, crystal clear water, well a heck of a lot warmer and clearer than Halifax harbor that's for sure. Unfortunately, underwater cameras were not common back then, so I don't have any photos.

Royal Navy Dockyard, Ireland Island, BERMUDA

HMCS Port St Louis   Heading into a little rough weather

During that operation, Bermuda was being threatened by a hurricane, which meant all vessels would make a run for it. Our dive boat was so small, that it was easily pushed around by the seas. That is when a hammock comes in really handy.

I lucked out a got one from Dan McLeod off the Cape Breton before the weather hit. It was the only one onboard and was never vacant. You didn't dare get up to go for a piss.

Typical hammock rigging

Dive Crew HMCS Port St Louis
Back Row: Cripps, Goulard, *Voutor,* Fenn,
Front Row: *Lukeman,* Lafontaine, Melonson, *me & Kettle*

Those listed in *blue* were clearance divers from the class of '62.

I designed the Ship's plaque 'Hell and Deep Water' with a little help from Bill Lukeman.

As luck would have it, while I was stationed at the Royal Navy Dockyard, Dan just happened to be stationed on HMCS Cape Breton, a supply ship that spent most of the winter months alongside in Bermuda. On weekends, we'd borrow a Zodiac and go around the island diving for conch shells and other pretty things.

It was during this deployment that a serious incident occurred.

On the 10 April 1963, the USS Thresher, a US Navy nuclear submarine (the second to be named after the thresher shark) sank during deep-diving tests off the coast of Boston killing all 129 crew and shipyard personnel aboard in the deadliest submarine disaster at the time. It was the first nuclear submarine lost at sea.

The 10th was a Wednesday and as per navy custom the afternoon was a 'make and mend' at sea or the afternoon off when ashore. I was at my girlfriend's house when I got the emergency call back to the FDU(A) to standby in case we were needed.

At the same time Capt George Bond, USN (the father of saturation diving) at the US Naval Submarine base in New Haven, Connecticut received a phone call: *"George, Thresher is reported missing and maybe sunk. Hold your best divers aboard. We may get a chance to rescue those men."*

The USS Thresher sank in 8,400 feet of water, beyond crush and recovery depths. With all hands lost, official reaction at the top was immediate.

This incident precipitated the Man in the Sea project - Sealab - and the birth of Saturation Diving.

Later that year, I was transferred back to FDU(A). Being shore-based, gave me the opportunity to try out for the navy football team. In the fall of '63, I played for the Stadacona Sailors who were part of the Maritime College Football League, along with Darby Mathews and Ken Whitney, both also clearance divers. Darby Mathews, a champion boxer in his own right, would later become the mayor of Esquimalt BC and Ken Whitney, judo master and one of the most notable football coaches in the maritime provinces.

One of the other players on the team was Moe Levesque. Moe would turn pro and play for the Montreal Alouettes.

Also on the team was Chucky Worser, a navy PE instructor - the only guy I've ever known who could do 1,000 sit-ups in one go. You didn't dare punch him in the stomach because you'd break your hand.

1965 Football card

'The Clearance Diver'

As seen by Navy Department
An overpaid, over-rated, insufferable tax burden who is indispensable because he has volunteered to go anywhere and do anything as long as he can booze it up, brawl, steal jeeps, corrupt women, lie and wear a Rolex diving watch and a K-Bar knife.

As seen by his Commanding Officer
A fine upstanding specimen of an honest, fun loving, athletic, provident, woman appreciating, improvising, completely misunderstood by the shore patrol/military police, navy department and his wife. But has however, signed the temporary loan car for a Rolex diving watch and a K-Bar knife.

As seen by his Shipmates
A whining, moaning, complaining, overpaid excuse for a sailor who works less often than his Rolex diving watch and is about as witty and sharp as the handle on his K-Bar knife.

As seen by the Shore Patrol
A drunken, brawling, jeep stealing, woman-corrupting liar, who wears a Rolex diving watch and a K-Bar knife.

As seen by his Wife
A little known, hung over member of the family who comes home once every six months with a ruck-sack full of dirty laundry and a hard-on. Wearing a rusty K-Bar knife and is never on time because he pawned his Rolex diving watch.

As seen by Himself
A tall, highly trained deep diving, double crimping, bomb disposal expert and professional killer who is a world-renowned female idol, ballroom dancer and bare-knuckle fighter easily identified by his exquisitely designed, extremely accurate Rolex[4] diving watch and keenly honed K-Bar knife.

[Source: Unknown]

---

[4] *I believe I was the first Clearance Diver to own a gold Rolex watch circa 1969 – my first year as a saturation diver and five years after leaving the navy. But I lost my K-Bar knife.*

Son, someday you will make a girl very happy, for a short period of time. Then she'll leave you and be with new men who are ten times better than you could ever hope to be. These men are called Clearance Divers.

[From RANCD reunion card]

Linden would be discharged from the navy just before the end of the year (1963). He went to Montreal and got a job as a commercial diver with KD Marine and rented a place in the same boarding house as my Mom.

I left HMCS Granby FDU(A) in March 1964 and returned to Montreal with every intention of re-enlisting and being back onboard a month later. However, it wasn't meant to be.

Shortly after my discharge from the navy, the Sealab experiment hailed the birth of saturation diving.

20 July 1964 Start of US Navy Saturation Program - SEALAB

SEALAB I was lowered off the coast of Bermuda on July 20, 1964 to a depth of 192 feet (59 m) below the ocean surface. It was constructed from two converted floats and held in place with axles from railroad cars. The experiment involved four divers (LCDR Robert Thompson, MC, Gunners Mate First Class Lester Anderson, Chief Quartermaster Robert A Barth and Chief Hospital Corpsman Sanders Manning [5], who were to stay submerged for three weeks. The experiment was halted after 11 days due to an approaching tropical storm.

SEALAB I was commanded by Captain George F Bond, also called "Papa Topside", who was key in developing theories about saturation diving. SEALAB I proved that saturation diving in the open ocean was viable for extended periods. The experiment also offered information about habitat placement, habitat umbilicals, humidity, and helium speech descrambling.

SEALAB I is on display at the Museum of the Man in the Sea in Panama City Beach, Florida, near where it was initially tested offshore before being deployed. It is on outdoor display. Its metal hull is largely intact, though the paint faded to a brick red over the years. The habitat's exterior was restored as part of its 50th year anniversary, and now sports its original colors.

[From Wikipedia]

Bond's Saturation Theory

True scientific impetus was first given to the saturation concept in 1957 when a Navy diving medical officer, Captain George F Bond, theorized that the tissues of the body would eventually become saturated with inert gas if exposure time was long enough. Bond, then a commander and the director of the Submarine Medical Center at New London, Connecticut, met with Captain Jacques-Yves Cousteau and determined that the data required to prove the theory of saturation diving could be developed at the Medical Center.

[Source: scubish.com]

---

[5] *I would eventually get to work with both Manning and Barth when they came to work for Taylor Diving & Salvage (TDS). I have a signed copy of Bob Barth's book 'Sea Dwellers' and a copy of USN Capt George Bond's book 'Papa Topside'. Both are highly recommended reading.*

Chapter Three 1964 - 69
Commercial Diver

Surface Air & Mixed Gas
Challenging the Pressure Zone

North Sea 1966 - with Desco Air Mask and Landry phone (marked by arrow)

March 1964

When I returned to Montreal, I caught up with Linden and also went to work for KD Marine. That was where I was introduced to the Constant Volume Suit. Looked like a Sladen (Clammy Death) Suit to me.

We did a few jobs around Montreal and that summer worked on a major contract in Burlington, Ontario - installation of a concrete pipeline extending out into Lake Ontario. Linden and I rented a beach bungalow and settled in for a good summer of diving. Near the end of summer Linden had had enough and decided to take a break. Keller & Dibbly, the "K & D" hired Walter Wolf to take his place. More about him shortly.

In Burlington, we ran into Mike Williams who was also involved with some underwater projects. One of which had him in discussions with a diving company in New Orleans. This company was in some way connected with the locating and recovery of the wreckage of Eastern Air Lines Flight 304 in Lake Ponchartrain.

Eastern Air Lines Flight 304, a Douglas DC-8 flying home from New Orleans International Airport to Washington Dulles International Airport, crashed on February 25, 1964.

All 51 passengers and 7 crew were killed. The water was only 20 feet (6 m) deep, yet only 60 percent of the wreckage was recovered because the breakup was so extensive.

[Source: Wikipedia]

Location of wreck

The Pressure Zone by Mike Cooke

Our friend had convinced them he could be of valuable assistance. They flew him to New Orleans. He in turn suggested there might be some work for us. So, we decided it might be a good move to head south.

The Gulf of Mexico - clear blue warm water - hey it was a no brainer - it was the end of summer and the water was starting to get a little cool in Lake Ontario. Time to leave KD Marine in the hands of Walter Wolf.

I did a couple of dives with him before heading south. He had other things on his mind. He was the first Canuck to own an F1 racing team and gave Linden one of his formula one racing jackets. There are a couple of interesting articles on the man in the Globe and Mail:

https://www.theglobeandmail.com/news/world/walter-wolf-international-man-of-mystery/article12758965/

He worked odd jobs, mostly in construction but also as an elevator engineer and as a pilot, and taught himself English by watching Western movies. He then moved to Montreal, where he worked as a diver for KD Marine installing intake pipes and building bridge foundations, ultimately landing a loan from the Bank of Nova Scotia to buy a 33-per- cent stake in the then-fledgling marine company.

https://www.theglobeandmail.com/news/national/who-is-walter-wolf-and-why-is-he-wanted/article13330221/

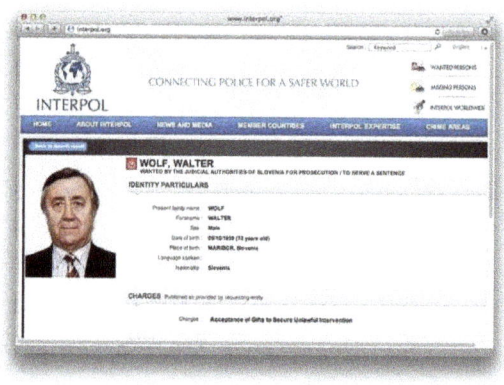

Interpol, the world's largest international police organization, posted his head shot to its website in March with this caption: Wanted by the judicial authorities of Slovenia for prosecution/to serve a sentence.

KATHRYN BLAZE CARLSON
PRITCHARD, B.C.
PUBLISHED JULY 20, 2013
UPDATED MAY 11, 2018

Now back to the real story.

On Monday 31 August 1964, I wedged into the shotgun seat in Linden's VW Beatle (Bug), which was loaded down to the gunwales with all our gear and headed south to New Orleans. By Monday night we'd crossed the border at Detroit and checked into the first available motel. We were Stateside.

On the road, bright and early the next morning hoping for a good start. But the only time we could make any decent head way on the Inter-State highways was to fall in behind a semi-trailer and let it act as a wind brake and run interference. Unfortunately, we were so close to the back of the trailer that we couldn't see the overhead road signs and ended up way out of our way in bourbon country – Kentucky. Awesome detour though - rolling hills, thoroughbred white fencing surrounding blue grass fields and a different distillery in every valley. Magic.

On 2 September, while driving through Tennessee, we heard that American WW1 hero and Medal of Honor winner Sergeant York had passed away in Nashville. You couldn't turn on the radio without hearing about it. Gary Cooper had starred in the 1941 movie honouring him - *'Sergeant York'*.

It was a hell of time to be heading down south. Here we were, a couple of young white guys from up north, heading south during the end of *'The Summer of 64'*. Many years later (1988), a movie was made about what happened during that time. *'Mississippi Burning'* was based on the murder of three civil rights workers in June 1964 - a local black and two white Northerners.

Once we'd crossed the Mississippi State line, we were escorted through every town by the local sheriff driving a big white Buick:

> 'Hey boys, where y'all headed? New Orleans huh? Well, you make sure you behave yourselves and keep headin' south and don't bother stopping. My brother-in-law will be waitin' for y'all at the next town to make sure you do. Y'all have a safe trip ya hear.'

It was a trip that would be the start of an amazing adventure and diving career.

On Wednesday evening 2 September 1964, we left Mississippi and crossed the stateline into Louisiana and entered N'awlins (New Orleans to the uninitiated) to the sounds of Eric Burdon and The Animals *'The House of the Rising Sun' (recorded on 18 May 1964)*. An auspicious start – *'There is a House in New Orleans...'* – we figured it was a good sign.

We arrived on a cool southern evening. A pleasant time to cruise and see if we could locate the diving company. Went out by the lakefront - Lake Pontchartrain. The building was dark, so time to find a motel. Checked into a place on Airline Highway.

Next morning, we got the shock of our lives. Opened up the door of our air-conditioned room and almost got bowled over by a wall of hot humid air – welcome to the deep south!

It was time for a closer investigation of the diving company our friend had referred to us – Taylor Diving and Salvage Co Inc (Taylor). I had no idea at the time, that I'd be with them for the next 21 years.

Taylor Diving & Salvage Co. Inc.
7600 West End Boulevard, New Orleans, Louisiana 70124

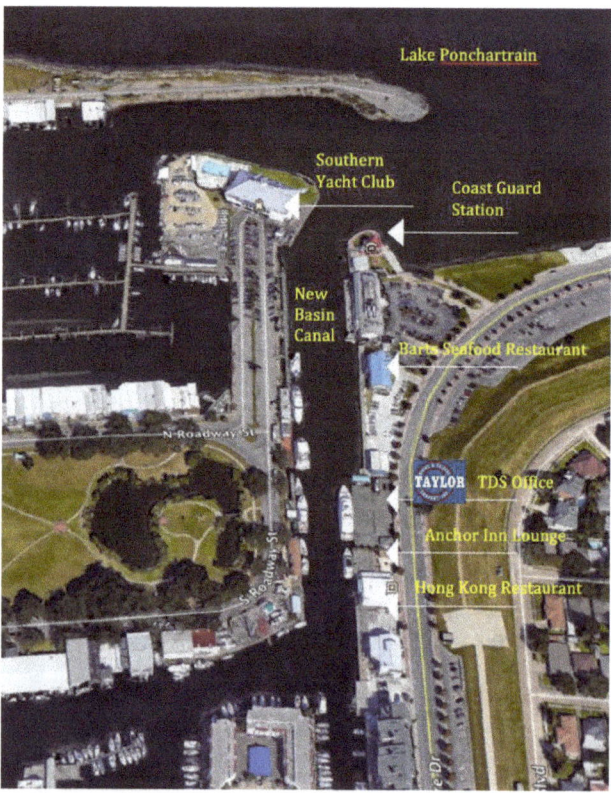

What an awesome location for a diving business. It didn't seem real. Two doors down from a bar (The Anchor Inn Lounge), a two-minute walk to one of the best seafood restaurants (Barts) in New Orleans (NOLA), two minutes the other way to some of the best Chinese food in town and across the canal was the Southern Yacht Club where there were more great seafood restaurants. Talk about class. Could it possibly get any better?

Pulled into the parking lot and introduced ourselves. Being close to the Labor Day weekend there was only one person in the office who just happened to be the manager. In fact, he was the MAN. Not Mark Banjavich, one of the owners, but Mitch, the guy who ran the show. Mitch would become a very close friend and mentor.

Mitch mentioned they were always looking for good divers, even if they were bad speakers (Canadian, eh). He recommended a hotel on St Charles Avenue in the Garden District and suggested we do a little reconnoitring of the French Quarter. He said to come by after the weekend and meet more of the staff and in the meantime, if anything came up, he'd give us a call.

Sure enough, the phone rang on Friday 4 September and the next morning I was heading to Intracoastal City (the term city is a misnomer). Three days after arriving in NOLA, I was out on a job. I was lucky - I'd been the one to pick up the phone.

Intracoastal City's facilities include a heliport, a shrimp boat docking facility, and crew boat docks. As it stands on the coast of the Gulf of Mexico it is somewhat remote from major settlements.

Mitch said "Take this route and when you run out black top – you're there." No shit, I couldn't go any further as there were cows in the way. I checked into the Brown & Root (B&R) office (port-a-camp) and then boarded the crew boat that would take me out to the B&R lay barge M211 in the Gulf of Mexico (GoM). My first day of work for Taylor.

Once onboard I introduced myself to the lead diver, Archie Weiss, who I would work with on several jobs that year. Five years later, in 1969, he would be one of the saturation divers on my first sat dive.

I was out there to relieve Archie's tender, Chuck Peel, who had a medical problem and required a penicillin shot? I didn't even have to get wet. That was when Archie gave me the most important advice at the start of my commercial diving career – "if you're a diver, don't come out here as a tender". That was it, I went back to Taylor the next day and told Mitch if you don't need a diver, don't give me a call.

The Pressure Zone by Mike Cooke

He replied, "If you want to dive then get your gear and move into the bunkroom. That way you'll be on call and you can earn some coin doing other things". On Tuesday 8 September I moved into the bunkroom.

Taylor Diving & Salvage
7600 West End Blvd

Top floor: Banjavich apartment
Lower floor: Bunkroom (canal side), office, dive shop and wet/dry (pot) chamber

7600 West End Blvd became my address for the next year.

Living at the 'shop', I got to meet most of the diving personnel working for Taylor. The boss, Mark Banjavich and his wife Henri, lived in the top floor apartment above the bunkroom. Some of the diving staff I would meet were dive superintendents George Morrissey and Bob McArdle - both ex-navy master divers. Other members of the diving crew were Louis Giacona and Carl Goring, who would be my first diving supervisors in the North Sea. Joe Schouest, who taught me all about dredge barges and how to hand jet – burying pipelines and risers. Neil Landry, who built the Landry dive radio, for Taylor. (I have a recent model dive radio from Desco – sure looks like a Landry one - shown in the photo on page 48).

Neil would be my Sat/Bell partner in Hawai'i in 1971. Fred Miller, 'The Legend' - my longest-running saturation diving partner - we made the first bell run on Shell Cognac and deepest dive in the GoM – 1,025 ft in 1976. Buddy Eglin, second longest bell partner. Boyd Vassey, Red & Whitey Paterson, Dick Ransom, Jim Stern (who unfortunately I didn't know for long as he got killed in a car accident coming back from a job), Pete Fitzmorris, Frenchie Collins, Ted Operchal, Frank Brock, Harry Rude, Art Herman and Jay Jones to name a few.

Didn't get to see Jay that often, he basically had Venice and the Mississippi Delta area covered. Not too deep but a lot of work. I asked Mitch where's Venice? He said, "man, you don't want to go there that's where they put the enema!"

And then in 1965, my life coach and mentor, Tom Duncan entered the scene.

Taylor was also supporting B&R operations in the Middle East. Got to meet Jesse Robie when he came back to NOLA. He had a diving accident over there - lost part of his hand working on an underwater pipeline flange. Didn't stop him from returning in style. Pulled up to the shop in his brand-new Cadillac Eldorado convertible. Now that's class and in the immortal words of Tom Duncan, "If you ain't got class, then you ain't got shit."

I was obviously working for the right company with a great bunch of guys.

The original home of Taylor was the schooner Justin II built in Maryland in 1923. Taylor was formally incorporated aboard the vessel near the Coast Guard station at the mouth of the New Basin Canal. Thanks to the efforts of Bob McArdle, the main mast of the Justin II would eventually find it's way to Taylor's new offices as the flagpole in Belle Chasse.

Justin II

The company was co-founded by Mark Banjavich, Edward (Hempy) Taylor III and Jean Valz. Both Mark and Hempy were ex US Navy divers and shipmates aboard the submarine rescue vessel 'Skylark'.

Jean was a French born American who was widely known for his piano playing at Lafitte's Blacksmith Shop as a vocation and skin diving as an avocation. David Levy would also be a part owner and investor.

I would get to know Mark, Jean and David.

By the time Linden and I arrived at Taylor, the Justin II had been leased and towed to Houma. Hempy had already sold out his share of the company, strapped on a side arm and headed to the Orinoco and Amazon rivers in search of gold.

Jean Valz & Mark Banjavich

I asked Buddy one day, how come the company was called Taylor and 'Hempy' was already gone? He said that when it came time to name the company Mark said "there's no way those Texans are going to hire a company called Banjavich Diving or Valz Diving". It needed an Anglo-Saxon name like Taylor Diving. Hempy agreed as long as he didn't have to be president. In 1957, Mark Banjavich became president of Taylor.

By the early 1960s, Taylor claimed leadership in the advancement of commercial diving. Taylor established a close bond with Brown & Root beginning in 1960. Eight years later, B&R's parent, Halliburton, purchased Taylor. During the 1960s and 1970s, B&R and Taylor worked hand-in-glove to pioneer the movement of the offshore oil industry into ever deeper water. (See Appendix for more details on Taylor).

Staying at the shop, I got to see Mark and Henri on a regular basis. Catching up with Jean was a whole different story and an awesome introduction to the French Quarter.

Mitch sent me to Jean's to get some checks signed. He lived at 927 Bourbon Street, just a couple of doors from Lafitte's Blacksmith Shop where he played piano at night.

Jean and Ethel had the ground floor apartment by the pool and Mark had the upstairs apartment. Louis Giacona had the ground floor apartment across the patio and David Levy had the apartment that opened on the street. The three owners of Taylor each with an apartment. Louis was a long-time employee, close friend and son of a well-known New Orleans character.

The house was a French Quarter classic. I rang the bell at the wrought iron gate, got buzzed in. With check book in hand, I headed down the side of the house to the courtyard and swimming pool in the back. Jean, showing his French heritage, met me eating a raw onion like an apple, and introduced me to everyone. That was when I almost dropped the check book in the pool - all the gals were topless - that was a first for me - and what an introduction it was. Back then, a bunch of Playboy Bunnies from the Playboy Club would visit regularly. A good time was had by all.

Let the good times roll'

At the end of September, I got my first paycheck - wow. Earlier that year, I left the navy earning $100+ a month, went to work for KD Marine making $100+ a week, then joined Taylor and started making $100+ a day. Not a bad lark this diving.

When I wasn't making trips to the Quarter or doing other work around the shop, I was busy putting together my own diving kit. For call-out shallow jobs you were expected to have your own equipment: compressor, diving hose and radio and your own vehicle.

The radio made life so much easier.

Before the advent of radio, divers used hand signals or predetermined pulls on their hose: two pulls for this, one pull for that, and the universally acknowledged four pulls which translated to: "Get my ass out of here now!"

Yep, the radio made diving easier and safer. Among other things, it made it possible to complete a job without the diver having to make several trips to the surface to explain what needed to be done. Not only was it possible to talk to the support people but an alert, experienced tender could tell, simply by listening to the radio, if his diver was getting into trouble.

Air Compressor

Diving Rig (Hose)

Rigged and ready to go

Since I was living at the shop, I used one of their pickups.

September and October were busy months and a great introduction to offshore diving. Spent a lot of time on the bury barge M-228 with Joe Schouest, Fred Miller and Boyd Vassey.

B&R Dredge (Bury) Barge M-228 with Jet Sled/Dredge (claw) hanging off stern

But it was on a call-out to the M-211 where I had my first diving accident, which could have ended my diving career.

To understand how the accident happened, let me explain a little about how pipeline installation works.

The M-211 was a first generation lay barge.

B&R LE Minor – first generation pipe lay barge similar to M-211

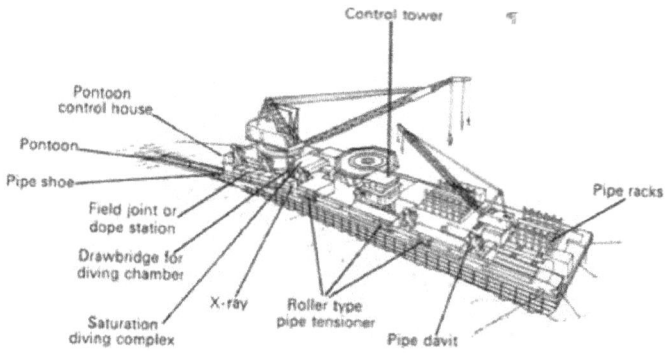

Brown & Root Pipe Lay Barge - BAR 324 (built 1972)

The BAR 324 is a first generation type pipe lay and derrick barge similar to M-211 (built 1956) and Hugh W Gordon (built 1966).

All had starboard side pipe welding stations and pipe ramp leading to the pontoon 'Stinger' at the stern. I worked on the M-211 in the GoM and both BAR 324 and Hugh W Gordon during my 12 year (1966-78) stretch in the North Sea.

B&R S-Lay Pipeline Installation

When performing S-lay pipeline installation, pipe is eased off the stern of the vessel as the barge moves forward. The pipe curves downward from the stern through the water until it reaches the "touchdown point," or its final destination on the seafloor. As more pipe is welded in the line and eased off the barge, the pipe forms the shape of an "S" in the water.

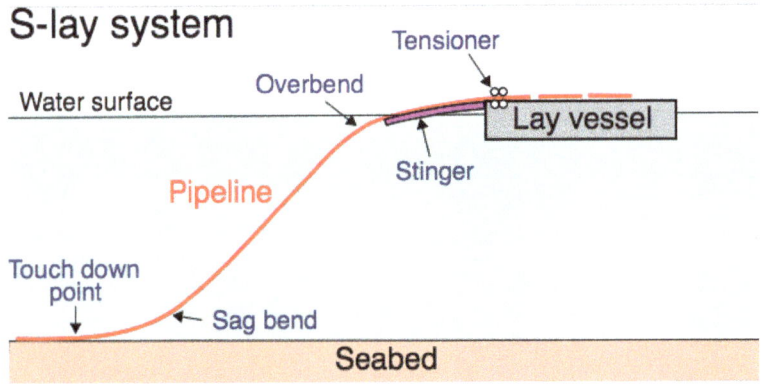

Stingers, measuring up to 300 feet (91 meters) and longer, extend from the stern to support the pipe as it is moved into the water, as well as controlling the curvature of the installation. Some pipe lay barges have adjustable stingers, which can be shortened or lengthened according to the water depth.

Wiring up the M-211's 728 ft (222 m) stinger to lay pipe for Shell's Marlin system

Stinger alongside starboard side of lay barge

The above photo (left) is of the same stinger which pinned my leg against the barge.

Proper tension is integral during the S-lay process, which is maintained via tensioning rollers and a controlled forward thrust, keeping the pipe from buckling. S-lay can be performed in waters up to 6,500 feet (1,981 meters) deep, and as many as 4 miles (6 kms) a day of pipe can be installed in this manner.

[Source: www.nord-stream.com]

Pipe being lowered into the water via a stinger for S-Lay installation

The white arrow is pointing to a steel bar ladder fender supported on either side by square, long heavy wood beams. These are used to fender off other vessels and also provide access to the barge by the ladder. For example, getting out of the water after a dive or working on the surface and getting back on board.

This is where the 'stinger' is located when alongside the barge fenders and hooked up to davits.

Now back to my story.

> *Hurricane Hilda was the most intense tropical cyclone of the 1964 Atlantic hurricane season and ravaged areas of the US Gulf Coast, particularly Louisiana.*
>
> *In addition to causing impacts inland, the hurricane greatly disrupted offshore oil production, and at its time was the costliest tropical cyclone for Louisiana's offshore oil production. Originating near Cuba, the cyclone intensified while moving through the Gulf of Mexico, and became a Category 4 hurricane in the Gulf of Mexico before striking Louisiana in early October.*
>
> *Hilda led to significant damage to oil platforms in the Gulf of Mexico, as well as $126 million (1964 USD) in damage, and 38 deaths.*
>
> [Source: Wikipedia]

On receipt of a hurricane warning, it was time for most vessels to take evasive action - head for cover in protected water. Prior to leaving site, the lay barge would need to run out from under the pipe and lower the pipe and stinger to the bottom.

This is what the barge M-211 did when notified of incoming Hurricane Hilda. Once the hurricane had passed and the water had calmed, the barge would head back out to location to resume laying pipe. But first, it would need to get the stinger hooked up and the pipe back onboard. This was going to require a beefed up dive crew and diving supervisors. Enter George Morrissey, retired Navy Master Diver who joined Taylor in 1963 as superintendent, becoming the diving industry's first full-time diving supervisor. I was part of the dive crew that George had onboard. He made me promise to tell everyone I was 24. I told him "George I'm having a tough enough time convincing 'em I'm 22!" Just another cross to bear when you're young and good-looking!

I caught the crew boat and made it out to the barge. It was a rough ride out. I was beat. Needed sleep. With the extra crew there were no spare bunks and being the new kid on the block, the best I could manage was a block of Styrofoam in the deck decompression chamber. I went out like a light – got decompressed three times.

The next morning, I was suited up in a wet suit standing by. Archie was in the water hooking-up wire slings from the davits to the stinger which was on the surface and alongside the barge. The water was choppy and Archie was getting thrown about. George hollered "Somebody get in there and give him a hand." Next thing I knew I was in the water giving him a hand. We got the sling hooked-up. It was time to get outta there. The stinger was rough riding up and down alongside the barge and every now and then a surge would smash it against the ladder fenders. Getting out of the water was gonna be tricky. Timing had to be right and movements fast. I picked my time at the top of a surge. I was able to grab the ladder and get my left foot on a rung before the stinger dropped and left me hanging. Before I could get both feet on the ladder another surge came in, lifted the stinger and slammed it against the barge fenders. My right thigh got caught and crushed between the wood fender and stinger – did that smart. I fell back into the water and Archie gave me a hand to get out.

Lucky for me, I was wearing a wetsuit which provided some protection and the stinger hadn't caught me a little higher and crushed my pelvis or worse. My leg started to swell and my wetsuit had to be cut-off me. I was in some serious pain but at least I got a bunk in sickbay (barge clinic). It would be 6-8 hours before I'd get a crew boat into shore. From there, I had to drive myself back to Marrero where Mitch lived. It was the weekend and thank god he was at home. I got out of the truck and keeled over in the driveway. The pain was exruciating and my leg had swollen to twice it's normal size. Mitch rushed me to a clinic on West Bank Expressway. A doctor placed me on a metal table with raised sides and made an incision in my right thigh – whoosh – fluid everywhere. There was a lot of drainage. He inserted a gauze wick about 2 feet long into my thigh to allow it to drain for the next couple of days.

That was mid-October. I wouldn't be cleared to dive for another six months. May as well spend Christmas with my sister and friends back in Canada.

1965

While I was recuperating in Montreal, Linden and Joe Schouest were testing out Taylor's concept of bell diving with deck decompression.

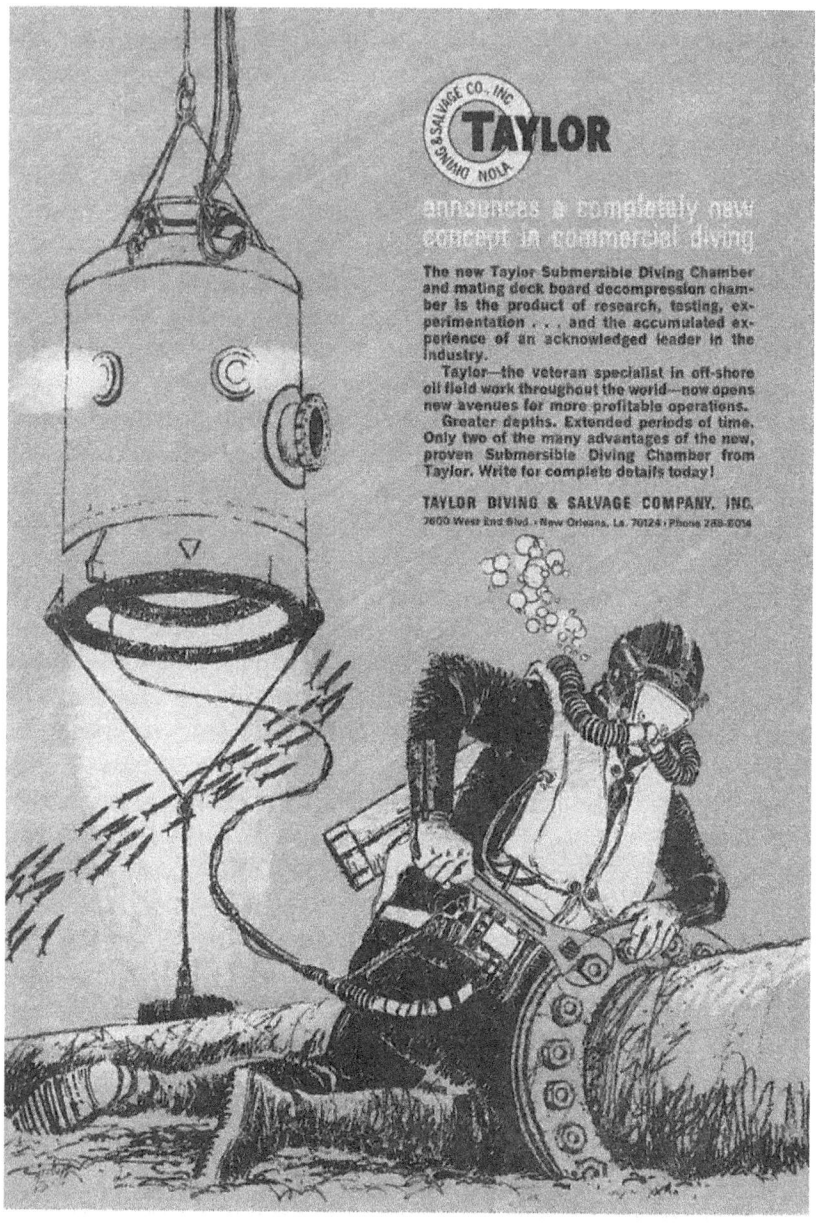

Taylor Diving advertisement in the February 1966 edition of *Offshore*

In March my leg had healed sufficiently for a doctor in Montreal to give me the all-clear. By then I'd run out of money. Time to call Mitch for some airfare. He told me "I'll send you $50, take a bus, leave the flying to us." I caught the Greyhound and headed south. Arrived in N'awlins with a dime in my pocket and two phone numbers - one for the shop the other for Mitch at home. If I made the wrong call, I had a heck of a long walk to the shop. As luck would have it, Mitch was at home, came and got me at the bus station and took me to the bunkroom – I was home.

Things were happening at Taylor. Platforms in the GoM had extended past the 200ft (60m) depth. The implications for the diving industry were clear: 1) divers would have to improve methods of overcoming decompression sickness, and 2) they would have to use mixed gas (helium/oxygen) for deeper dives. Because there was really no equipment available at that time to go to those depths, Taylor developed its own, designing the first 'recompression chamber' employed in the commercial diving industry and modifying the gear worn by divers.

Enter George Morrissey again, who was in charge of developing commercial helium-oxygen (HeO^2) equipment. He started training men at the research facility (Taylor's shop), providing divers and equipment to work in the open sea at 200+ feet. Living at the shop, I was one of the first in the barrel (diving gear).

We tested and evaluated a few different rigs:

Dave Clark Helmet

In the mid 1960's, David Clark from Worcester, Massachusetts, entered the diving suit manufacturing business. They borrowed information and designs from space helmets and applied it to diving helmet design.

The early hats were very unpopular as they were clumsy, too buoyant, and had poor visibility through the rounded, curved faceport. They used chest and back weights that were suspended from straps attached to the helmet neck ring. Very uncomfortable.

Boyd Vassey and I tested a suit that resembled this one. We looked just like astronauts

This diving helmet, if memory serves me correctly, is similar to the one I tested at Taylor
Photo courtesy of Leon Lyons

The firm got completely out of the diving manufacturing business in the early 1970's.

The Pressure Zone by Mike Cooke

Jerry O'Neill's Mark-VI recirculating breathing apparatus

Diver Hank Anderson wearing the Mark-VI on the Smith Mountain Dam total saturation job in Virginia. This was the world's first **commercial** application of saturation diving techniques. [Source: 'Cast a Deep Shadow' - Gary L Harris]

This system was used by Taylor for a limited time in the GoM.

It was turning out to be a busy pre-season testing out all this new gear.

The next unit we tested and the one which was used both for surface mixed gas and saturation diving was the Divex rig – the Swindell Hat.

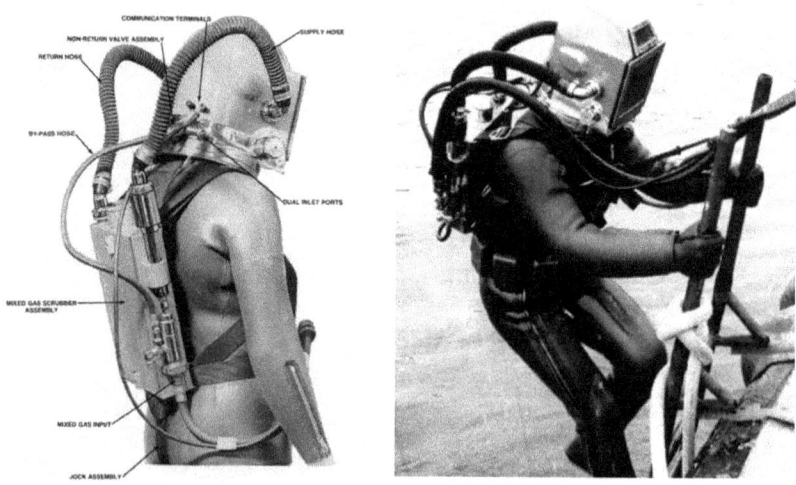

Swindell Hat with CO_2 absorbent backpack cannister

The progression from compressed air to helium-oxygen necessitated evaluating this new equipment. Because pre-mixed helium-oxygen was costly and exhaled in greater volumes with increasing depths, divers were equipped with a rebreather apparatus that recirculated helmet gas using a venturi jet taking suction from a carbon dioxide absorbent cannister. "In this manner," said Dr. Robert Workman, the diving physiologist in charge of the NEDU, "exhaled carbon dioxide is removed, and the oxygen level maintained in the helmet by a lesser volume of supply of gas than would be required by ventilation with supply gas alone." In designing Taylor's helium-oxygen gear to make it more lightweight, Morrissey replaced the heavy metal helmet used in conventional dry dress diving with a US Navy modified Mark-6 partial rebreather. It was a plastic bubble helmet that resembled those used by the Apollo astronauts. The lightweight apparatus proved to be twice as effective as the heavy gear on long duration dives. In place of the standard carbon-dioxide scrubber cannister, Morrissey substituted a compact, lightweight rectangular crossflow cannister which "proved to be 200 percent more efficient than previous models."

By the mid-1960s, Taylor Diving achieved a day-to-day working capability in the 100-200-foot depth range. But could they go deeper? To do so, diving companies had to find a way to handle greater decompression requirements and enable divers to have greater effective bottom times. The introduction of saturation diving as a solution to these problems revolutionized the commercial diving industry and in the process, established Taylor Diving as prime innovator in this technology.

[Source: *Offshore Pioneers* – Brown & Root p 141-142]

During this period there were basically three types of diving jobs:

1. Call Out Diver – could be a one to two day job or replacement offshore on a barge or any other jobs that might be needed around the shop, ie testing and evaluating equipment and procedures.
2. Regular Barge Diver – usually spent the season (6 - 8 months) in GoM.
3. Overseas Contract Diver – signed an 18 month contract. Which meant you stayed overseas for 510 days or job completion, which ever came first. It also had something to do with tax benefits.

Living at the shop, I was a handy call out diver. It also put me in a good position to become a regular barge diver, which happened that year. I became a barge diver with Boyd Vassey and Joe Schouest on B&R Dredge (Jet) Barge M-228, a first generation trenching barge.

Linden had secured a position on Lay barge M-211. Not bad for a couple of 'Johnny Canucks'.

A bit about Dredge (Jet/Trenching) Barges.

Trenching barges are also called 'jet' or 'bury' barges. Their function is to excavate a trench for a pipe or cable in order to protect the pipe or cable from damage and stabilize it on the seabed.

The depth of the trench required can be anything from 0.5 m to 5 m (1-15') depending on the area. The infilling of the trench is normally left to the natural movements of the seabed.

The amount of infilling that eventually occurs varies with the area and the nature of the bottom. The sleds used to produce the trench differ considerably in design depending on the nature of the seabed conditions and the policy of the operator. They may use high pressure water jets with air-lifts, water extruder or a proprietary ploughing system. Divers may be needed to check the physical characteristics of the trench, the status of the pipe and sled, set the sled and assist with any problems that may arise.

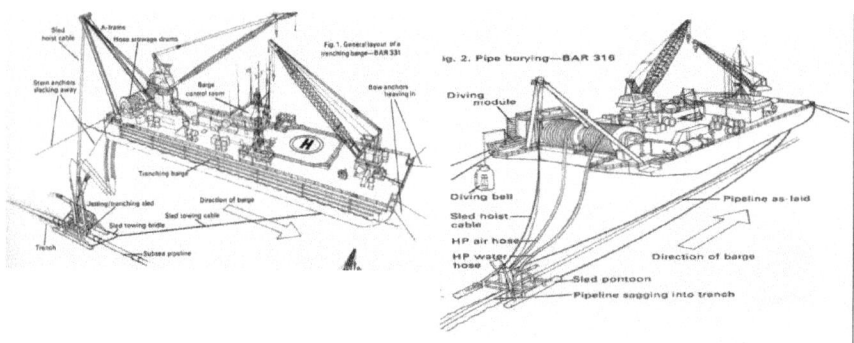

B&R Jet Barge BAR 331

B&R Bury Barge - BAR 316
Saturation Unit on the stern (Note: diving bell)

B&R Dredge (Jet) barge next generation.
Built in Rotterdam for NS pipeline jetting/trenching operations.
White arrow points to the jetting/trenching sled (claw) the size of a small two-story house.

The diver had to set/guide the sled over the pipeline by holding on to the bottom of the suction tubes and stand on the pipeline while the sled (small house) rotated up and down above him.

This is quite a dangerous operation, one wrong move and the diver could get hurt very quickly.

Joe Schouest lost half a hand while setting the claw in the North Sea (NS). And yes, guess who took his place and made the next dive.

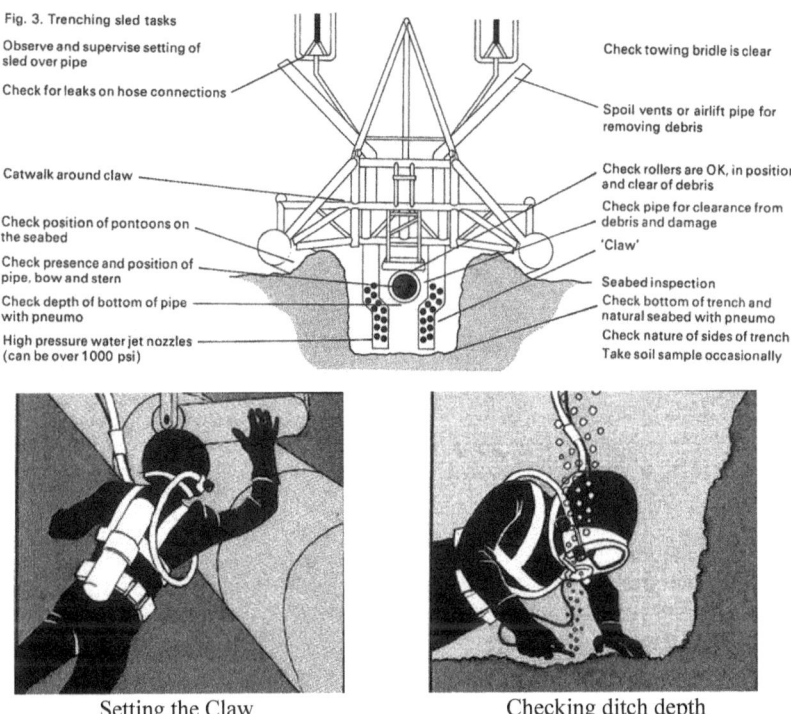

[Source: The Professional Divers Handbook – Submex Limited]

The M-228 was where I did most of my diving that year. This barge was a first generation bury barge and was sent to the NS the following year to bury the first offshore pipeline. Both the M-331 and M-316 would be introduced into NS operations thereby replacing the M-228. More on that later.

Back to GoM. Although I spent a fair amount of time diving on the M-228, I was still a call out diver and so got to do other diving jobs.

One of the more interesting ones was in the early part of April and Ted O and I were working the 'gator-infested swamps around Cameron, Louisiana. A 20 inch pipeline was being laid across ten miles of this treacherous marsh. The cement-coated steel pipe was welded together in 40 foot joints, snaked off the end of the barge and pulled by two marsh buggies through a flooded ditch.

To make the heavy pipe more buoyant and easier to handle, 55 gallon drums were strapped with steel bands. What an awesome sight this steel vertebrae monster presented, slithering across miles of endless swamp.

Once the pipe was fully laid, our job was to cut the barrels off allowing the pipe to sink to the bottom of the ditch and be buried. This was usually at one of the many bayou crossings, too deep for the marsh buggies, which criss-crossed the swamp in a devil's maze of water ways.

The swamp was part of the huge wildlife sanctuary in this area. The only thing that outnumbered the many different types of birds were the mosquitoes. And hardly a day went by that we didn't get to see the majestic head of a deer knifing through the surface of the water in its pursuit for dry land. They seemed about as much out of place here as we were. Of all the creatures that made this boggy mass their home, there was no doubt in anyone's mind who was the undisputed boss here and that was the damn 'gators.

Having spent the better part of two weeks in this varmint-infested paradise, we were in a hurry to get back to civilization. We didn't have that much smooth skin area left to offer these buzzing predators. We were hoping to finish up that day. With both of us in the water, it would be a snap. Cutting barrels is a relatively simple job, and one I was sure Ted could handle without any problem. However, we didn't count on his royal highness taking his family sunbathing and what better place than a 55 gallon drum. There they were, big as life, with their grotesque bodies draped over several barrels in the middle of the crossing, soaking up the rays. Well, first we kinda' eyed the 'gators, you know ... stare 'em down a little bit, then we looked at each other, then back at the 'gators, but looking wasn't going to move 'em, so with eyes as big as saucers, we both hit the water. He on one side of the crossing, I on the other. Both working toward the center and those damn 'gators. Ducking below the water, I became extremely aware of my feet dangling behind me. As was the case most of the time there was no visibility.

The sooner we got this over with the better. So I started cutting and barrels started popping to the surface. Somewhere around the middle, I felt something bump me. With a fright, I started up, shot out of the water and glanced frantically about me. There several feet away was Ted, my fear mirrored on his face. Then we both broke into a grin, realizing we had bumped into each other. With a sigh of relief, we gave the 'thumbs-up' signal that all was OK. Swimming back to the bank, I was thankful to be heading home and leaving that god-forsaken place with all extremities intact.

Another event in August which had a major impact on my life was a fire at Taylor.

I'd just come back to the shop, where I was still staying in the bunkroom, and noticed the place on fire. I went to check and see if everyone was OK. Mark and family still lived on the second floor.

Mark and his wife Henri weren't there, however their baby daughter Fredricka and maid Enola, were. I got them outta there and took them to George Morrissey's house.

Once the fire was put out, I spent the rest of the night stationed in the doorway to the apartment to ward-off any intruders. Mark & Henri were most appreciative.

The major damage was downstairs at ground level and to the bunkroom.

Time to look for new accommodation. Linden and I salvaged whatever we could and moved into the Imperial House Apartments.

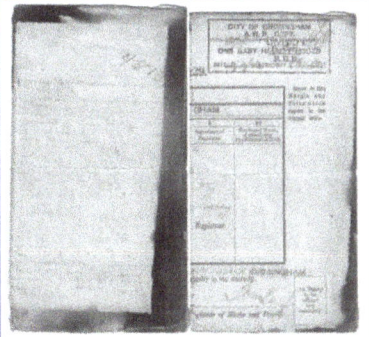

My scorched birth certificate is the only reminder left.

Imperial House Motor Hotel and Apartments
North Causeway Boulevard, Metairie, Louisiana
Greater New Orleans newest Motor Hotel located just fifteen minutes from famous French Quarter
Restaurant – Rooftop Cocktail Lounge – Swimming Pool
Luxurious Rooms and Suites

'A' - Lower level corner apartment facing pool – 4 graduate nurses
'B' - Lower level corner apartment facing pool – 2 horny divers
[Source: Postcard]

Also moving into another apartment was Buddy Eglin and Frank Brock. We all had one good time! Little did we know back then how famous or infamous the place would become:

US Court of Appeals for the Fifth Circuit - 478 F.2d 1171 (5th Cir. 1973) May 15, 1973

Appellants "Frenchy" Brouillette and Joan Clemens were convicted of violating 18 USC § 1952. This section prohibits the use of interstate commerce in promoting, establishing or managing an unlawful activity.

In this appeal, Brouillette and Clemens challenge the validity of a search warrant under which certain items, later admitted into evidence against them, were seized. After careful consideration of their claim, we are compelled to agree and must remand this case to the district court for a new trial.

The Factual Setting

Mr. Brouillette and Ms. Clemens are allegedly the "managing partners" of a prostitution ring headquartered in Metairie, Louisiana. While it seems virtually admitted that they indeed operate in the "world's oldest profession", the question in this federal prosecution centers on the commission of a federal, rather than a state, offense. To bring the appellants within the grasp of federal authorities, the government alleges that they have caused, or perhaps more accurately aided and abetted, one of their "girls" to "attend" a convention in New York City and there to ply her trade.

In the process of preparing its case, the government sought and obtained a search warrant for Apartment 224 at the **Imperial House Motor Hotel in Metairie, Louisiana**. *This location was the alleged nerve center of the prostitution ring's operations. A search warrant for the above address was signed on April 8, 1971. The federal agents duly executed this warrant on April 12, 1971 and seized a number of items allegedly used in furtherance of the prostitution activities. These items included various address books and files, bankbooks, pictures, and documents. Many of these items were introduced against appellants at trial.*

Diving continued at the normal hectic summer pace. The 'shop' was only about five minutes from the apartment. If your pager was working and you didn't get a page – might be time to look for another job. Out in the Gulf work was going full bore until…

Hurricane Betsy slammed into New Orleans on the evening of September 9, 1965. 110 mph (180 km/h) winds and power failures were reported in New Orleans. The eye of the storm passed to the southwest of New Orleans on a north-westerly track and hit the New Orleans area from about 8pm until 4am the next day. Hurricane Betsy was, for its time, the costliest and deadliest hurricane in US history. As the first hurricane with damages over a billion dollars, it earned the nickname "Billion-Dollar Betsy." It killed 76 people in Louisiana.

Prior to Betsy's arrival preparations were being made offshore:
- the dredge barge M-228, which I was working on at the time, pulled up the jet sled getting off the pipeline and out of the trench and headed for protected water.
- the pipelay barge M-211 'ran out' from under the pipeline and laid it and the pontoon on the bottom.

Ashore preparations were also being made – filling bathtubs full of ice, booze, water, whatever, taping and boarding windows and sliding glass doors, bringing in from outside anything that could get blown away. But most important of all was to find out where the best 'hurricane party' was gonna be.

The nurses knew of one that was in the French Quarter across the street from Jackson Square and next to St Louis Cathedral where I parked – should be pretty safe. We spent the night drinkin', gettin' to know our neighbours better, and listening to Betsy raise hell outside.

We spent the night on the second floor across from Jackson Square

Damage down river – houses washed up on the levee

By 8am things had settled down so it was time to take a ride, pick up something to eat and check out the apartments.

I must have picked a sweet spot to park. Mine was the only car amongst many that didn't have any broken glass. When the hurricane came through, it pulled a vacuum and sucked in just about every car window. Luckily, I'd left one of my windows slightly open – didn't even get rain damage. On the drive back the only place open was 'Crystal Burgers' (25 cents). There were damaged trees all over the road but not too much flooding.

All was fine back at the apartment and I started dating one of the nurses, Mary Lee Couvillion.

Once things had settled down, it was back to work again. Needed to get the pipeline and stinger off the bottom and connected to the stern of the barge M-211.

I was on the bottom connecting a shackle and crane sling to the stinger eye pads. This is all done by feel. The GoM may have some of the prettiest and clearest water in the world but 10-15 ft from the bottom down it's just a muddy cloud – NO VISIBILITY.

The Pressure Zone by Mike Cooke

With my hand wrapped around the wire splice the barge surged, the sling shot up – I was left with a 4 inch gash down to the tendons in my left palm. Just another palm lifeline I still have today.

I got another morphine pill from George Morrissey and another ride to the hospital. This time my diving tender, Larry Huff, did the driving. What is it with hurricanes and the M-211? Two accidents, two hurricanes, same barge.

After getting stitched up, I wouldn't be working for a while so Larry and I headed to Montreal for a couple of weeks. It was time to put my new car, Pontiac GTO, to the test.

Back in New Orleans, Karl Bock (who lived in the apartment next door) and worked for James Dean Diving, was involved in the salvage of a barge of chlorine that sunk in the Mississippi River just south of downtown Baton Rouge during Hurricane Betsy.

The hat (helmet) he's wearing is a Joe Savoie original. I never did get the chance to own one. Also on that job was another Canadian Navy Clearance Diver – Jim Onion (the class before ours – I didn't catch up with Jim until 1969).

Karl Bock of New Orleans climbs from the Mississippi River after another dive to prepare the lifting harness for a barge of chlorine that sunk in the Mississippi River just south of downtown Baton Rouge during Hurricane Betsy

[Source: East Baton Rouge Parish Library]

When we got back to NOLA, it was getting close to Christmas and the weather was starting to pick-up in the GoM. Not much offshore diving, with just the odd inshore call out job.

That year I made some good friends and contacts and a decent diving reputation. According to George Morrissey – 'he can be counted on'.

Also met another one of my mentors – Tom Duncan – a first class character. Taught me a few things about life – like, his wonderful saying, "if you ain't got class, you ain't got shit". Tom was a good 20 years older, and a whole world wiser. Picture a guy that had a moustache and gut like Pancho Villa, with two inches of crack showing above his jeans and a pair of size 13 black brogans. This was a guy that made life interesting.

Got to make friends with some good barge hands (crew) especially on the M-228: Barge Supt Johnny 'Bear Track' Clawson; The Natchitoches 4: Joe 'Rollie' Perot, Billy Smith, 'TT' Hicks and Jack McBride.

Didn't work on the M-228 that winter (1965/66) as it was undertow to the North Sea. I would join it in England where I'd catch up with everyone.

That winter I got engaged.

Meanwhile, the US Navy was proceeding with their saturation diving programme with the introduction of Sealab II.

1965 - Sealab II

SEALAB II was launched in 1965, and unlike SEALAB I, it included hot showers and refrigeration. It was placed in the La Jolla Canyon off the coast of Scripps Institution of Oceanography/UCSD, in La Jolla, California, at a depth of 205 ft (62m). On August 28, 1965, the first of three teams of divers moved into what became known as the "Tilton Hilton" (Tiltin' Hilton, because of the slope of the landing site).

Each team spent 15 days in the habitat, but aquanaut/astronaut Scott Carpenter remained below for a record 30 days. In addition to physiological testing (described in the book by Radloff & Helmreich), the divers tested new tools, methods of salvage, and an electrically heated drysuit. They were aided by a bottlenose dolphin named Tuffy from the US Navy Marine Mammal Program.

Aquanauts and Navy trainers attempted, with mixed results, to teach Tuffy to ferry supplies from the surface to SEALAB or from one diver to another, and to come to the rescue of an aquanaut in distress. There were plans for Tuffy also to take part in SEALAB III.

The first commercial saturation dives were performed by Westinghouse to replace faulty trash racks at 200 feet (61 m) on the dam in 1965.

[Source: Wikipedia – Smith Mountain Dam]

I would get to work with three members of that Westinghouse crew: Winston Chee, Engineer, Jerry O'Neill, Chief Engineer and Art Pagett, Diver.

1966

I knew I would be going overseas that summer but wasn't sure for how long, so do I or don't I get married? So who do I turn to for advice but none other than Mitch – "Hell, get married man, there ain't nothing else happening - now's a good time."

Got married on 16 April. Mitch was best man (Linden was doing his own thing in California). Mark hired a twin-engine plane and he, George and Mitch flew to the wedding. On the flight up to Marksville, one of the engines conked out. George started showing a little bit of concern when the pilot turned around and assured him in his best Cajun accent "Ma cher, I'm here too, ya."

Joe and Buddy also attended. It was the social event of the year – at least in Marksville.

Mary Lee's Dad, Bascom, roasting four 'Cochon de lait' (milk feed pigs)
The church is in the background

From 1964-66, I did quite a bit of diving in GoM. Mainly surface air, some mixed gas (HeO^2 – Helium/Oxygen) and open bottom bell bounce diving. Would not do any saturation diving until I got back from the North Sea in 1969.

1966 – 1968: North Sea

That summer, I signed my first 18 month overseas contract. We flew to London and caught the train to Great Yarmouth. I caught the crew boat out to the barge M-228 and my wife moved in with Paddy and Netta Mansfield until we could find a place of our own. Paddy, another ex Navy Master Diver, was Taylor's General Manager in Great Yarmouth. We would become close friends and he would be Godfather to my son Michael.

Taylor's facilities were in the Marine Base on South Denes Rd near the mouth of the River Yarre.

We were working on the first pipeline to be laid in open water in the North Sea. The B&R Hugh W Gordon (HWG) was the lay barge and the M-228 the bury barge.

A little North Sea History:

The North Sea (NS) lies between Great Britain, Scandinavia, Germany, the Netherlands, Belgium and France, on the continental shelf of northwest Europe. It is over 600 miles long and 360 miles wide. While in the southern NS, the ocean depth averages 30 - 150 ft, in the northern part, this increases to 650 ft. Along the Norwegian coast it plunges to 2,200 ft in the Skagerrak trench.

It experiences much harsher weather patterns than other areas traditionally worked by the offshore oil and gas industry.

Especially in the early years, the often-stormy conditions meant work was perilous and risky. Underestimating wave heights and unreliable information about NS climate patterns contributed to the dangerous conditions experienced in developing the region.

1965 - First well is drilled
BP discover gas. Conoco's first fixed platform in the UK North Sea is set in 90 ft of water 50 miles off Great Yarmouth. The jack-up rig, Mr Cap, moves to Great Yarmouth.

1967 - Gas flows from Leman
The first gas comes ashore from the Leman field. Discovered in 1966 and in production by 1968, it remained the biggest offshore gas field in the world for the next 20 years.

During this time, Brown & Root increasingly used Taylor Diving. In 1968, Halliburton took over Taylor Diving and made it part of Brown & Root.

With that support, Taylor Diving was able to develop techniques such as saturation diving and hyperbaric welding and in the 1970s it became the largest diving company in the world.

> *The Birth of a North Sea Gas Industry*
>
> *In November of 1965, BP discovered a large deposit of natural gas at West Sole - 55 miles from Conoco's original drilling site - in UK waters off the southern coast of England. After several years of high hopes and false starts, the North Sea had finally yielded commercial quantities of hydrocarbons ...*

Brown & Root dominated offshore construction in the North Sea during this initial gas boom, building the bulk of the platforms required to produce this gas and most of the pipelines needed to carry it to markets onshore. The company boasted an impressive fleet built primarily in Holland for use in the North Sea, including the Global Adventurer, the *Atlas* and its sister vessel the *Hercules*, the *HW Gordon* (a pipelay, combination barge), the *M-228* (a bury barge built in the United States), the *BAR-279* (another bury barge), and five cargo barges. Indeed, until the early 1970s, Brown & Root enjoyed a near monopoly on the ownership of large modern construction vessels in the North Sea.

Moreover, the company brought to the region a solid reputation among the major oil companies active there, long experience in other offshore provinces, and the early presence established in its joint venture with Heerema. Even for a company as experienced as Brown & Root, however, the North Sea would bring special challenges.

[**Barges** I worked on].

That the North Sea was demanding and unforgiving was evident in the first flush of excitement brought by the discovery of the West Sole field ... The hard clay bottom and the rough waters of the North Sea also required improvements in pipeline laying equipment. George Brown said: "Some months we are able to work only three or four days. Any sea can get rough, but the North Sea lays it on. During one period we expected to lay forty miles of pipeline. We laid only nine." Brown & Root had to adapt to such conditions to maintain its traditional leadership in offshore pipelines in this new environment. One writer concluded in 1973 that Brown & Root had conducted "the lion's share of North Sea pipelaying." Hugh Gordon gave more personal testimony: "We tended to specialize more in the pipeline side than the offshore platform side. We did a lot of that, but we pushed the pipelines harder just because we liked it more."

In 1965, Brown & Root had laid a short pipeline from a loading terminal in the North Sea to a Shell refinery in Denmark, but the company's work at West Sole marked the first substantial North Sea pipeline work in the open sea. The 45-mile, 16-inch line from West Sole to the onshore facilities of the British Gas Council at Easington, East Yorkshire, lay under up to 105 feet of water ...

With the completion of this 16 inch trunk line, Brown & Root laid a 24 inch pipeline for almost 2 miles under the Humber River. The entire system delivered gas from West Sole field into the British Gas Council's existing onshore pipeline grid in the fall of 1966, marking the first commercial development of North Sea oil or gas ...

George Brown acknowledged that burying [the pipelines] was non-negotiable in the North Sea: "The pipelines must be buried to avoid ocean travel in that shallow water. The minute rough weather comes, boats drop anchor and the anchors drag right over the pipelines. So we have to dig a ditch on the floor of the sea and bury the lines."

[Source: *Offshore Pioneers* – Brown & Root. Extracts from pages 212- 217]

The sea bottom was proving to be difficult for dredging operations with many sections of stones, gravel, pebbles and shells. A lot different from the silty clay bottom of GoM. The bury barge M-228 was too small for the NS and its trenching equipment didn't cope well with the harder clay bottom of the NS. Needless to say, the water jet cutting of a ditch was having its toll on the jet sled (claw). We were pulling into Grimsby on a regular basis to undertake repairs and seek shelter during foul weather. Just about anything from force 6 and above on the Beaufort Scale. During the laying of the pipeline in the rough sea conditions it got buckled, requiring a number of flange repairs.

While repairs were being undertaken there wasn't much diving needed so we got to spend some time ashore.

My wife would catch the train and come up to Grimsby where we would get to spend some time in the seaside town of Cleethorpes at the Kingsway Hotel.

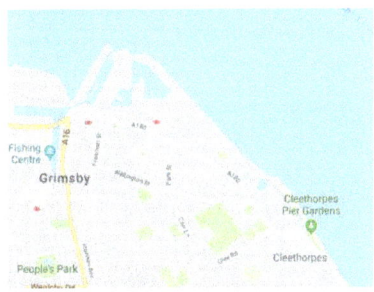

Kingsway Hotel - Circa 1965

If we were going to be in port for several days, we (Joe 'Rollie' Perot) and I would rent a car and drive to Great Yarmouth. I was in good hands. Rollie was the barge Superintendent – the guy in charge – if he said jump, you said 'how high?' and if he said shit you replied, 'how much and what color?'

Pictures of the first pipeline to be laid in open waters North Sea:

Pipe being welded on HWG

Pipeline leaving stern of barge, going down the pontoon

Pipeline pulled ashore, lay barge in background

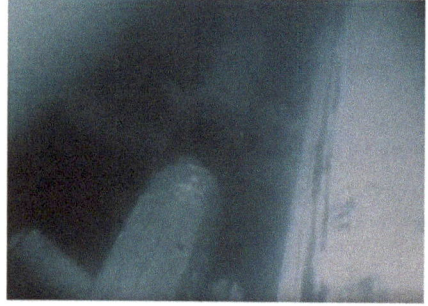 

Pipeline underwater in the pontoon

Taylor barge diver (Vic Becker?)
- checking pipe and pontoon

Note: Jack Browne (Desco) air mask

I was on bury barge M-228 when these photos were taken.

Offshore Ship in heavy storm, North Sea [Source: You Tube]

Me on the stern of bury barge M-228 getting ready to check the ditch and West Sole pipeline for possible buckles. Note: Jack Browne (Desco) air mask with Landry Radio (communications) on post.

My tender Pete Bradley helping me out of the water after setting the claw. Note: white water turbulence caused by airlift suction.

It's a small world - Pete Bradley, my first UK tender, happened to be from Bedford and lived at No 10 The Embankment, which was directly across the River Ouse from St Mary's Abbey, where I first lived.

Stoppin' for a cuppa

Barge M228 'claw' at stern

The Pressure Zone by Mike Cooke

Had to stay occupied during rough weather. So while Linden was up in Cook Inlet, Alaska, working for Taylor, my artistic talent got flowing:

    WHERE EVER THERE IS WATER
        AND A JOB TO BE DONE
    THE NORTH SEA DIVER
        IS SECOND TO NONE

    WETHER THE DEPTH BE 4 OR 400
        YOU CAN COUNT ON US
    TO GIVE THE VERY BEST
        WITH A MINIMUM OF FUSS

    WE'VE TRAVELLED THE WORLD OVER
        LIKE WAVES ON THE SEA
    AND THERE IS NOTHING WE CAN'T DO
        TO A CERTAIN DEGREE, NOT A DEGREE

    FROM THE "SEVEN SEAS"
        AND OTHER NOTABLE PLACES
    WE'VE GATHERED A CREW
        OF QUITE REMARKABLE FACES

    NO JOB IS TO GREAT TO HANDLE
        FOR THIS WELL SKILLED BUNCH
    THE ONLY THING WE ASK FOR
        IS A "TOT" BEFORE LUNCH

    HAVING HEARD FROM ALASKA
        ABOUT THE CURRENT AND THE COLD
    THEY MAKE IT SOUND ROUGH
        BUT WHAT ABOUT THAT GOLD

    TO OUR BUDDIES IN THE NORTH
        THE SOUTH, EAST, AND WEST
    WE CAN'T HELP BUT SAY
        WE THINK WE'ER THE BEST.

The artwork above ended up on the outside end of our deck decompression chamber.

TDS Offices – North Sea Area

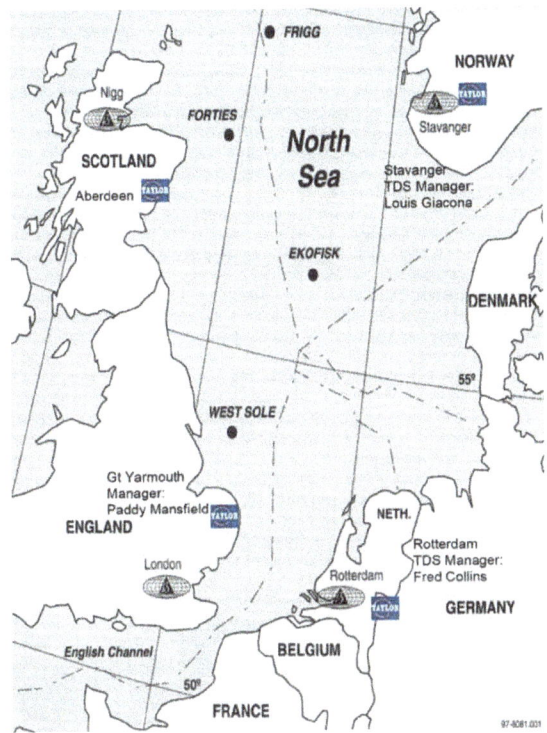

It wasn't all work and no play. That first winter, I probably spent as much time ashore as I did at sea. It was enough time to get settled in and rent a house on Beccles Road just outside of Great Yarmouth on the way to Burgh Castle.

Great Yarmouth was a great spot, a great location, great times and AWESOME memories.

Marine Parade – Great Yarmouth

The Tower was a hotel and casino complex. It was where we stayed my first night ashore in Great Yarmouth. It didn't matter if it was summer or winter, the weather seemed to be the same – cold! Needed a nice warm room and a nice warm bed.

The room was freezing, called the front desk and was told to put 20p in the room heater – 20p for 20 minutes which had to be renewed every time – welcome to England.

THE TOWER, MARINE PARADE   GREAT YARMOUTH

In 1965 the first offshore oil and gas wells were drilled off the coast of East Anglia. *American giant Conoco built their first fixed platform just 50 miles off Great Yarmouth and by 1967 gas was being piped ashore from the Leman field. The Duke of Edinburgh opened the Bacton Gas terminal in 1968. Senior company directors from Texas and the Gulf of Mexico virtually took over Great Yarmouth, bringing the mighty dollar and prosperity in their wake.*

Over the following year over 10,000 American families settled in the Great Yarmouth area. Although everyone struggled to understand each other's accents, the incomers brought with them many benefits but especially business. The region was booming.

With money to spend and time on their hands, they were keen to discover the tourist hotspots of London, Cornwall, the Lakes and especially Shakespeare Country ... Everyone in Great Yarmouth hoped the oilmen and their deep pockets were there to stay.

[Source: Web. © Escaping Hitler by Phyllida Scrivens 2016]

When not working and spending time ashore our favourite meeting place was Molly's Bar at the Carlton Hotel.

Paddy Mansfield and Buddy Eglin would each marry a receptionist from the Carlton and Joe Schouest and Alan 'Crazy Al' Anderson also married local girls.

> One time we were working on some pipelines that connected a gas field off the coast with a terminal at Bacton, a small village just north of Great Yarmouth. As usual, whenever we got the chance to get ashore it was pull out all the stops and worry about the bills later.
>
> The Carlton Hotel was the best hotel in town had the necessary credentials for attracting the diving crowd.

Carlton Hotel

It was also a very proper hotel with a proper staff that wasn't quite certain what to make of these not so proper invaders who would order bathtubs to be filled with ice and stocked with champagne or for breakfast a case of Mateus and two dozen hard boiled eggs - peeled.

This type of carrying on certainly attracted attention and naturally stirred up the curiosity of the hotel staff as to what those crazy divers were going to do next.

The burden for finding out this information fell on the shoulders of a couple of cuties who worked on the reception desk and switchboard. As is the case in most hotels, the switchboard operator is usually the first to know about anything and everything. Well, the situation got to the point that you couldn't be sure of the privacy of your phone calls.

The girls still weren't sure how to treat us but they were finding out fast and for obvious reasons we just weren't getting the attention we'd been receiving in the past. Was the game up? No way! Just fall back and regroup. Something desperately needed to be done to get things back to the way they were, and Tom Duncan came up with a classic plan.

He sent himself a telegram, knowing full well that when it arrived the mystery and importance of it would have the girls in a fit. He was right, it hadn't been out of the messenger's hands and the receptionist was calling his room informing him of its arrival.

"Hello, Tom," came the sweet voice of the operator, "a telegram has just arrived for you, would you like me to have it sent up?"

"No, don't bother, I'll come down and get it when I get up," Tom replied casually.

Let 'em get a good bite on the bait and dangle a little bit.

"Are you sure, it seems terribly important" she stressed.

"Well, I'll tell you what, why don't you just go ahead and open it and read it to me?" he asked.

"Are you sure?" she asked excitedly.

"Sure, go ahead."

"Ah, it says, 'HI TOM WILL BE OVER FOR OPENING OF LONDON CLUB STOP KEEP EYE OPEN FOR FUTURE BUNNIES STOP SEE YOU IN TWO WEEKS STOP HUGH".

"Thanks hon, you can throw it away now."

"Er ... Tom...this ... ah...it's from ah, Hugh Hef ..."

Click, he hung up.

Attention? Did he get attention? Hell, after a stunt like that it was nothing but carte blanche and the best-looking broads for twenty miles around. Yep, you had to get up real early in the morning to put one over on Tom.

[Extracted from my original story]

The Playboy Club's history dates back to the swinging 60's and the legalisation of gambling in the UK after WWII. The club on Park Lane was the first in Europe - opening in 1966.

The hotel was also the gathering spot for many of the singing and acting personalities that performed in town during the summer, at places like Wellington Pier and Winter Palace which were just across the road from the Carlton.

Wellington Pier

One of the special guests was popular singer, the attractive Anita Harris who naturally wanted to stay in a suite. As it would happen, Joe was already checked into the suite she was interested in. Mr Chittleborough asked Joe if it was alright to show Ms Harris the suite. He said sure, go ahead.

Ms Harris looked around, found it to her satisfaction and said she'd take it. Mr Chittleborough asked Joe if that was OK for Ms Harris to move in. Joe naturally agreed.

Mr Chittleborough said he'd fix Joe up with another room. Joe replied, "Whoa, hold on a minute I'm not going anywhere, if she wants to use this suite she's more than welcome to move in." Sadly for Joe, she refused his offer.

Another guest who stayed at the hotel was well known comedian Benny Hill who was performing at The Wellington Pier. He and Tom hit it off from the start, both being fun loving characters, with the same sense of humour and love of life.

Benny was scheduled to do some filming in the countryside and Tom thought it might be a good idea to surprise him with a visit on location. The Surprise – buy a case of Mateus Rose, 50 plastic cups and rent a helicopter. Buddy called me and asked if I wanted to join him and Tom. Of course, I agreed. Little did I know at the time, Buddy and I would be sharing the cost of the chopper. Hell, Tom never had any money.

So we rented a chopper. Three passengers, a case of wine and 50 plastic cups! We were certainly doing it with style. Like Tom always said "If you ain't got class, then you ain't got shit".

We flew out to the village and landed in the local church yard. Asked a couple of amazed locals if they knew where the filming was taking place. "It was right here but they left awhile ago". They were shooting to take advantage of the early morning light. Bugger.

By the time we got back to the hotel, Benny Hill was sitting very comfortably in the lounge chatting with Mr Chittleborough.

The Pressure Zone by Mike Cooke

Benny could not believe the story we had to tell - he was amazed that we'd do something like that. Well at least we didn't have to pay for any beers that night.

Much as I liked Great Yarmouth, it was not my idea of a summer resort. The postcards of the beach showed girls in skimpy bikinis but if you looked a bit closer, everyone in the background was rugged up in overcoats and parkas.
OK, did we do any work? Heck yeah, a lot. From June '66 through November '68, I spent a lot of time offshore. This was all air diving in wet suits, comprising a vest, 7mm long johns with jacket plus a 3mm jacket on top of that and you still got cold. Because of the strong currents, most diving occurred during slack (high/low) tides with a change approximately every 6 hours and a dive window of 1-2 hours.

The type of work consisted of dive support for pipe lay barges, pipe bury barges and derrick barges. Pipeline installation, pipe burying, pipeline and ditch inspection and pipeline repair (bolted flange).

The largest dive crews were needed during pipeline repairs:
- the buckled (damaged) pipe had to be physically located
- concrete removed with high pressure water jet blaster and
- the pipeline cut using underwater burning
- each section was then brought to the surface to have a flange half welded to each end, then placed back on the bottom to be bolted together.

This required a lot of diving time in and out of the water. Diving on the tide, surface decompression, get something to eat, hit the rack (bunk) for 1-2 hours, up again for the next tide, standby diver and supervise.

Initially this was just a 4 diver/4 tender crew. Constant work and no rest was taking it's toll. We contacted Paddy, Taylor General Manager, in Great Yarmouth, and he came out with Carl Goring and Frank Brock, who would become full shift (12 hours on/12 hours off) diving supervisors in charge of diving operations.

It was on one of these shifts, after a repetitive dive, that my right leg cramped and I stumbled while heading to the chamber for decompression. The bends – could be. Paddy treated me for it and the whole dive crew got 24 hrs off – no diving, needed the rest big time. After that, all 4 diver/4 tender dive crews had a supervisor.

One of my most memorable moments occurred when I was diving off the bury barge and the dredging operation came to a complete stop. The pressure gauges were reading high and the barge was unable to move forward. On checking the sled and pipeline, I discovered they were wedged up against an unexploded WWII bomb. After cautiously removing the claw and having the barge move off to one side, the Royal Navy was called in to remove and explode the bomb. This little incident provided more diving work for us.

Now, in addition to checking the dredging progress and trenching depth and cover, we had to walk ahead of the claw to check to make sure there were no bombs in the way. This walking (diving) the pipeline was done from one of the barge tugs and was commonly referred to as 'live boating'.

The tug wasn't stationary - it was under power the whole time, which made life interesting. There was another benefit of checking ahead of the dredging. We could not only check the pipeline for armaments, but big lobsters liked to hide underneath the curve of the pipe on the bottom. A few of which would end up on board for dinner.

April '67, Linden & Greta get married in Algiers, LA.

Taylor Diving undertakes first saturation dive in St Lawrence river, Montreal, Quebec. My hometown and I'm stuck in the NS. It was also the year of 'Expo 67'.

1968

Possibly one of the most dangerous jobs at that time in the NS was setting the claw.

The diver had to set/guide the sled over the pipeline by holding on to the bottom of the suction tubes and stand on the pipeline while the sled (the size of a small house) rotated up and down above you.

One wrong move and the diver could get hurt very quickly.

Joe Schouest lost half a hand while setting the claw. And yes, guess who took his place and made the next dive. I just happened to be on beach enjoying a little R&R when Paddy Mansfield called and said they need you out on the barge to set the claw – Joe's had an accident.

After a choppy ride out to the barge I got on board and Joe Perot was waiting for me. He said "Hope you can set this thing."

"It's a bit choppy" I said.

"Crawfish" he said "there's a very thin line between caution and chicken shit."

Next thing I know I'm in the water, setting the claw.

Linden & Greta also moved to Great Yarmouth.

(L-R) Dinner at the Carlton Hotel with Linden, Greta, Mary Lee and me

Another of the Taylor fraternity living in Great Yarmouth was Jim Pickle Nicholson. He was a fairly religious fellow and he and his wife would take their young son to church on a regular basis. Sitting down in the front one day, his son looked up at the crucifix on the wall and asked his Dad about it.

"Dad, what's that up there?"

Jim, in a quiet voice explained about Jesus and the crucifixion. His son sat there quietly, staring at it. The Priest got up and started the sermon. Halfway through, Jim's little boy yelled out:

"Jump, Jesus jump!"

His interjection was roundly appreciated by the whole congregation.

Diving work was increasing with more pipelines being laid, buried and repaired. Work as usual. However, I spent enough time ashore for my wife to become pregnant. Fortunately, as fate would have it, my 18 month contract would be completed in November. We were able to return to the States just in time for my son Michael to be born (16 November), one week after returning. Mary Lee had to promise the airline she would not have the baby mid-flight.

1969 - *SEALAB III*

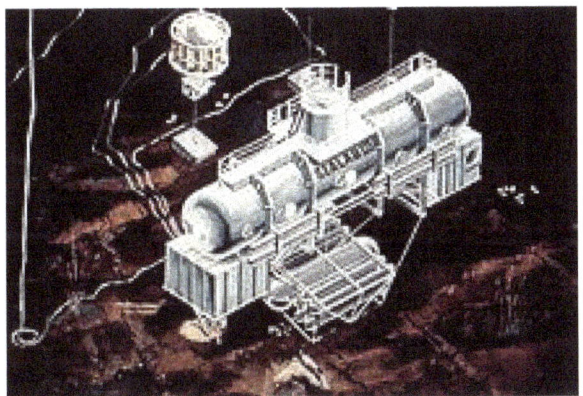

SEALAB III, artist's impression

SEALAB III used a refurbished SEALAB II habitat, but was placed in water three times deeper. Five teams of nine divers were scheduled to spend 12 days each in the habitat, testing new salvage techniques and conducting oceanographic and fishery studies. Preparations for such a deep dive were extensive. In addition to many biomedical studies, work-up dives were conducted at the US Navy Experimental Diving Unit at the Washington DC Navy Yard. These "dives" were not done in the open sea, but in a special hyperbaric chamber that could recreate the pressures at depths as great as 1,025 ft (312 m) of sea water.

According to John Pina Craven, the US Navy's head of the Deep Submergence Systems Project of which SEALAB was a part, SEALAB III "was plagued with strange failures at the very start of operations". On 15 February 1969, SEALAB III was lowered to 610 ft (190 m) off San Clemente Island, California. The habitat soon began to leak and four divers were sent to repair it, but they were unsuccessful. On the 17 February during the second attempt, aquanaut Berry Cannon died. It was found that his rebreather was missing baralyme, the chemical necessary to remove carbon dioxide. Surgeon commander John Rawlins, a Royal Navy medical officer assigned to the project, also suggested that hypothermia during the dive was a contributing factor to the problem not being recognized by the diver.

The SEALAB program came to a halt, and although the SEALAB III habitat was retrieved, it was eventually scrapped. Aspects of the research continued, but no new habitats were built.

[Source: Wikipedia]

A summary of the development of the US Navy's saturation program follows:

The Sealab undersea habitats were groundbreaking experiments conducted by the Navy between 1964 and 1969. Navy scientist Dr George F Bond developed and led the Sealab projects to test and demonstrate the concept of saturation diving. Bond's experiments with saturation diving were born from a desire to improve the length and efficiency of deep sea dives.

While divers work underwater, their body tissues fill with atmospheric gases that can cause decompression sickness if they do not allow the gases to safely leave their tissues through decompression. Divers using surface-supplied breathing systems often had to spend many hours decompressing after only minutes of bottom work time. Bond postulated that after 24 hours at a particular depth, a diver's tissues would saturate with atmospheric gases, capping the amount of decompression time the diver required. Divers could thus remain underwater for days or weeks and still decompress for the same amount of time. Bond proposed the idea of saturation diving in 1957 and conducted a series of laboratory experiments over the next six years to establish gas mixtures and decompression schedules. These controlled experiments culminated with Project Genesis, which applied Bond's findings to human subjects.

The next step was to demonstrate the viability of saturation diving in a non-controlled environment. Under Bond's supervision, in July 1964, four aquanauts spent nine days at 192 feet living in and working from Sealab I off the coast of Bermuda. The divers conducted extensive oceanographic research, returning to the pressurized 40ft by 9ft habitat between tasks, before an approaching hurricane truncated the exercise. The success of Sealab I established saturation diving as an efficient method of working underwater.

Sealab II was designed and built at Hunter's Point Naval Shipyard in San Francisco. Fifty feet long with a 12-foot diameter, it contained four separate areas: an entry, a laboratory, a galley, and living spaces. The redesigned exterior of Sealab II featured two end bells that were fashioned through explosive metal shaping, a very technologically advanced method at the time.

After a one-inch thick piece of flat steel was placed over the concave side of a dome-shaped die, one hundred pounds of C-4 plastic explosive were attached to the steel. The C-4 was detonated at 30 feet underwater in the San Francisco Bay, forming each end bell in 0.004 seconds.

Sealab II was designed to work at a similar depth as the first Sealab, but extended the length of the aquanauts' stay and expanded the type of work they performed.

Between 28 August and 14 October 1965, three teams of 10 divers spent 15 days each at 205 feet off the coast of La Jolla, California. Aquanauts tested underwater tools, raised a sunken fighter jet, conducted geological studies, set up a weather station, and worked with a porpoise trained to carry tools and messages between the habitat and the surface.

The Sealab II structure was modified to operate at a greater depth for the third Sealab experiment. Rated for 600 feet, the habitat was lowered to the ocean floor off San Clemente, California, in February 1969.

The project came to an abrupt halt after experienced aquanaut Berry Cannon died of carbon dioxide asphyxiation while repairing a helium leak underwater. The tragedy put a swift end to Sealab III and other saturation diving experiments.

Despite this terrible accident, the Sealab projects conclusively demonstrated the principle of saturation diving and its potential application in Navy (and civilian) underwater operations. The Navy went on to create saturation diving systems like the transportable Mark I fly-away system and the more sophisticated Mark II system with personnel transfer capsules and deck decompression chambers. Today, they continue to advance saturation diving techniques through ongoing research programs at the Navy Experimental Diving Unit and the Navy Submarine Medical Research Laboratory.

[Source: US Naval Undersea Museum website @ https://navalunderseamuseum.org/endbell/]

The Sealab saturation programme consisted of three teams.

I later worked at Taylor with a number of members of the Sealab programme: including Bob Barth, one of the four members of Sealab I and the only diver in all three experiments; Sandy Manning (Sealab I); Charlie Coggeshall and Billy Meeks (Sealab II); and Frank Reando and Don Risk (Sealab III).

In the navy, I also worked with Bill Lukeman and Mike Lafontaine, Canadian Navy clearance divers who were members of the Sealab III team (photo page 43).

This was the end of direct US Navy involvement in the development of saturation diving, which was then taken up by the commercial diving industry.

Chapter Four 1969
Saturation Diver

> *"We stand today on the edge of a new frontier"*
> [President John F Kennedy Inaugural Address 1960]

1969 - The year I became a Saturation Diver

20 July 1969 is remembered in history as the date man first walked on the moon.

However, it wasn't the only frontier being challenged that day. While Neil Armstrong and his fellow astronaut were doing their lunar two-step in outer space, back on earth a group of daring aquanauts were intrepidly leaving their footprints on the ocean floor and challenging the limits of inner space.

I was onboard the M-280 in the GoM doing a saturation dive in support of a dry hyperbaric weld in 213 feet of water – the first time this had been attempted at such a depth.

The dives made in the azure blue waters of the Gulf of Mexico that historical summer would anchor in a new and exciting era – the commercial use of saturation diving.

This new technology, saturation diving, would allow man to work underwater at greater depths and for longer periods of time than previously thought possible. Unlike in the past where the duration of most dives was logged in minutes and hours at depths less than 100 ft, dives were now being recorded to depths greater than 1000 ft and lasting days, weeks and even extending to a month or more.

These dives were pushing the envelope for duration, depth and perseverance and just like any other risky ventures into the unknown, came with their own set of hazards.

It was a time when the world's seemingly insatiable demand and dependence upon petroleum products was forcing oil and gas exploration to the remotest locations on the planet. Of all the areas being developed, none was more challenging, demanding and treacherous than the rough, menacing, cold waters of the outer continental shelf. With the increasing demand for sub-sea energy, exploration was moving further and further offshore into deeper and deeper water.

Extracting oil and gas from reserves trapped many thousands of feet beneath the seabed requires large sums of capital, fleets of vessels, massive equipment and machinery, the latest technology and considerable daring. Although often overlooked, the success of many offshore operations depends on the assistance of divers. The commercial deep-sea diver has a key role in the quest for subsea energy. His is probably the most daring and demanding of all offshore occupations.

There is a saying among divers:

"There are old divers and there are bold divers, but there are no old, bold divers."

With the advance of technology, a new generation of complex diving equipment and sophisticated methods were being developed. The deep dive system and saturation technique were a part of this expansion allowing man to conquer the depths and cope with the increasing pressure.

It is difficult for someone who has never dived to imagine the dangers faced when one enters the alien environment beneath the sea surface. Dangers that multiply as the depth and pressure increase, posing an ever-greater threat to one's life.

This is a story about those dives and the divers, who lived, worked and sometimes died in the pressure zone……this is my story.

The above is part of my original draft that was put to paper over 40 years ago and was written in both long hand and typed during many saturation dives between 1969 and 1978.

Offshore Pioneers provides an excellent description and analysis of the development of saturation diving, particularly as it affected me, working with Taylor.

Saturation Diving – Taylor Diving

Saturation diving, pioneered by the Navy, proved to be a timely development for deepwater construction. It resulted in the spectacular growth of commercial diving. Following the Navy's celebrated "Sea Lab" tests in 1964, Taylor Diving developed its own saturation systems, built a new research facility, and extended the technology to record depths in the late 1960s and 1970s. Mark Banjavich's colleagues regard him as a "visionary" who appreciated the value of saturation diving. Anthony Gaudiano said that "he could see down the road that this technique could be put together and made commercially viable and a fair amount of revenue could be generated from it."

The distinction between conventional and saturation diving was a matter of depth and duration. In conventional diving, also known as "bounce" diving, a diver is on the bottom for a relatively short period of time (usually less than one hour) and then decompressed, which may require a period of several hours. Most working dives are completed in less than one-half hour. The 400 ft dives that Banjavich performed for the Navy off Panama in 1949, for example, lasted no more than about ten minutes, but required about twelve hours of decompression. Naval scientists discovered that body tissue becomes "saturated" with whatever gas a diver breathes at given depths for longer periods until the tissues cannot absorb any more. Because of the large quantities of gas absorbed and the slow rate that it can be expelled, decompressing a saturated diver requires much more time, a matter of days rather than hours. As a rule of thumb, a diver spent a day of decompression for every 100 feet of saturated depth.

Researchers found that the time to reach saturated condition decreased at greater depths. They calculated that saturation decompression was required after a diver spent about one hour at depths of 300 to 400 ft and after about one-half hour at depths of 400 to 600 ft. Thus, a diver who worked at these depths for any significant amount of time would need long periods of decompression.

Although decompression time did increase with the length of the dive, saturation diving offered important advantages. It permitted great economies in deep-water work by vastly increasing the ratio of bottom time to decompression time. Once a diver became saturated at a certain depth, decompression time remained the same regardless of time spent at that depth.

<u>As one engineer put it, "The decompression period is as long for two hours at 600 ft as it is for one year at 600 ft."</u> In deep water construction, particularly pipelining, saturation diving presented opportunities to do weeks of intensive work.

Banjavich said, "We never would have gone any place if we had not used saturation diving. We would have never progressed out into deep water. You had to get down there and had to be able to stay there, of course."

The US Navy had experimented with principles involving tissue saturation as early as the 1930s. In the early 1960s, the Navy's Sea Lab experiments, directed by Captain George Bond, verified saturation diving principles on both animals and humans.

In 1965, Marine Contractors Inc and Westinghouse Inc applied saturation diving for the first time commercially at Smith Mountain Dam in Virginia.

Taylor Diving: SDC mated to DDC

As their Gulf of Mexico dives were getting deeper and their jobs lasting longer, Mark Banjavich and George Morrissey sensed that saturation diving would be the wave of the future in the industry. So they designed a two-person diving bell or submersible diving chamber (SDC) that could be mated to a deck decompression chamber (DDC). This allowed divers to be transferred between the two while under pressure.

In operation, two divers were locked in the SDC, which was then pressurized to bottom pressure at a rate of 75 ft per minute. It was then lowered by winch to within a few feet of the bottom. The divers breathed through their helmets, which were fed a helium-oxygen gas mixture from the deck. The chamber was equipped with a carbon-dioxide scrubber and a heating unit to condition the environment and keep the divers comfortable.

Once on location, the divers opened a bottom hatch in the SDC and connected their breathing gear to special umbilical lines that led to the surface. Since the gas pressure inside the SDC equaled sea pressure, the interior of the SDC did not flood. One diver exited the SDC to go out and work up to three to four hours, which was a significant breakthrough in work time. The second diver tended the first diver's umbilical while inside the SDC.

The divers changed places and continued working for another three to four hours. "So, we were able to get an eight-hour shift out of two divers," Banjavich explained.

When work was completed, the SDC was winched to the surface and mated with the DDC, where the divers were replaced by two others. By using a six diver, three-team rotation, the group could put in 24 hours of continuous work for several days before they were all decompressed in the DDC. "The diving bell was just an elevator. It was always under the same bottom pressure." The SDC-DDC system offered significant improvements in saturation diving. SDCs allowed divers to work in rough weather and descend through strong currents without exposure. Working out of a controlled environment made possible greater depths and extended work time at the bottom. The Equitable Equipment Company out of New Orleans built the first partial saturation diving chambers for Taylor. They were used aboard Brown & Root's lay barge, the M-210. In the summer of 1967, Taylor made its first total saturation dives to install risers for Shell Oil's Marlin System at 320 ft in the West Delta field of the Gulf of Mexico.

"Everything, really, we had to develop as we went along because there was nothing available," said Banjavich. New problems were encountered as divers reached greater depths under prolonged conditions.

Life support systems on the diver and in the SDC had to be redesigned. "It was one thing to just take divers down to depth. It was another thing to keep them there and comfortable so they could work." The technological advances to permit humans to live underwater matched some of those that permitted habitation of outer space. "Just one was going under pressure, and the other was reducing pressure," pointed out Ken Wallace. "You had a lot of similar problems and life support activities, they were quite similar."

Using helium-oxygen mixtures at increased depths presented difficulties in keeping divers warm.

Because helium has a six-fold greater thermal conductivity than air, divers would be seriously affected by small variations in temperature. "Once you get beyond about 400 ft, the water is just above freezing," Banjavich said. "If you cannot keep those divers warm because the helium is such a conductor of heat or cold, in a matter of minutes, they're frozen out." Taylor Diving addressed this problem with heated suits. The company took the space suits designed for astronaut John Glenn's pioneering trip into outer space and modified them for inner space. Initially, the suits contained plastic tubing with perforated holes for ventilation. Later on, rubber tubing was attached to wet suits. Taylor simply pumped hot water (106 to 110 degrees Fahrenheit) from the surface into the tubes of the hot water suit. The water was heated and pumped with 250,000 BTU/hour heaters. It flowed through an insulated hose to the SDC, and then to the diver through his diving umbilical. The hot water suits worked fantastically well, allowing divers to spend many hours in cold water.

"By early 1967," wrote Ken Wallace, "rapid advances in saturation diving were being made almost on a monthly basis." With the increase in bottom working time, communications with divers became important. Helium atmospheres, however, often caused unintelligible speech transmissions. As anyone who has ever sucked helium out of a balloon can testify, the gas makes one's speech sound like the quacking of Walt Disney's cartoon character, Donald Duck. Radio and electronic communication systems employed by divers had evolved from homemade devices to laboratory designed underwater telephones.

In 1967, several electronics corporations researched the "Donald Duck effect," which led to the commercial development of helium voice "unscramblers" that became widely employed in the industry beginning in 1968.

During this period, Taylor Diving engineers improved atmospheric control capabilities in the saturation diving systems (DDCs). They designed environmental controls that enabled divers to live for extended periods in a saturated state.

The main lock in the DDC contained toilets, supply locks, bunks, and individual environmental controls. Each DDC had an external control house from which an operator could control power generation and pneumatics in the main lock. Constant monitoring of the gases inside the main lock was crucial.

At greater depths under hyperbaric conditions, the threat of gas contamination increased. "Very small contaminants of gases at depth which you could tolerate up here forever," noted Mark Banjavich, "would kill a person instantly at depth." The saturation systems were equipped with oxygen monitor/controllers to regulate oxygen levels. Under higher than atmospheric pressure, oxygen percentage had to be lowered to prevent damaging levels of oxygen in one's central nervous system. The effect is known as "oxygen toxicity." Air contains 21 percent oxygen, but under pressure equivalent to 200-foot depths for example, the oxygen level in breathing gas could not rise above 4 percent.

Temperature and humidity control also was mandatory. The Taylor units used cold water and hot water exchanger coils in the environmental control systems. The environment in the chamber was circulated over the coils to condense out excess water vapor and to reheat the gas to comfortable temperatures. Exhaled carbon-dioxide and other gases also had to be removed or "scrubbed out" of the atmosphere. "We scrubbed out everything, including personal body odors, with filters containing potassium permanganate and soda lime," remembered Banjavich. "We changed the whole atmosphere every three minutes."

Taylor engineers also designed an entrance lock through which medical personnel could enter the saturation system in case of emergencies. On one tragic but, in the end, fortunate occasion, an entrance lock on one of Taylor's systems saved a diver's life. That diver almost died when he carelessly opened the discharge valve on the commode while he was still sitting on it. The pressure of the discharge locked his buttocks onto the toilet and pulled several feet of small intestines out of him. The diver had been severely injured but could not be rushed to surface pressure because he was totally saturated at about 250 feet. Taylor officials found surgeons who were experienced in handling war casualites in Vietnam. They were quickly sent through the entrance lock and into the chamber to perform an operation. Because they were in highly controlled, hyperbaric conditions, no ether or anaesthesia could be used. The surgeons kept the diver alive for fifteen days while he was being decompressed. Miraculously, he survived to tell about it. The accident reminded everyone of the dangers of working in a highly pressurized, saturated environment at great depths.

(Note: see my comments about this incident later regarding Donald Boone).

It also stood out as an exception to Taylor Diving's remarkable safety record. As Banjavich told his people at the time, "If we're going to go into these deep waters, one thing that would kill the program is if you start injuring or killing people. You have to go to the nth degree of safety to make sure nothing happens."

In 1967-1968, as Taylor started making total saturation dives into deeper water, the company expanded rapidly, building up its research capabilities and training programs.

Saturation diving had demonstrated its utility and cost effectiveness to the offshore oil industry. In 1967, Gulf Oil officials estimated that in repairing two Gulf of Mexico production platforms in 210 feet of water, saturation divers required 33 percent fewer hours than surface divers would have, at a 36 percent cost savings.

In 1968, Mark Banjavich sold 80% ownership of Taylor Diving to Halliburton Company, Brown & Root's parent. The sale gave Taylor greater financial resources and organizational support to enlarge its personnel, equipment, and research.

Several individuals from the Naval Experimental Diving Unit (NEDU) joined Taylor, including Ken Wallace, a diving supervisor who would become Taylor's president, and Dr Robert D Workman, a Navy physiologist whom Mark Banjavich called the "grandfather of saturation diving." Workman had enjoyed a distinguished career with the US Navy Medical Corps. As head of the NEDU, he had developed the Navy's decompression tables. Banjavich, who was a close friend of Workman's, recruited the doctor first as a diving consultant and then convinced him to join Taylor full-time when Workman retired from the Navy in 1970. "Everyone was after him," said Banjavich. "He is the reason we could do these very, very deep dives ... the great safety record we had with the deep saturation diving was attributed directly to Dr. Workman and his expertise. He just controlled all the dives, all the experimental dives that we did."

Innovation in deepwater diving shifted from the NEDU to private industry - and to Taylor Diving. In 1968, Taylor began construction on its new world headquarters and underwater research facility at Belle Chasse, Louisiana, next to Brown & Root's pipe yard. Anthony Gaudiano said, "It was obvious from the feedback we got from Brown & Root, the pipe diameters [would] get larger and the water [would] get deeper. And this was going to happen very quickly." Taylor's depth simulator, the first not owned or controlled by the government, maxed out at 350 feet. They needed a facility that could push the limits of deepwater exploration. Completed in 1969, the research center housed a three vessel hyperbaric complex, described by the company as "the largest existing facility of its kind in the world."

It became the second depth simulator not owned by the U.S. government. The main vessel consisted of a "lower wet pot" and "upper igloo" capable of simulating wet and dry environments similar to those encountered undersea. Although initial research programs were planned to simulate dives under depth pressures of around 1,000 ft, the vessels were designed to withstand pressures equal to 2,200 ft. The Belle Chasse hydro-space research center became the site for state-of-the-art research into underwater diving that pioneered many stunning achievements in offshore construction in the 1970s.

[Source: Offshore Pioneers – Brown & Root pages 142 - 147]

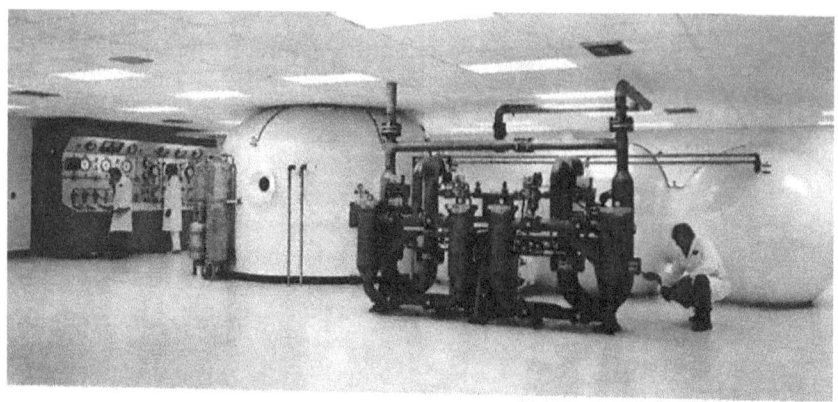

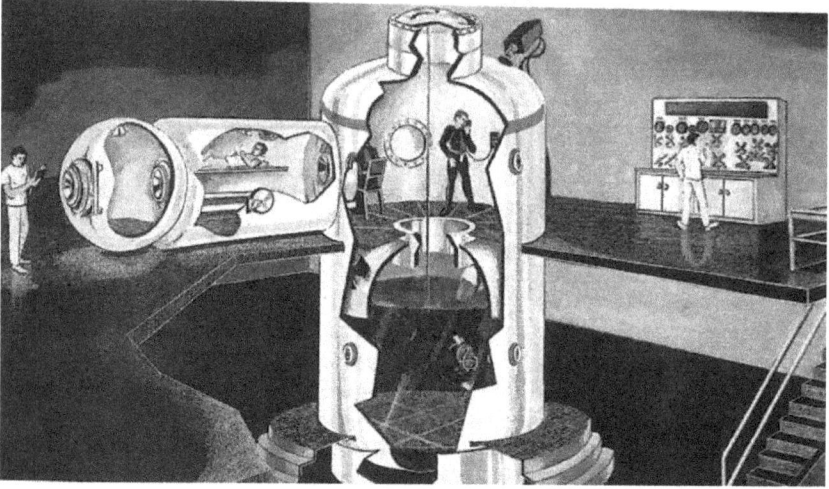

Taylor Diving's main research complex with control console, (Bob McArdle top far left talking to divers in chamber), igloo (top of wet and dry chamber – lower level), annex living compartment, and entry lock. In foreground are environmental controls.

The US Navy undertook a 1,600 fsw (488m) dive in 1973 in this complex which was then the world's largest hyperbaric facility.

I made a 1200 fsw (366m) (wet saturation dive) in this complex 3 - 20 December 1976.

The following is the abstract of a Research Report by Dr Robert Workman:
[Source: https://apps.dtic.mil/sti/pdfs/AD0620879.pdf]

U. S. NAVY EXPERIMENTAL DIVING UNIT

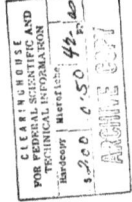  

U. S. NAVY EXPERIMENTAL DIVING UNIT
WASHINGTON NAVY YARD
WASHINGTON, D.C.

RESEARCH REPORT 6-65

CALCULATION OF DECOMPRESSION
SCHEDULES FOR NITROGEN— OXYGEN
AND HELIUM— OXYGEN DIVES.

PROJECT NO. SF-011-06-05

TASK NO. 11514, SUBTASK 5

BY

R. D. WORKMAN, CAPT, MC, USN

26 MAY 1965

SUBMITTED:

R. D. Workman

R. D. WORKMAN
CAPT, MC, USN
SUB. MED. RESEARCH

APPROVED:

C. H. Hedgepeth

C. H. HEDGEPETH
CDR, USN
OFFICER IN CHARGE

ABSTRACT

This report presents the theoretical basis for calculation of decompression schedules for nitrogen-oxygen and helium-oxygen mixtures used in diving. It includes definitions, theory of exponential saturation and desaturation, and theory of limiting values of excess saturation permitted at various ambient pressures with helium and nitrogen. An attempt has been made to simplify the presentation of the calculation procedure to implement the theoretical method. The necessary tables and worksheets used in calculations are presented, together with sample calculations of dive schedules. The discussion describes and appraises other methods of calculation developed in recent years.

I made my first saturation (Sat) dive in the summer of 1969 on B&R's Barge M-280. It was Taylor's first full saturation hyperbaric welding dive with a 7 man Sat crew (2 diver/welders – Archie Weiss and Lyle Stockdale, 4 Sat divers – Buddy Eglin and yours truly. I can't recall the other two – could have been Boyd Vassey and Fred Miller and a Sat tender - Pete Weichert, if memory serves me right.

With three 2 men crews we were able to provide 24/7 diving at a depth of 213fsw (65m). This would allow us to undertake approximately three 8 hour bell runs a day. That was ideal, however depending on the task, bell runs could take longer, say 10-12-14 hours. My longest bell run was 16 hours. I was the one qualified to take the pipe weld X-rays.

The films had to be sent topside for developing and approval – which all took time. Buddy and I thought this was a long bell run but we still had a while to go to beat Archie and Lyle's 22 hour bell run. They were the only qualified diver/welders.

> *In training individuals for hyperbaric welding, Taylor enjoyed the most success with welder-divers. "Underwater welding is a precise science that isn't quickly assimilated by every candidate," said Bob Dykes, training director for Taylor Diving, "so it helps to start with men who are already expert welders." Because pipelining was one of Brown & Root's special areas of expertise in the offshore industry, the company employed many excellent welders who were practically artists with the welding rod. Banjavich brought some of the more experienced welders into the company and "taught them the basics of diving, but always <u>kept experienced divers</u> with them* [the likes of Buddy Eglin, Fred Miller, Boyd Vasey, Linden and I were needed] *to keep them out of trouble." When Taylor started training welders for saturation diving, Banjavich confessed "I picked the best welders Brown & Root had" and offered the welders "huge sums of money, so they actually all wanted to come on." Construction managers at Brown & Root, understandably, resisted giving up their best workers to Taylor, but they relented in the spirit of mutual cooperation and common purpose. "The beauty ... between Brown & Root and Taylor," said Banjavich, "was how well we worked together as a family."*
> [Source: *Offshore Pioneers* – Brown & Root page 154]

During this Sat, while we were working in the habitat on the bottom, Hurricane Camille swept through and delayed the operation by 13 days. As a result, the total time from start to finish was 44 days, with 13 lost to Hurricane Camille when the barge headed for protected water and we were decompressed and sent ashore.

> *Hurricane Camille was the second most intense tropical cyclone on record to strike the United States. The most intense storm of the 1969 Atlantic hurricane season, Camille originated as a tropical depression on August 14, south of Cuba, from a long-tracked tropical wave ...*
>
> *Emerging into the Gulf of Mexico, Camille underwent another period of rapid intensification and became a Category 5 hurricane the next day as it moved northward towards the Louisiana - Mississippi region. Despite weakening slightly on August 17, the hurricane quickly re-intensified back into a Category 5 hurricane before it made landfall a half-hour before midnight in Bay St Louis, Mississippi.*
>
> [Source: Wikipedia]

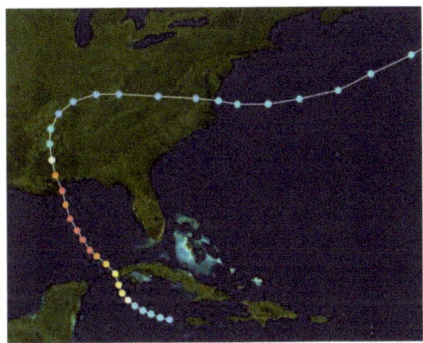
Hurricane Camille path

Barge location: Main Pass Block 298
[Source: Wikipedia

Hurricane Camille: Ships washed ashore

Running for shelter

Trinity episcopal Church: before

… and after

[Above four photos - Source: Times Picayune]

On 17 August 1969, 16 people took refuge from Hurricane Camille in Trinity episcopal Church in Pass Christian, Mississippi. After the storm, all but one perished.

[Source: Times Picayune]

I'd just bought a new house which luckily survived OK.

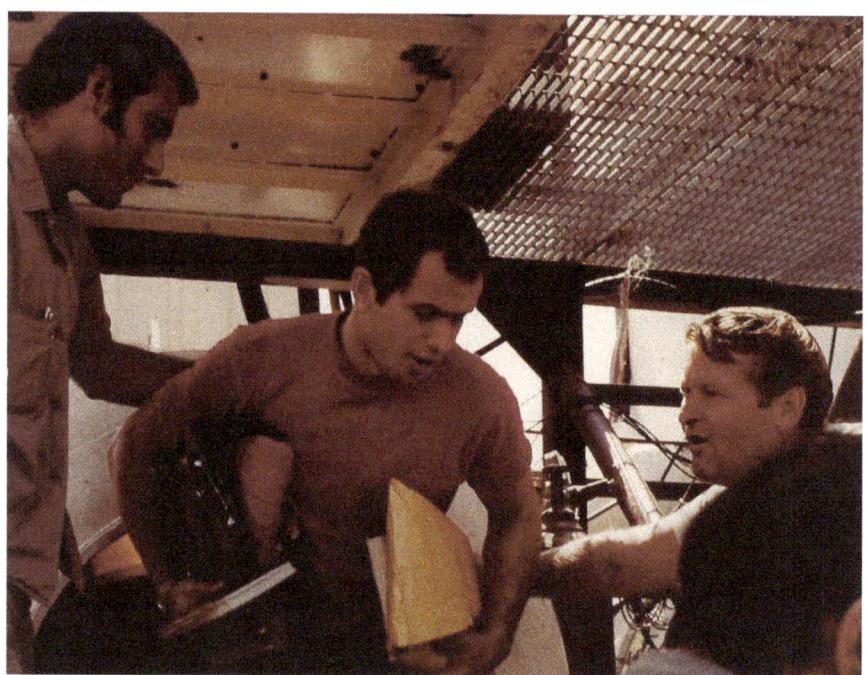

Reaching the 'surface' and leaving the chamber after my 1st saturation dive. Charlie Duff is on the right.

Charlie Duff played a major role in saturation diving during the next Sat dive on the M-280.

Charlie was at Taylor until my departure in 1985. We became good friends and were invited to his house many times – he made the best Italian meatball 'po-boy' sandwiches and had a fine collection of cars - a Studebaker Advanti and a classic Porsche 911.

A bit about Charlie.

> *The arrival of saturation diving led to the requirement for a new category of employee, the diving technician. Charlie Duff, the first and certainly one of the best qualified, arrived at Dick Evans Divers in the spring of 1968 having just retired from the navy. Duff had a background in medicine and nuclear submarines, he had learnt helium diving in first-class diving school and he had ended up at NEDU: just the sort of person McDermott needed. Evans put him on the payroll, but with the tri-sphere complex not yet complete he had nothing to do.*

> *After eight months of twiddling his thumbs, and needing something to occupy him, Duff accepted an offer from his former navy colleagues at Taylor. Almost immediately, he began going offshore, overseeing the divers in saturation from the control van and providing medical attention when needed.*

As he had done at NEDU, he made up his own medical kits, which contained everything he might need to treat a diving accident, including solutions for intravenous drips.

The most alarming accident Duff dealt with occurred on one of Taylor's early hyperbaric welding contracts. Daniel Boone, an experienced diver in his mid-thirties, was reading on the toilet in one of the chambers. The procedure for flushing the toilet was to open a valve, then knock on the chamber wall to signal for the opening of a second valve on the outside. Opening the second valve sucked the contents of the bowl into the holding tank, which was at atmospheric pressure. Except when flushing the toilet, the inside valve was to be kept closed, and instructions were posted in the chamber to that effect. Boone, however, failed to check the valve was closed. Either he called for a flush when he was still on the toilet, or more plausibly a diver in an adjoining chamber called for a flush and the tender flushed the wrong toilet. The toilets did not have seats, and although Boone was by no means overweight his bottom made a seal with the toilet, with the result that the violent pressure drop sucked out his small and large intestines.

Duff was on the barge but away from the complex. When he heard what had happened he locked into the chamber, which was pressurized to the working depth of 240 feet.

The divers had laid Boone down on his side, his intestines hanging out. He did not appear to be in extreme pain; mainly he seemed to be suffering from shock. Duff administered a sedative and called ashore for a surgeon. While he waited, he kept the intestines moist with a clean towel and saline solution.

Mark Banjavich, who was in his office, telephoned the company doctor, Dr Lynwood Carter, and told him to get hold of an ex-Vietnam War field surgeon experienced in operating under battlefield conditions.

Carter lined up Dr Victor Tedesco, and together they flew out by helicopter from the hospital where Tedesco worked.

When Carter and Tedesco locked into the chamber, they told Boone that unless Tedesco operated at once he was going to die. Decompression from saturation at 240 feet would take approximately 60 hours; he would not last that long. There would be no general anesthetic. With a piece of plywood across the bunks on either side of the inner lock for an operating table, they gave Boone an intravenous anesthetic to deaden the pain. Then cut him open from his breastbone to the top of his pelvis.

Thus was performed, by hand-held diving light, the world's first and only hyperbaric colostomy. (A partial colostomy in fact, since the colon was not removed. After decompression the colostomy was completed at a New Orleans hospital.) According to Banjavich, the operation was videotaped and subsequently reported in The American Journal of Medicine.

Surprisingly, Duff reported that as far as he knew Boone was never in any great pain during the ordeal. On the other hand, Dr Carter is said to have commented that it was the worst experience of his life.

After the accident. Taylor installed a seat on every chamber toilet, arranged so that it automatically closed the flush valve when it was put down.

[Source: The History of Oilfield Diving by Christopher Swann, pages 258-259]

The type of toilet was more like a urinal funnel in a similar shape to the photo (left). The seating area - having no toilet seat - made for a perfect seal.

Drawing at right showing toilets and valve positions.

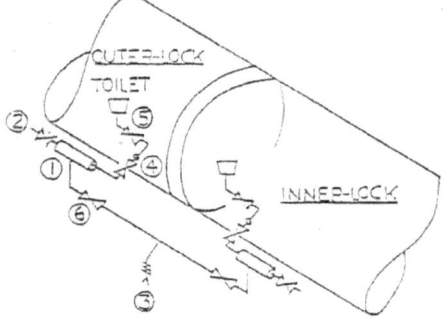

Valve type and disposal tanks for inner and outer lock

As in a case like this, there had to be a lawsuit somewhere, but it came from a surprising quarter:

> 341 F.Supp. 628 (1972)
>
> 2
>
> Linwood Hugh CARTER, Plaintiff,
>
> v.
>
> TAYLOR DIVING & SALVAGE COMPANY and Brown & Root, Inc., Defendants.
>
> 3
>
> Civ. A. No. 71-161.
>
> 4
>
> United States District Court, E. D. Louisiana, New Orleans Division.

5

March 29, 1972.

6

ALVIN B. RUBIN, District Judge:...

9

A doctor who suffered a heart attack as a result of his exertions in saving the life of a mutilated diver invokes the Good Samaritan doctrine. The question presented is whether the doctrine extends to injuries sustained only indirectly from the perilous situation by a professional who was compensated for attempting the rescue.

10

Boone, a deep-sea diver, was injured in part due to the negligence of his employer, Taylor Diving, and in part due to his own contributory negligence. Boone was one of a group of divers who lived in a pressurized tube, six feet in diameter, for seven days during the course of which they made deep-sea dives. Living in the chamber made it unnecessary for them repeatedly to adjust to pressure and to be depressurized. They ate and slept, rested and relaxed, in the chamber between dives. The chamber was aboard a barge in the Gulf, off the Coast of Louisiana.

11

While living in the chamber, the divers used a toilet that flushed to the outside. When the toilet was flushed, the lower outside pressure sucked the atmosphere from the chamber. To prevent escape of pressure as well as danger to the divers while using the toilet, the toilet was controlled by two valves. When the diver was ready for the toilet to be flushed, he opened the inside valve, and, using a two-way speaker, asked personnel outside the chamber to open the outside valve and flush the toilet.

12

On this occasion, Boone left the inside valve open when using the toilet. While he was on the commode, the toilet was unaccountably flushed from the outside. Boone was partly eviscerated, a portion of his anus was ejected, and his condition presented the likelihood of his death if there were not immediate surgical treatment.

13

After a first aid man entered the chamber and diagnosed the problem, Taylor Diving telephoned and then sent a helicopter for Dr. Carter, a physician who was expert in medical diving problems. Dr. Carter was 46 years of age, and, although he had suffered from cardiac problems for a number of years, he continued to offer his services for offshore cases ...

17

After viewing the preliminaries of the hospital operation, Dr. Carter went to another room in the hospital to have a cup of coffee. Shortly after he arrived, he suffered a heart problem, which was later diagnosed as early congestive heart failure, atrio-fibrillation, and physical exhaustion.

18

... Dr. Carter, who had previously been consulted by Taylor Diving, as well as by other companies in the diving business, had raised his fees to $100 per hour for medical services in his office; and $200 per hour for services outside his office, portal to portal, and an additional $100 per hour for all time spent in diving chambers. ...

35

It may be said that a humanitarian spirit would reach out to recompense the injured doctor. But dollars paid as balm for his hurt may not properly be extracted by the force of the law from the employer who did no negligent act toward him and who engaged him to save Boone without dickering on fee in advance. It may be said that the result of this case deters physicians from undertaking to render treatment, but it is evident that a contrary conclusion might well cause the employers of injured persons to hesitate before paying high prices to "Professional Samaritans" assuming known risks. It is the injured worker whose succor is society's first concern, and the result here will encourage providing aid to him without regard to the expense of experts' fees.

36

For these reasons, judgment will be rendered for the defendant.

After Boone's accident, I was part of the next Sat crew. Same chamber – safer toilets with new seats.

A Taylor saturation system ready for shipping (*Collection of Drew Michel*)

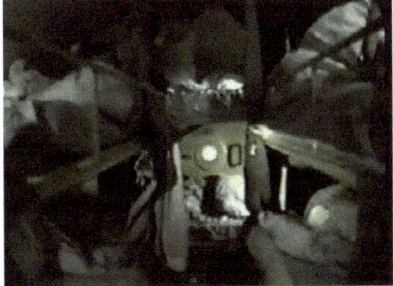

Typical bunk layout in Sat chamber – crowded but cozy

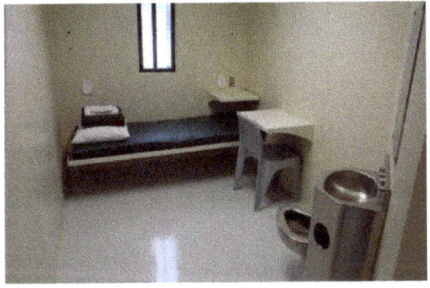

One person modern prison cell: toilet is similar to the one used before Boone's accident - no toilet seat. Sink in 'Sat' was just a stainless-steel bowl

Typical Sat crew. I am third from left.

The balance of 1969 and most of 1970 was spent in saturation preparing pipelines and risers for hyperbaric welding. This would include some of the following:

- Locating pipeline and moving into position
- Removing concrete and mastic from pipeline using high pressure water blaster
- Rough cut pipeline with oxy burning torch
- Line up ends of pipe to be welded
- Set SPAR over pipeline
- Using SPAR hydraulic clamps, line up pipe ends
- Set habitat UWH over pipe ends to be welded
- Seal UWH and pipe ends – blow habitat dry
- Prepare pipe ends for welding with WACHS cutting machine
- Install and line up 'pup joint'
- Weld both pipe ends to pup joint (this was a job for certified diver welders)
- Take x-rays
- Clean up UWH
- Remove seals from UWH, unclamp SPAR from pipeline
- Bring SPAR with UWH to surface
- Move to next job

But for all the work there were also some amusing stories. While bell diving was unquestionably safer, it didn't protect us from everything.

> Like that time we were working out of Empire, Louisiana in the South Timberlier area in about 320ft of water.
>
> The job involved searching for a 300ft double pontoon that had been torn off the stern of a pipe laying barge. Although the pontoon was 300 ft long, 10 ft high, and 10 ft wide, due to the limited visibility it was like looking for a needle in a haystack. Plodding along in the soft, slippery, muddy bottom, we would virtually have to run directly into it before we'd find it.
>
> We spent several days stirring up grey clouds of silt and clay that hung suspended in the water all around us blocking out all light and making any artificial light useless. This was a real 'stab-in-the-dark' routine. The only thing we seemed to keep bumping into was a colony of the biggest damn jewfish we'd ever seen. These guys were truly the heavy weight contenders in their class. The largest, being several times bigger than a diver and weighing several hundred pounds, we named Ol' Silver. Along with his size, blotchy battled-scarred body and aggressive nature, he was easily distinguished as the leader of the pack.
>
> The pack would form a welcoming committee every time one of us would leave the bell to descend to the sea floor. There they were, a brooding bunch of silent sentinels stationed around the perimeter of faint yellow cone of light that filtered down from the bells lower hatch.

Were they guarding Davy Jones locker or just checking out lunch?

We were always stumbling into them as they seemed to be forever in the way. Every now and then as you emerged from a dark cloud of silt, there was Ol' Silver, bang, right in your face. Enough to scare the piss out of ya - which was usually resolved by giving him a sharp whack on the snout. This was only effective for a while, since Ol' Silver would wait outside in the murky water under the perimeter of the light and then decide it was payback time. As you were climbing back in the bell, he would make his move.

On one dive, he headed straight for John's dangling feet. Feet were flying, jaws snapping, adrenaline racing, and all kinds of hollering over the radio. There's no way you can keep quiet with half a leg inside the jaws of an angry jewfish. John finally managed to kick himself free and reach the safety of the bell but not before Ol' Silver had gotten his huge jaws up to John's knees. John was back in the bell, a little shaken but safe. Topside then called down.

"Let's change out divers."

"Change out divers?" Lee queried.

Obviously, there had been a breakdown in communications. The diving supervisor just didn't understand what had happened.

"Hey, topside" Lee called out. "John's in here on the verge of heart failure and Ol' Silver's out there and he's roaring mad. I'm in here and I don't think it's wise to upset Ol' Silver any more. The hatch is closed and waiting for a seal."

The bell was brought back to the surface and mated with the chamber. John and Lee crawled out of the bell and into the chamber. Topside called down.

"Next two divers in the bell."

[Extracted from my original story]

Guess who they were – Buddy and me. I was first out of the bell, dropped down to the bell weight and got sorted. When I peered out of the cone of light below the bell, all I saw were pairs of eyes – I was totally surrounded by a pack of large curious jewfish. I had to just ignore them and get on with it.

When I wasn't offshore, I spent some good times with 'My fella' in 1969.

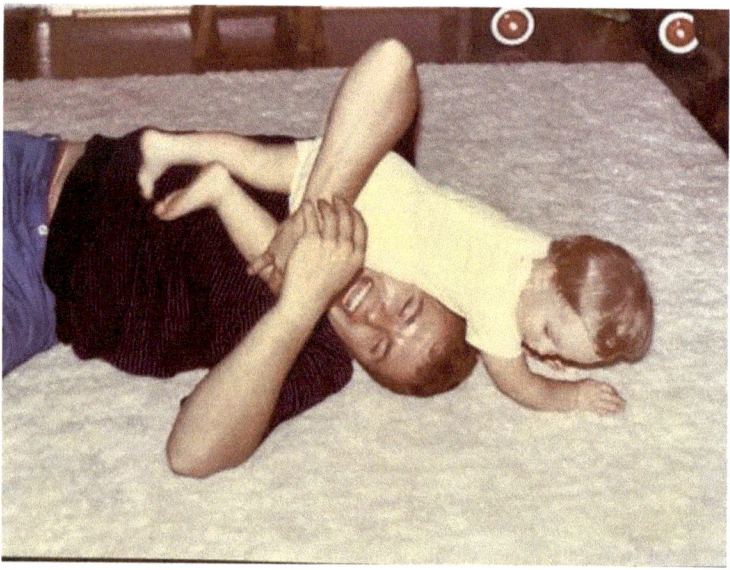

Winter of 1970 had me signing another overseas (18 months) contract. Back to the North Sea but this time it was the Norwegian Sector.

1970/71
Norway / Ekofisk

It was the start to Norway becoming the 'Trillion Dollar Baby', as Paul Cleary put it in his book of the same name.

The Discovery of Ekofisk

The oil jackpot was long in coming, but proved to be worth the wait. In the 1960s, 200 exploratory wells in the region yielded no commercial quantities of petroleum. Norwegian waters alone witnessed thirty-three dry holes in these lean years. When the bit finally found oil at Ekofisk in late 1969 and early 1970, however, it found a giant field. Through 1980, the field produced more than 575 million barrels of oil and 1.4 trillion cubic feet (Tcf) of gas. The cost to develop Ekofisk and the six nearby fields (West Ekofisk, Cod, Toe. Eldfisk, Albuskjell and Edda) reached almost $6 billion, making this project second only to the Alaska pipeline as the largest private commercial engineering project completed up to that time.

As in Alaska, the harsh environment contributed to this high cost. A Brown & Root engineering report noted that, "With the acceptance of the Ekofisk project, we encountered the most severe environmental conditions for design that our department had experienced up until that time. These conditions included water depths of 230 feet, a 78-foot design wave, and a 126-mile-per-hour wind. Additionally, it was estimated that an average of only 50 hours per month could be used for offloading of supplies during the winter months. A Brown & Root engineer said it more simply: "One of the things we had to do early was to learn how to stay offshore and be able to handle the storms."

Ekofisk held out hope that Europe might someday achieve energy independence ...

In late fall of 1969, Phillips Petroleum neared the end of its patience with the North Sea. As the weather worsened and the work season neared its end, Phillips decided to give it one last try before abandoning the site for the winter and perhaps for good. This last try proved historic. Drilling at Ekofisk 1-X during September 1969, Phillips's crew found traces of oil in the circulating drilling fluid at 5,500 feet. Technical problems forced the abandonment of the well. In December, a new well on Block 2-X about six-tenths of a mile from the original site found no oil at the 5,500 foot mark but detected signs of oil at 10,000 feet.

The volume of oil increased as the drill bit dug deeper. These solid indications of oil came from a promising strata of chalky, highly fractured limestone with good porosity. Phillips had tantalizing hints that it had found an epoch-defining discovery in the North Sea, but it would have to sit out the inclement winter weather before it could learn more about its find.

In the spring of 1970, Phillips returned to the site and confirmed that new field contained a giant oil deposit, which measured eight miles by four miles and consisted of a 690-foot thick, porous, pay zone of carbonate rock.

Initial estimates placed reserves in the seven billion barrel range, making this the largest oilfield ever discovered in Western Europe. The field, named Ekofisk, was a few miles east of the British-Norwegian offshore boundary adjacent to a large block of uncommitted acreage. Its proximity to Stavanger made that Norwegian city the logical location for Phillips's Ekofisk headquarters. As oil and gas production in the Norwegian sector of the North increased over the years, Stavanger became the center of the Norwegian oil and gas industry.

The Ekofisk discovery sent a lightning bolt through the oil fraternity. There was oil, and lots of it, in the North Sea ...

Phillips called on the resources of the worldwide offshore industry to push its project forward. Brown & Root was among those responding to the Phillips's call, and it played an important role in the initial phase of the field's development ...

Phillips had not yet proven the field at Ekofisk, but the company decided "go ahead and produce the wells that they drilled during exploration, just look at the viability of the field," said Bill Golson, Brown & Root's project engineer on Phase 1 of the Ekofisk project. Phillips hired Brown & Root to search for the most efficient way to get started at Ekofisk and suggested converting the 300-foot jack-up rig Gulftide, which they had under lease, into a temporary production facility. Golson and his colleagues at Brown & Root were pessimistic: "How in the hell are we going to make a production facility out of that thing?" Still, they forged ahead with feasibility studies, which indicated that a specially designed caisson might be used to convert the Gulftide into a temporary production platform. Golson said, "We were really out in the wild blue yonder with this one," but he also acknowledged that Phillips "was reaching on out there themselves." Time was money, and Phillips was willing to flaunt convention in search of a quicker route to oil production from Ekofisk. Brown & Root was more than willing to follow. As one Brown & Root engineer recalled, "We were given the go-ahead by Phillips to go after it."

Phillips wanted to "get after it" immediately, despite the obvious difficulty of working 200 miles from land in the central North Sea in the middle of winter. When Brown & Root reminded its client that "this is the worst time of the year, particularly at this place.

It's absolutely lousy weather and our downtime might be 60 percent," Phillips responded: "If your downtime is 60 percent and if we can produce for two months, we've paid for it all." For the first time, Brown & Root then ventured out into the North Sea winter and stayed out, far from shore, for months. On Ekofisk Phase 1, Phillips ordered Brown & Root to go full-speed ahead. Clyde Nolan remembered: "There were not enough hours in the day. You just worked your tail off and it didn't make any difference how many hours or whatever it cost, you just did it" ...

The jack-up drilling rig 'Gulftide'

Converting the Gulftide into a temporary production platform capable of supporting an array of production, processing, and transportation equipment was a daunting task. Golson recalled that "The challenge that we had using the jack-up rig, of course, was trying to get the oil from the seabed to the deck of the Gulftide, which was setting up at the maximum elevation of plus 89 feet above mean sea level. And it was set up that high because of the waves." The removal of all drilling equipment from the Gulftide's deck created space for custom-made separators, meters, pumps, and an elevated flare stack [and also room for a TDS Sat Unit].

Critical to the success of the conversion was the placement of wellhead equipment on four subsea wells, the connection of these seafloor wellheads to the production platform, and then the connection of production pipelines from the platform deck back down to the ocean floor and outward to two single buoy moorings for loading oil tankers. One Brown & Root engineer explained that the basic challenge of Ekofisk was to "perform constructive offshore pipelaying in fully exposed areas, where return to sheltered water is impractical in severe weather, even in the most hazardous season." None of this had been done before in such deep water or under such harsh conditions.

The oil flowlines, hydraulic lines, and control cables had to be connected at depths of more than 200 feet, which required precise positioning to assure secure connections. Brown & Root's engineers designed and fabricated a unique 44-ton subsea landing base which divers helped install on the ocean floor between the legs of the Gulftide to form a base for flowlines and loading lines ...

The underwater connections at Ekofisk placed heavy demands on divers. Even before the Gulftide arrived on site, divers had prepared the way by making the first subsea wellhead completions in the North Sea. Connecting these wellheads to the pipes and cables in the caisson and tying in the single moorings kept the divers busy throughout Phase 1. Winter weather made conditions extremely difficult, but Phillips had asked the divers "to stay out during the winter and get every hour we could work." This made for a lonely winter, with more waiting than working, "but we had to stay out and get them hooked up, and it paid off in the end."

Taylor Diving Company completed this difficult and dangerous underwater work in almost unbelievably harsh conditions. The divers plunged to 230-foot depths to weld underwater pipeline connections, repair platform jackets, connect flowlines to platforms, and assist in pipeline trenching and burying.

To make the underwater connections, divers used a combination of hydrocouples, hydraulic expansion sleeves, misalignment unions, and swivel joints. During later phases of Ekofisk's development, Taylor divers spent thousands of hours making saturation dives and hyperbaric welds to connect the system's pipelines.

Phase 1 at Ekofisk required much trial and error to create a temporary production system, but little time was lost to experimentation. Phase 1 began during the winter of 1970-71.

[Source: *Offshore Pioneers* – Brown & Root pages 226 - 232]

The development plan for the test phase shows "Gulftide" in the middle with the four production wells connected to the platform via pipelines. Two loading buoys (SBM – Single Buoy Mooring) are connected to the jack-up platform.

With this work, TDS introduced saturation diving into the NS. It had saturation units on both the Gulftide and B&R pipelay / derrick barge 'Hugh W Gordon' (HWG).

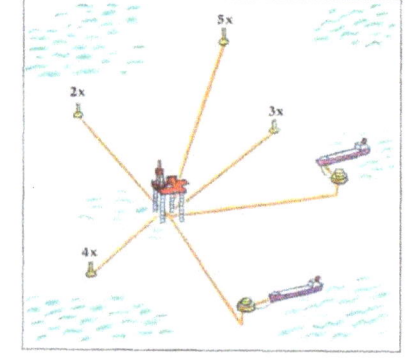

I was part of the first saturation dive team to arrive on the Gulftide around 5 December 1970. The first Sat dive consisted of Archie Weiss, Boyd Vassey, Buddy Eglin and me. It was a rather interesting and new experience not only to be confined in the Sat chamber for 30 days at a time but also restricted to the limited space onboard the rig. In the GoM, once you completed a Sat dive it was generally possible to catch a crew boat and go ashore (home) until you were needed again. It wasn't like that in the NS. You signed the contract (18 months), you do the time.

Merry Christmas. Just happened to be out of Sat for Christmas Eve - a good time to try and make a ship to shore call home. This would have to be made through the rig's radio room via VHF to a shore station which in turn would connect to the local telephone exchange. There were two major things to remember when making this type of call: 1) it cost $12/minute, 2) say 'over' after talking so the person who you called could reply and 3) most importantly, watch what you say because the whole world was listing.

For instance, don't let your loved one to get all excited about you coming home and start explaining the wonderful things she was going to do!

It was during this radio room visit we overheard a radio conversation between a drilling supply ship and the rig it was delivering 40 ft sections of drill pipe to. The weather was nasty and the ship started taking on water. The Captain started to evacuate his crew using the rig's crane suspended personnel basket.

He was able to get everyone off except for himself before the vessel took one last gigantic wave and rolled over. The Captain was giving a blow-by-blow description of what was happening - wished everyone a Merry Christmas and goodbye. The radio room went silent - that was it, he went down with the ship. We were stunned.

Just as we were trying to grasp what had just happened the radio squawked back to life – "I'm back" and the Captain proceeded to explain what happened. The more the ship rolled the more drill pipe rolled off. Once all the drill pipe had rolled off the ship it righted itself. It was a gonna be a good Christmas after all.

After spending over five months on the Gulftide, three of which were in Sat, Buddy and I had had enough confinement and asked head office if we could change out and we'd pay the transit fee for our reliefs. Head office agreed. Left the Gulftide on 8 April 1971.

When we got back to Belle Chasse (Taylor's head office) they wanted to know what was wrong, why didn't we want to stay out there? We told them that everyone else out there - tugs, rig and barge crews - were rotating on a monthly or bi-monthly basis with the dive crews being stuck for the duration of contract. After hearing this, Mark discussed the matter with B&R and agreed that a minimum overseas contract would now be for 120 days (four months instead of 18 months).

Also, we didn't have to pay the transit fee for our reliefs or our own way back home.

Major, major benefit. Something I feel responsible for and really good about.

After that, I got into the habit of programming myself into a four months on / two months off routine whenever possible.

1971

I spent another four-month hitch Sat diving in the NS. After that hitch, I returned home and checked into the office in Belle Chasse. Oh, what a surprise I was given. I was offered the sweetest job ever. Taylor was contracted to provide the US Navy with a Sat Unit in HAWAI'I – no shit - awesome.

As a dive location, it don't get no better than this. - if ya gotta work, den dis be da place to be, yeah.

And it sure wasn't all work and no play……. Hey, it's Hawai'i!

We were billeted in a hotel on Lewers Street about a block and a half from Waikiki Beach. The room was paid for with per diem allowance and had enough room for my wife and son. We would celebrate his third birthday at Stuckey's Pizza Parlor. And did he celebrate, decided to try my beer through a straw, one sip – talk about one wired kid – never again.

Our hotel 'The Pad' on Lewers

Aerial view of Waikiki

Waikiki, Honolulu, Pearl Harbor and Wai'anae mountains in the distance as seen from Diamond Head

We were within walking distance of so many good spots:
- International Market Place – Trader Vic's – best Mai Tai in town
- Sheraton Hotel – Kon Tiki – right around the corner
- Hawaiian Hilton – Benihana's – great introduction to Japanese food
- Ala Moana Shopping Center – Patti's Chinese Kitchen – best noodles ever – opened 1967, closed 43 years later. On one of our shopping trips to Ala Moana, Webb introduced me to Kim Chee, and I still keep a jar in the fridge.

- Crazy Shirts – I had some 'T' shirts designed and made for our crew – 'Team 69' – "No sea to ruff, No muff to tuff", "We dive for five".
- Dennis Webb was the Saturation Diving Superintendent. This was not his first trip to Hawai'i. He was in the US Navy and stationed at Pearl Harbor on 7 December 1942, the Day of Infamy, when the Japanese attacked Pearl Harbor. Needless to say, he didn't like going back - brought back too many bad memories.

I still top up my wardrobe from Crazy Shirts. I'm their No.1 Haole.

One adventurous day, Neil and I decided to rent a car and take our wives for a tour - circumnavigate the island. This was going to be one heck of a daring and exciting adventure.

Daring – the northwest area, Ke'ana Point, was out of bounds and not covered by the rental contract. No official road.

Our Team '69 logo was similar to this

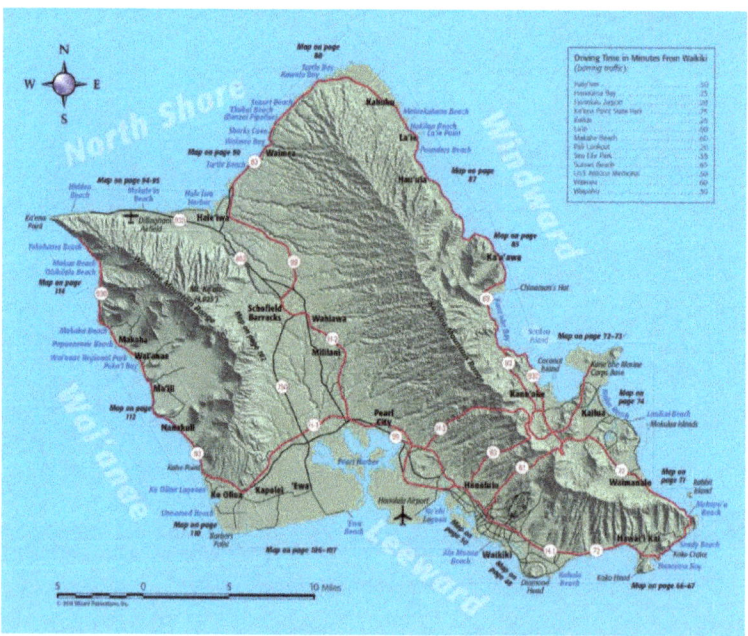

Ka'ena or Kaena Point is the westernmost tip of land on the island of O'ahu. The point can be reached on foot from both the East (via O'ahu's North Shore Mokulē'ia) and Southeast (via Wai'anae Coast). An unimproved track extends some 3 miles (4.8 km) along the coast from the end of the paved road on the east side, where a gate prevents entry of all except authorized vehicles. On the southeast side, at Ka'ena State Park, a paved road passes a beach before terminating into an unpaved road.

It continues for a few miles, after which the road is washed out, and further travel must be on foot. It is not possible to travel around the point in a vehicle as the route is better described as a "path" in most places, and is lined on one side with a cliff and on the other with basalt rocks which are quite capable of damaging vehicles.

In Hawaiian, ka'ena means 'the heat'. The area was named after a brother or cousin of Pele who accompanied her from Kahiki. The State of Hawai'i has designated the point as a Natural Area Reserve to protect nesting Laysan Albatrosses and wedge-tailed Shearwaters, Hawaiian monk seals, and the fragile (to vehicular traffic) native strand vegetation that has been restored there. Some ancient Hawaiian folklore states that Ka'ena Point is the "jumping-off" point for souls leaving this world.

[Source: Wikipedia]

Kaena Point

Exciting, scary and possibly foolish but we made it around safe and sound with mc (drawing the short straw) driving and the other three walking and guiding just in case the car decided to go over the edge.

We made it, got to circumnavigate the whole island.

Road? Trail? Track

Not so lucky

Taylor had a contract with US Navy to provide saturation support for the 'AEGIR'. The AEGIR was berthed alongside Makai Pier.

Makai Pier, Makapuu Point Waimanalo, HI (above and following page)

AEGIR – Submersible Habitat (follow on from SEALAB Program)

With Gosta Fahlman, Pryor developed Aegir, an undersea habitat, which accommodated six persons and was successfully tested at 600' depth for two weeks at ambient pressure off Makapuu Pt in 1968. I would initially get to meet Gosta when he came to work for Taylor.

AEGIR

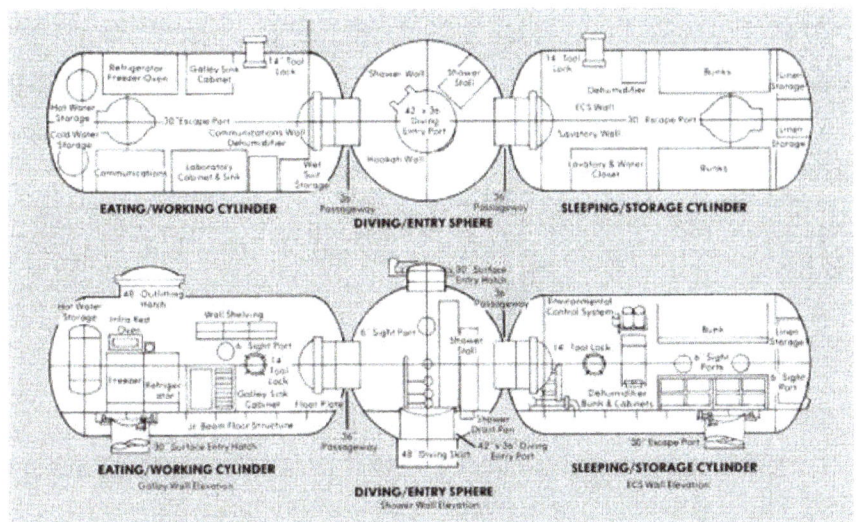

AEGIR layout

AEGIR at sea

MAKAI RANGE PROJECT – HAWAI'I September 1971 – February 1972

TAYLOR DIVING & SALVAGE Co Ltd provides saturation diving support to US Navy onboard YRST 1

DIVERS: Mike Cooke, Neil Landry, Buddy Eglin & Jeff Sherry
DIVING SUPT: Dennis Webb
DIVING SUPVS: Fred Biggers & Fred Collins

YRST 1 Alongside Pearl Harbor

The following is from:

Harbor Clearance Unit One Log Report for Calendar Year 1971
OPNAV Report 5750-1

US Navy Harbor Clearance Unit 1 (HCU 1)

1. Even before the arrival of the YRST-1 in Pearl Harbor, plans were being made to use the craft as the surface support platform for the Navy/Makai Range Calendar Year 71 Dive Project off Makapuu Pt., Oahu, Hawai'i. Work began in earnest in September and continued at a fast pace until the dives commenced in November. All dives were completed by early December in time to decompress the Aquanauts for Christmas.

2. Preparations of the YRST-1 for surface support was a long, arduous task for the sailors of HCU-1. The YRST-1 was expected to provide surface support including power for the ocean floor dive system AEGIR, provide a platform for the Taylor Diving System, provide space for the research and recording equipment required, and to provide living, berthing and messing facilities for the multitude of embarked personnel. In October the YRST-1 went into the Pearl Harbor Shipyard for removal of the Monorail System on her fantail and installation of the Taylor Diving System which was to be used as a rescue chamber in an emergency. Installation of this system included an "A" frame and personnel transfer capsule, a large double-lock decompression chamber mounted on hydraulic-powered skids and capable of mating up with the PTC, a large Sakgit Winch for lowering the PTC and a 27-ton tube trailer which contained the Helium gas used by the TDS divers. Transformers were installed to provide correct power to the AEGIR and extra bunks were installed to provide sleeping accommodations for the many embarked personnel. HCU-1 personnel devoted many extra hours - working weekends, holidays and into the evening, to make the YRST-1 ready for this important project.

3. The dive sequence was originally scheduled to be in three phases. First, a series of 80 ft. training dives to familiarize all personnel with the operation functions required. Then a short 200 ft. dive in preparation for the final dive of 10 days at 520 feet. A team of 2 civilians, 3 U.S. Navy and 1 Royal Navy personnel were trained to submerge in the OFDS.

4. YRST-1 was underway behind the USS GRAPPLE (ARS 7) on 2 November for Makapuu Pt. and the 80-foot dive sequence. Heavy seas hampered getting secured in the 5 legs of the moor and it wasn't until evening of the 3rd of November that YRST-1 was completely moored.

The AEGIR conducted several training dives on the 5th and 6th, including practice evacuations into the Taylor System which was lowered from the YRST.

[Neil Landry and I were the two Sat Divers for Taylor onboard YRST-1. We made the bell run and secured a travel line between the SDC (PTC) and AEGIR to assist in practice evacuation.]

The 80 ft. dive sequence was successfully terminated on the afternoon of the 6th with all major goals being met, and YRST-1 was returned to Pearl harbor. These dives proved very beneficial to the members of HCU-1 as they provided invaluable training for all hands.

5. On the 17th, YRST-1 was again towed to Makapuu Pt., this time for the 200-foot dive. However, Mother Nature disagreed with the timing, and extremely adverse weather conditions prevented the YRST-1 from entering the moor. All units returned to Pearl Harbor that evening after a rough day at sea.

6. YRST-1 was again underway behind USS GRAPPLE (ARS 7) on the 20th bound for the 200 ft. dive site. Although the weather conditions were still poor, the experience gained on the 80 ft. dives enabled the crew to get YRST-1 positioned in the moor the next day after a night of steaming.

On Monday the 22nd, the AEGIR was brought out for the 200 ft. dive. All appeared to be going well until AEGIR finally submerged when shortly after leaving the surface, all communications were lost. Investigations disclosed that upon submerging, the AEGIR had planed over and hooked the starboard quarter mooring leg of YRST-1 severing the communications umbilical. The AEGIR was brought to the surface, returned to port and the dive temporarily suspended.

7. YRST-1 remained in her moors for the next 8 days awaiting the continuation of the dive.

[Taylor divers, Neil Landry & I, remained under pressure in the Sat chamber.]

During this time the weather continued to deteriorate. However, the morning of the 30th of November dawned calm enough to continue, and the AEGIR was brought out, moored astern of YRST-1 and submerged to 200 ft. without incident. For the next 4 days, the Aquanauts performed a series of tests and projects, completing all major events scheduled for the 200 ft. dive.

Neil and I would each make a bell run and excursion dive to the AEGIR proving the practical and safety aspect of Taylor's saturation system. Should it have been necessary, the crew inside AEGIR could have been safely transferred under pressure using Taylor's system.

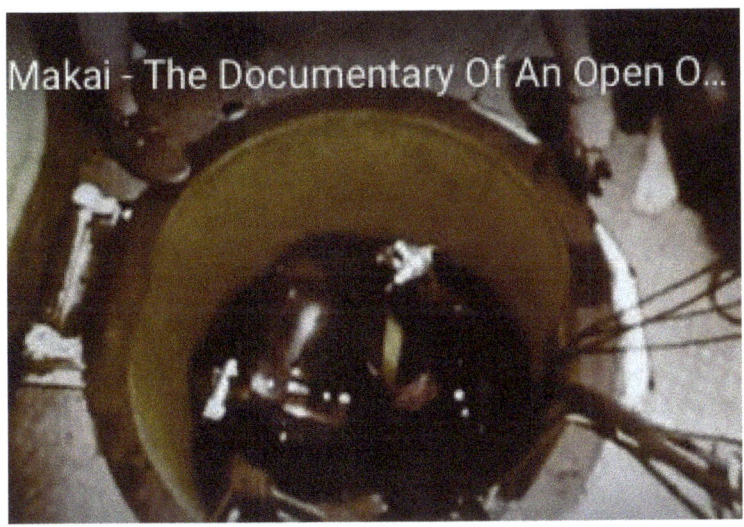

Diver entering/returning to AEGIR

On the morning of 3 December, the AEGIR surfaced, YRST-1 broke the moor and was towed back to Pearl Harbor. Decompression of the Aquanauts completed the 200 ft. dive.

8. Preparations to commence the 520 foot dive in January or February continued until 20 December when word was received that due to the probability of further deteriorating weather, the high cost of continuing and the fact that much of the sought after information had been gained during the 200 ft. dive, the 520 ft. dive had been canceled. Removal of major equipment from YRST-1 was not scheduled until after the New Year, so the members of HCU-1 settled down for the Christmas holiday, and a well-deserved rest.

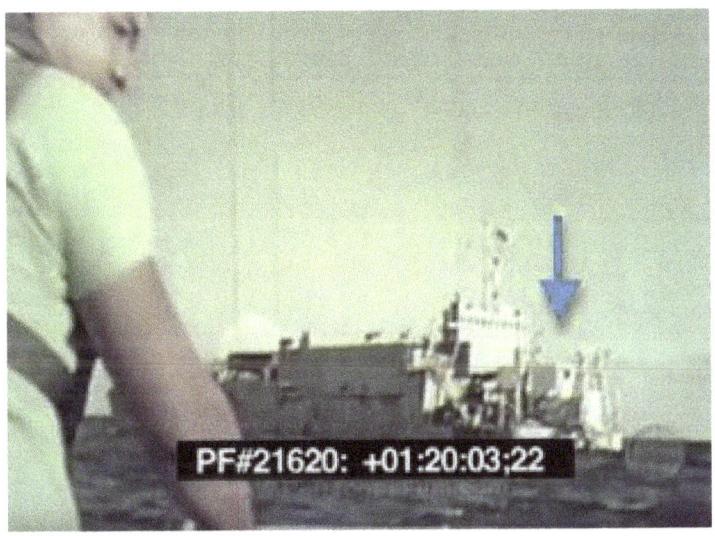

Blue arrow points to Saturation Diving System

Blue arrow points to Saturation Diving System

It wasn't always calm.

This photo and the ones on the preceding page are from *Makai - The Documentary of an Open Ocean Dive* which was produced by the Department of the Navy in 1973. The focus is on preparation and employment of a mobile saturation dive off the coast of Oahu, Hawai'i.

Spectacular underwater photography is combined with descriptions of diving research sponsored by Bureau of Medicine and Surgery, Office of Naval Research and Navy Supervisor of Diving.

The documentary is available on DVD or can be viewed on You Tube at: https://www.youtube.com/watch?v=AN6PLmO4kGw

Taylor also had to demonstrate that one of its Sat systems could be airlifted and placed on a salvage vessel enabling expanded capabilities in salvage and rescue operations – deeper depths & longer bottom times. Enter the USS GRAPPLE.

1972

Aloha – back to Hawai'i to demobilize the saturation diving equipment off the YRST-1 and then install it onboard the fantail of USS GRAPPLE ARS 7.

On mobilization of Taylor's crew, a tragedy happened. Neil Landry was killed in a car accident on his way to New Orleans airport to catch the flight to Honolulu.

Buddy Eglin would become my bell partner. The test/task was quite simple and standard. Shackle a line from topside to an anchor which had been placed on the bottom. The bell (SDC) was lowered to the bottom, bell pressure was equalized with the depth, bottom hatch opened; I entered the water. The most beautiful blue and unbelievable visibility I'd ever experienced.

Looking for the anchor – no problem – it was close by. The line was shackled, and I was back in the bell within a 10 minute period. Job complete. We'd sailed from Pearl that morning and were back alongside for pizza that evening.

After decompression it was back to New Orleans. Although I'd return to Hawai'i every so often, it would be almost another 30 years before I'd get to dive those beautiful waters again.

USS GRAPPLE – ARS 7 alongside

The Pressure Zone by Mike Cooke

With TDS Sat Equipment installed on fan tail (stern)

Jim Trotter, who had just retired from the Navy and still lived on Oahu, joined the team as a training supervisor. It was the start of a long career with Taylor. His daughter, Debbie was in high school and would 'baby sit' my son.

Hawai'i was a trip (job) of a lifetime and one I'll never forget.

Spent the rest of 1972 working out of Bahrain (Louie Giacona was the Area Operations Manager), NS and the GoM. Busy year.

Even did a bit of supervising in the Persian Gulf.

On my return to Belle Chasse, I was assigned to the working committee of the American National Standards Institute for the formulation of proposed diving standards.

1973
Focusing on the Colossus

After spending several months in Sat, it was time to go back to Ekofisk and install the tank.

> *On the 14th of May in 1971, the Phillips Group signed a contract with the French company CG Doris for construction of a concrete storage tank for the Ekofisk field. The agreement marked the end of an intense decision-making process which went on during the first months of 1971. There were a number of questions in connection with this pioneer project - the most fundamental being whether such a tank would float, so that it could be towed from the construction site to the field.*
>
> [Source: Phillips Petroleum Report – A history of Ekofisk]

The tank did float and is seen here being placed into position.

Taylor had a Sat unit standing by waiting for it to be placed on the bottom. A bell run was made to confirm it was on the bottom. Ed Russell and Boyd Vassey were the bell divers and I was the Sat Supervisor on that shift. The barge was anchored in position alongside the tank leaving just enough space to lower the bell.

Ed was the first diver out to check. "On the bottom" the radio squawked in the familiar Donald Duck helium sound, "searching for the tank".
Then quiet. What's he up to?

"Hey Ed, what's up, have you located the tank?"

"Not yet still doing a circle search."

He was making a 150 ft radius circle looking for something 10 ft from the barge and bigger than a football field.

"Oh, Oh, I found it. It's about a foot over my head."

"Ed get back in the bell – now!"

With both divers safely back in the Sat chamber, the tank was flooded some more in order to securely sit on the bottom. The rest of the job went smoothly - releasing scouring mats and checking to see if the tank was firmly on the bottom.

I spent the remainder of 1973 and the better part of the next five years as a saturation diver in the NS and GoM, averaging four 30 day Sats a year, some a little longer – weeks, some a little shorter – days. With an approximate rotation schedule of 4 months on (2 x 30 days in Sat + 2 x 30 days standby onboard) followed by 2 months off, on the beach at home, I had ample time to write.

It was during the period between 1969 to 1978, during many saturation dives, that I wrote the original draft of *The Pressure Zone*, some in long hand, some typed. The original draft included a number of true events, some of which I have now extracted and placed in chronological order. What follows is a cut-down version of that story.

The Pressure Zone
(Original Draft written in Sat)

"It is noted that individuals who may demonstrate slightly neurotic characteristics in normal life might better adapt to a career of diving and underwater work than those who seem better balanced."

European Undersea Bio-Medical Society
Stockholm, June 1973

Chapter 1 – Day 31

Deep Sea Diving Services Inc
7600 West End Blvd
New Orleans LA 70014
USA
Tel: (504) 929 7600 Telex: 92747

Saturation Diving Log

Vessel: *Ocean Venture*	Sat Unit: *SDC/TL 12*		Max Sat Depth: *1000 ft*	
Date: *29 Oct 1977*	Time: *00:01*		Shift: *Midnight/Noon*	
Location: *North Sea NCS*		Weather: *Gale Force 8 - Rough*		
Chamber:				
Depth: *664 ft*	PPO2: *0.39*	CO$_2$: *0.4%*	Temp: *84 F*	Humidity: *63%*
Personnel in Sat:				
Inner Lock: *Divers*		Outer Lock: *Divers*		
Fred 'Dinger' Bell, Joe Rhodes,		*Matt Sims, Jeff Morgan, Al Rollins, Buddy*		
Tender/Medic: Pete Whiteshirt		*Walker*		
Comments:				
Seas rough, barge undertow. Sat unit decompressing – 4ft/hr. Chamber personnel asleep. Change out CO$_2$ canister and purafil (odor) when personnel awake – not urgent. Pete needs clean sheets for inner lock. Mail on crew boat due at noon if it can get alongside weather permitting. Buddy still suffering from sinus problems.				
Sat Tech	Diving Supv		Diving Supt	
James Vlassic	*Charlie Mussels*		*D W Spider*	

Our cold steel home shook uncontrollably from the force of another three-storey wave as it smashed into the bow of the barge ploughing through the heavy seas.

Several days ago, the waves had started out as wind-blown ripples on the sea surface. As the wind increased, the ripples turned into waves and swells. The longer and stronger the wind blew, the bigger the waves got. With a Gale Force 8 blowing 34-40 knots, the wind had turned the sea ugly. Deep dark troughs had formed with foaming white crested walls 30 feet high.

Mother Nature was at her mischievous best ensuring we weren't going to get a comfortable rest this night.

Having completed the work on the bottom almost four days ago, our saturation diving team settled into the monotonous daily routine of decompression. Unlike surface diving where decompression could be done in the water and/or in a topside decompression chamber for a relatively short period of time, say an hour or two, as 'Sat' divers we spent many days confined, decompressing in the relative 'comfort' and safety of the saturation unit. Even though the Sat unit was housed and secured to the upper deck, it didn't prevent our Sat crew from experiencing the full force of the raging storm.

Travelling (decompressing) at an ascent rate of 4 ft/hr and with a couple of scheduled stops on the way, the length of decompression required for working at 1,000 feet would take the better part of eleven days. If all went as planned, it would be another week before we would eventually get the chance to escape from our confinement and inhale their first breath of sweet fresh air.

Drifting in and out of sleep, I stirred slightly. Rolling over onto my side, I heard the automatic ascent system solenoid valve popping-off and the hiss of gas escaping from the chamber. Although there are times when the popping and hissing is annoying, it's persistent chatter was a comforting indicator that the decompression program was still on schedule - four days of decompression gone, seven to go. Trying to sleep, I wrestled with the bunk covers fighting to find a comfortable position (if there was such a thing).

My bliss was short lived, however, as the chamber shook violently from the force of the three-storey wave that crashed over the bow of the barge. The chamber shuddered uncontrollably as the barge plowed into the heavy seas being churned up by the raging tropical storm that had entered the area during the night. The storm was expected to last for several days, making it too rough for diving operations but a convenient time to decompress and change out with the standby crew.

There was a slight lull as the sea settled before building up again. The vibrating, rattling and noise inside the chamber subsided and the reassuring sound of the solenoid valve popping and hissing could still be heard.

Like me, the rest of the diving team was now awake and aware of the unsettling change to their pressurized confines.

From the outside, our pressurized world - with its boiler shape - looked more like the replica of a turn of the century railway steam engine, than a modern piece of engineering at the cutting edge of diving technology. This was one of the new breeds of super chambers designed with three locks (compartments), accommodation for 11-12 people (if a sheet metal bunk connected by two chain cables can be called accommodation) and good to a depth of 1,200 feet.

So, with a working dive crew of seven there was ample living room, or at least as much as one could expect to find in a tube 25 feet long and eight feet in diameter. However, it wouldn't be too much longer before some of the crew would be going ashore and heading home. For some, it would be their first visit home in at least four months. That is if everything went according to schedule.

Our ascent was controlled automatically, from the 'dog-house', at a rate of four feet an hour with several stops or waiting periods at designated depths on the way up. This slow rate of ascent allowed the saturated gases in our bodies to be released without any adverse effects such as the "bends". The periodic stops also aided our bodies to become more adjusted to the change in pressure. During decompression there isn't much for us to do but play the waiting game: eat, sleep, read, think, eat sleep, think, sleep, think, and think and think.

If one thing can be said about 'Sat decompression', it's that you have an abundance of time to think, dream, reflect and wrestle with mind games. Ample time to sort out all of life's little problems.

Lying in my bunk, my mind was revved up and kicking into gear trying to recollect when it all began. When was the first time I'd crawled into a saturation chamber? What is it that makes any sane, normal person want to be confined in a steel cylinder for weeks at a time? Are we a particular breed or cult? What is this irresistible urge that makes divers always want to go deeper to challenge the 'pressure zone'?

Is it knowing that when you leave the diving bell and stand on the seabed, there's a good chance that you're the first person to see, feel, and know what is actually down there – the first human ever to stand on this spot? Is it the adrenalin rush and buzz from daring the unknown? Is it the ego trip - the bravado? Or is it just the money? Maybe all of the above?

When did it all begin and how did we get into this profession known as "saturation diving"?

The majority of early diving work was in shallow offshore oil fields, but in order to meet the growing demand, the oil companies were being forced to expand their exploration activities further and further out to sea in deeper and deeper water. The effect of this expansion had a tremendous impact on commercial diving.

To meet the demand for deeper diving, beyond the practical working limit for compressed air in the 165 – 200 ft range, helium replaced nitrogen as the inert gas in the diver's breathing media.

Mixed gas diving, using something other than compressed air such as helium/oxygen, helium/nitrogen/ oxygen, or oxygen with still other exotic gases had been used before World War II.

But now, the commercial diving industry was being forced to go deep.

One immediate snag was the shortage of experienced personnel. Most, if not all, of the people with this kind of know-how, were master divers employed by the Navy. And so, the recruitment program moved into high gear. With the same fervour and tact of professional football scouts touring college campuses, commercial diving companies started scouring submarine bases and other naval establishments, sweet talking divers into a change of lifestyle by swapping their uniforms for substantially higher pay and the chance to wear a Rolex Submariner, solid gold no less.

In relatively short order, we were ready to start diving deep, down past the 200ft level. There was no SCUBA diving to these depths. Instead, it was done from the surface using an umbilical with safe gas mixes in place of compressed air. The diver's 'dress' was also changing in style. Compact fibreglass 'hats' were now the rage - replacing the awkward brass and bronze helmets with their strange valves and portholes - normally confined to the military or the old diehard pearl, sponge and harbour divers. One nifty outfit came directly from the NASA space industry. Heck, if it was good enough for Neil (Armstrong, that is) it was good enough for us. Although there are many parallels and comparisons made between the exploration of outer and inner space this was not one of the successful ones. It was sharp looking but had problems staying dry – it leaked. Therefore, never made it to the Top Ten List.

In addition to the new style of head gear, another noticeable change was the backpack, now being worn by the diver. This composed of canisters containing a Carbon Dioxide (CO_2) absorbent.

Due to its limited supply, helium is quite expensive. So it became necessary to contrive a way to conserve this precious gas. Since the diver consumed only a small portion of the gas supplied to him, with the bulk of it exhausting into the water, the natural question became – instead of wasting it, why not recycle it? Using a partial rebreather rig solved this problem. This allowed the diver to use (re-breathe) a major portion of gas and still have a continuous supply from above with a minimal amount of waste. However, this in turn created still another problem.

Now that the diver was rebreathing gas his susceptibility to carbon dioxide (CO_2) poisoning increased considerably. On inhalation, the diver uses up oxygen (O_2) and expels CO_2 on exhalation. What about the Helium (He)? Oh yeah, that. Its inert. It just took up space and cost a hell of a lot.

Carbon dioxide, though, is dangerous and potentially lethal. It is normally colorless, odorless and tasteless, in amounts encountered by the diver. However, too much of it will cause the diver to black-out and worse. To get rid of CO_2 build up, a granulated substance that absorbs this gas is used. This absorbent is carried by the diver in a canister, which can be a part of his hat or strapped to his back. Problem solved.

Ready for the murky depths, we were now able to meet the oil companies' demands.

Hold it right there! What's that garbled noise coming from the diving radio? The hurdles just keep on comin'. The sound was a cross between Donald Duck and Alvin the Chipmunk. We conquered the depths but just couldn't express ourselves too well. A major side effect of helium is that it plays havoc on the vocal cords and distorts the voice. Was the answer 'hand signals'? Not bloody likely! We could be heard, just not understood. So, some genius came up with the bright idea that if we can use pulls as signals on a diving hose why not use 'beeps' as signals over the radio. One beep for "no", two beeps (beep, beep) for yes. BEEP BEEP, and we thought Donald and Alvin were bad. Now we're sounding more like the Road Runner – BEEP BEEP!

It wasn't long though before someone solved the problem and developed the helium unscrambler. Back in action, just don't talk too fast. You might say the problem was half-solved but due to the demand, new and better equipment was being introduced daily.

Mixed gas diving was truly opening up a new and exciting frontier. Nowhere was this more apparent than in the Gulf of Mexico. Every day seemed to herald in a new depth record.

All along the gulf coast, from the mouth of the Mississippi River to Sabine Pass, in the lounges, bars and juke joints, in places like New Orleans, Morgan City and Lafayette, wherever divers were hanging out, the talk was about the deepest dive, the longest bottom time, the incidents of bends and always who was making the most money. This was the language of the 'neoprene knights', a whole new breed of adventurous young men, ready to wager their lives and reap the rewards for challenging the pressure zone.

Many a high roller calling, "a round for the house" knew that their ability to pay was due to their daring and disregard for danger.

THE NEOPRENE KNIGHT

*Artwork by Diane R.
compliments of Paul Kalman*

A very simplistic diving rule of thumb is the deeper the dive, the shorter the bottom time, that is working time. What this means is that the deeper the job, the shorter the bottom time and the more divers that were needed to complete the work. However, if the bottom time increases, conversely, so does the decompression time.

With more divers working, at greater depths and for longer times, the frequency of 'the bends/decompression sickness' cases was on the rise. In an effort to increase diver safety new decompression tables were formulated. These tables were a carefully guarded commodity and each diving company prided themselves on having the best set – the fewer cases of bends, the less amount of downtime, the less chance of a lawsuit, the less time in court.

Thinking about it, I couldn't recall ever knowing of anyone losing their life due to a case of bends. In fact, once decompression had been administered, most guys were back in the water the next day. It wasn't unheard of for some divers to be 'bent' several times a week. Not sure if it was because we were a hardy lot or maybe it was just the impetuosity of youth or simply because we just didn't know no better.

With the increasing depths the diver's hose, the umbilical, was steadily getting longer. In the past, what could be accomplished with a 300 ft air hose now required a 600 ft mixed gas rig. With more hose out, the risk of it getting fouled increased proportionately. Getting fouled was one of the hazards and a major cause for concern. With all the trash on the ocean floor it was always getting hung up on something.

I remember one time when a diver got his hose fouled by a cruising giant manta ray, more commonly known as a devilfish. The hose became entangled between the two horn like flukes protruding from the ray's huge head. The ray, a generally docile creature despite it's huge size, quickly turned the incident into a carnival giving the diver an underwater rollercoaster ride he'd never forget. The ray took off with the diver's hose trapped between his flukes. In what seemed like a matter of seconds the distance between diver and the ray's gaping jaws and thrashing body became uncomfortably shorter. Luckily, the fish untangled itself before any serious damage was done. With the thrashing white belly of the monster imprinted in his mind, a thoroughly terrified diver made his way to the surface. In the years to come, he'd have one helluva blood curdling fish tale to tell his kids.

A tangled hose rarely meant disaster, because the standby diver could usually be sent down to clear it if the troubled diver was unable to do so himself. One of the greatest problems however, was the current. Too strong a current and too much hose had the diver being swept off the bottom and left trolling with no control as to maintaining depth – which is a no, no and very dangerous. Sure the hazards were there and so was the incentive but to get the work done, diving needed to be made safer.

Enter the deep sea diving bell.

The diving bell or Submersible Decompression Chamber (SDC) is a steel cylinder or sphere capable of withstanding pressure and housing two or more people. The bell is used as a transport vehicle - a shuttle service - taking divers to and from their work, like an underwater elevator. Diving with the aid of a bell became a totally new experience.

The divers would enter the bell on the surface and once inside they donned their diving gear, did a communications check and with all systems 'Go,' closed the hatch and would be pressurized with compressed air to the equivalent working depth. The outfits they wore were not only hideous looking but horribly uncomfortable. What a relief it was to rip the mask from your face after a dive lasting several hours.

Inside the bell, once pressurized, it was necessary to keep masks on at all times. Due to the expense and short supply of helium, the bell would be pressurized to the working depth on air and only the divers would be supplied the mixed gas. The air atmosphere in the bell was toxic. The oxygen percentage in the air atmosphere would be too rich for this depth, causing anoxia (oxygen poisoning), while the nitrogen level would be so high as to cause acute narcosis.

After the bell was pressurized to the working depth, it was picked up by a crane and lowered over the side down to the work site. A nice safe ride if the sea wasn't rough. Upon reaching the assigned depth, the pressure in the bell would be equalized to that of the water pressure outside, thus allowing the bottom hatch to pop open so we could go to work.

One man would leave the safety and security of the bell while his partner stayed inside and tended his hose. If need be, the divers would take turns working and in the event of an emergency or some extenuating circumstance, both divers could leave the bell. Once the job was completed or the bottom time had elapsed (invariably the latter), the diver would return to the bell. Inside the bell, with the hatch secured and sealed, we were ready to be brought back to the surface to start the lengthy decompression that accompanied such long dives.

The bell was brought back onboard the work barge and mated to a decompression chamber. We crawled out of the bell into the larger chamber, put on the oral-nasal O^2 masks and settled back for the long journey to the 'surface'. Now that we were back in our steel living quarters, the bell could be separated from the chamber and used by a fresh team to make another dive.

Our bottom time (working time) was getting longer and the amount of decompression was already well beyond projections.

From the time a diver entered the bell, made a dive and finished decompression, he would have spent 12 to 16 hours under pressure and become partially saturated. Total saturation wasn't that far away.

We were diving deeper, but we also inherited the problems that go with it. In shallower water, it was possible to dive around the clock with six to eight divers.

Now to dive a full day, it took 12 to 14 divers and a score of support personnel. The complete crew included divers, tenders to assist the divers, technicians or life support operators to handle the gas, much gear, and a supervisor to get and keep it all together. From the original two-man diving team, we were rapidly expanding into a small army.

As this horde descended onto a barge, it wasn't unusual to hear the barge superintendent complain, "My God! Where in hell can we sleep and feed you all?"

He wasn't the only one with problems. The diving companies had their own. The oil companies were becoming increasingly concerned because it was taking more people, more equipment and importantly, more money to put a diver down another 100 ft deeper for one or two hours.

In any event, we were already doing partial saturation, so it was only a short jump forward to plant both feet firmly into total saturation.

Sat-u-rate: 1. to cause to be thoroughly soaked. 2. to cause to be so completely filled or charged that no more can be taken up.

A gas will be absorbed by a liquid (Henry's Law). The fluids in the human body absorb gas (breathing), but they will only absorb so much gas according to the amount of pressure (depth) applied. Once this level has been reached, the fluids have become saturated.

The objective we faced was to saturate the diver's body to whatever depth he was working and leave him there. Because our bodies were saturated, it would take that much longer for us to decompress, allowing the absorbed gases to escape slowly from our tissues and thus prevent bends.

No sane person was going to stay under water that long, so the solution became a pressurized home, a place where divers could eat, sleep and be comfortable. Under such conditions, we would be able to work on the bottom for as long as might be necessary.

With partial saturation, we already had chambers and bells in economy models. What we now needed were a few accessories to give us the deluxe model or the 'total saturation unit'.

I can still remember the first time I saw a saturation unit. In the fall of 1968, I'd returned from the North Sea where I'd been working for the past few years. The gas and oil discoveries off the coasts of England, Norway and Scotland were turning into a bonanza, but it would still be several years before we would truly infiltrate this area with dozens of drilling rigs and scores of production platforms.

The saturation unit I was examining was being outfitted in the company's warehouse in New Orleans. It was being readied for a job the following summer in the Gulf of Mexico in 320 feet of water. The diving supervisor who conducted the tour smiled and nodded: "After you."

It didn't take long to figure out what he found so amusing. It must have been the look of disbelief that registered on my face when I crawled inside that piece of pregnant pipe. I turned to him and said, "You're putting me on. Eight men living in here ...for 30 days?"

It was crowded with just the two of us. This I had to see. And I did .... many, many times.

The thing looked like a huge boiler with the insides ripped out and replaced on the outside. The chamber was compartmented into several sections called 'locks' because each section could be pressurized independently, thereby locking one from the other.

This was a triple-lock chamber including entrance lock, outer lock, inner lock and connected to the tunnel at the far end, the bell. The inner and outer locks were living quarters. The entrance lock was for emergencies and adding more personnel, if needed. The unit, as a whole, could be put on a barge or big work boat and secured to the deck with the bell being the only part of the unit to go into the water.

Inside the chamber, I was surrounded by metal folding bunks, four in each lock. The passageway between the bunks was hardly wide enough to walk. It was immediately evident that the majority of the space had been set aside for sleeping. However, there was still sufficient room to perform daily functions like eating, bathing, and an occasional bowel movement.

This chamber was a super deluxe model. It had two toilets - one in each lock. This fact is emphasized because from where I was standing, I could see both potties side-by-side, separated by a small partition. I asked quite pointedly: "What arrangements have been made to create a little privacy?" and was informed this was no time to be modest. The problem was solved later with a strategically placed curtain – originally made out of taped together large plastic garbage bags.

Several blower motors circulated the atmosphere inside the chamber. By blowing gas across heating and cooling coils, it was possible to control the temperature to maintain a comfortable environment.

I pointed to a large cannister above one of the motors and asked if this was for the Soda Sorb. The supervisor nodded affirmatively. There were two such cannisters filled with Soda Sorb, a white granular substance used to absorb carbon dioxide. With the tour almost over, I pointed to a small hatch on the side of the chamber. I was informed that this was the medical lock, a small tunnel used for sending in our daily needs such as food, mail, linen and diving gear. It would also be employed for sending the used stuff out. A pressurized dumb waiter, you might say, but once pressurized, it became one of only two communications links we had to the outside world. The other was talking over the speaker to the diving supervisor and support personnel in the Dog-house.

The Dog-house is a box-like affair bolted on top of the chamber. When a Sat dive is in progress, the Dog-house is manned 24 hours a day.

Here is where all the gauges and instruments are located to record and monitor the activities and the environment in the chamber below. There are depth gauges, O_2 and CO_2 recorders, temperature and humidity controls, an electrical panel of knobs and switches, one wall with a maze of valves and gauges for the automatic ascent system and, on top of this, back-up or redundant systems for the whole works.

It's no wonder that the person in charge of all this is called an 'instrument man'. His is a crucial job requiring know-how, understanding and a certain amount of compassion. Not only does he keep a constant, watchful eye on things 'below' but he is also in direct communication with the chamber. He is also usually the first to take the brunt of any complaint.

At first, the helium-distorted voices (Donald Duck effect) of saturated divers are difficult to understand and very trying on the dedicated instrument men. Within a day or two however, an experienced 'dog-houseman' grows accustomed to frequent requests.

You can often hear his voice bellowing over the PA system to one of the tenders: "Flush the shitter".

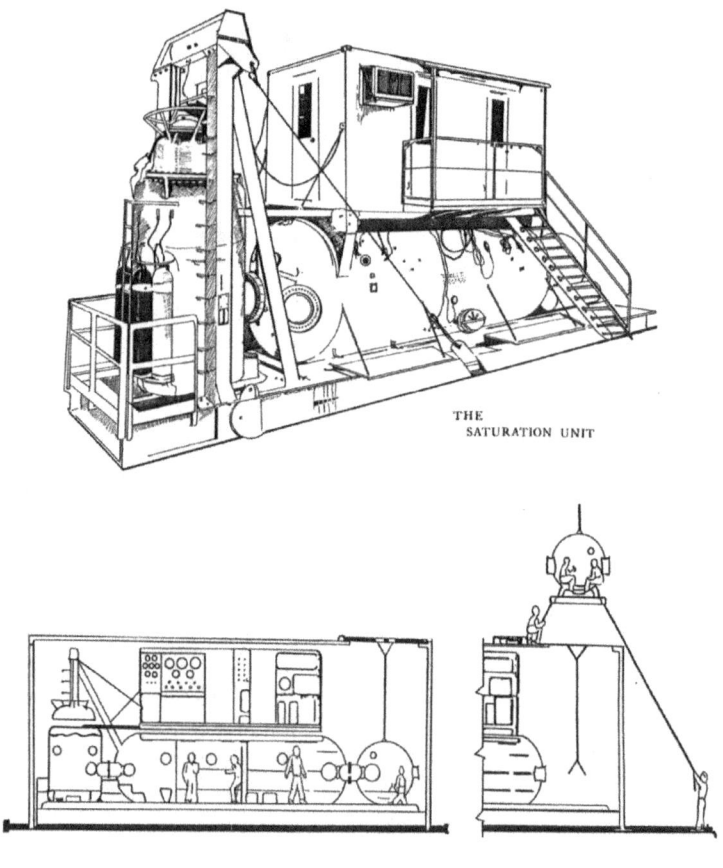

THE SATURATION UNIT

THE TRANSFER

Artwork by Diane R. compliments of Paul Kalman

> *"Believe me, if you've been shut up for a year and a half, it can get to be too much for you sometimes. But feelings can't be ignored ... I long to ride a bike, dance, whistle, look at the world........."*
>
> [Anne Frank 1942]

Chapter 2

Sat Log - Day 32 – Decompression Schedule – 1,000 ft Dive

Vessel: Ocean Venture   Sat Unit: SDC/TL 12

Date: 30 Oct 77   Time: 0100   Shift: Midnight/Noon

Depth: 564 ft

Confinement comes in many forms and many varying situations. Being incarcerated is confinement, stationed on a submarine is another form of confinement but nothing quite compares to the confinement and restriction of a saturation unit during decompression with a full complement of divers. The action of getting out of your bunk and going to the toilet can mean invading someone's space or disturbing their mental state – like being woken up from a beautiful dream. Sleep is sacred, it's killing time and during decompression time is the enemy. With such limited space – feelings can't be ignored.

I was wide-awake now as I tried to work up enough energy to leave the warmth and security of my bunk. The temperature must have dropped a few degrees during the night. It's probably 82F or 83F degrees, not much below a comfortable 85F or 86F, but in our pressurized steel home, a one or two-degree variation in temperature makes a big difference. The big difference right now is the slight chill which is playing hell on my swollen bladder. When you gotta' go, you gotta' go.

Trying not to wake the other guys, I got out of my bunk and headed toward the curtained-off section of the chamber, where the toilet, sink, medical lock and tunnel to the bell are located. This was the action area. Guided by the faint light seeping in through the partially covered port (window), I made my way down the narrow aisle between the two rows of bunks. I reached my objective and with a sign of relief and relieved my aching bladder of its burden. Turning to the speaker nearby, I called to topside, "Topside, what's the temperature?"

"82F degrees, I'm trying to warm it up now."

"How about a flush and send down a pot of coffee?"

"Roger, one flush and one coffee."

It would take about ten minutes for the tender on watch to get some coffee from the galley. While I waited, I wondered if the seas had calmed down any since last night. Outside of an occasional shudder from the chamber and checking with the Dog-house, events in the topside world were usually a mystery.

The outside hatch on the medical lock closed with a bang, and with a blast of gas the coffee was on its way. The inside hatch popped open as the two compartments equalized and the fragrant aroma of freshly brewed coffee filled the atmosphere. I poured myself a cup. Too hot to drink, I sat there with my hands wrapped around the steaming cup, feeling it's warmth cut the chill. Suddenly, the barge took a heavy roll to port as it broached the seas in an effort to change course. The chamber rocked from side to side while the two tugs, towing the barge, fought the pounding waves in their struggle to swing the barge around.

This recent bit of activity was enough to wake a few of the guys. I could hear one or two of them curse or mumble as they braced themselves for the next roll.

The rock and roll session ceased once the two tugs had swung the barge around and were heading into the seas. Things were back to normal.

I smiled to myself as I thought about one guy who wasn't having any problem sleeping, Matthew Sims, my hibernating bell partner. Everyone called him Matt. However, I'm not sure if it was just a shortened form of his first name or because of his affection for a mattress. This guy had no problem staying in the rack; 14 to 16 hours was a short stay. One of these days he is going to end up in a hospital for an amputation ... to get the mattress cut off his back.

I've known Matt for several years and working in a confined space, such as this, you get to know a lot about a person. He was a few years younger than I, which wasn't all that unusual. In a racket where 45 is considered ancient, by the time you're 33, you're a veteran. He and I had worked a lot of jobs together not only in saturation, but also in shallow water. Aside from his prowess for sleeping, he was a good hand in the water. Like a lot of commercial divers breaking out in the past few years, he'd received his basic training in the Navy. He'd done the UDT course, Seal Team and deployed to Vietnam before 'civi-street'.

It didn't take him long to find out that the abalone diving on the west coast was all sewed up and was a tough racket in which to make a buck.

Making the rounds, he'd heard that there was plenty of action in the Gulf of Mexico. What the hell, even if it was only rumor, Mardi Gras was just around the corner and being the world's greatest free show, it had to be worth the trip.

It didn't take too many nights of crawling around the bars and strip joints on Bourbon Street to get the feel and swing of the French Quarter. In his exploration of the finer points of interest on the tourist guide, it was only a matter of time before he found the local haunts of divers. I wonder how many of us, back then, used the Seven Seas as a place of residence. It must have had one of the most well-known phone numbers in town.

In the early 60's, it was common for a dispatcher of a diving company to call these joints looking for a diving crew. Jobs were still a little hard to come by at this time and answering the phone at the right moment could put rice and gravy on the table for that week. There were times though when answering that thing could be murder. Like the time Matt grabbed the receiver off the wall at 11 o'clock at night. He was finishing a Dixie beer, getting ready to change locations. He just happened to be the closest one to it when it started to ring.

"Yeah, Seven Seas," he answered.

"Is Bill Murphy there?" asked the voice on the other end.

"Hang on a minute, I'll check," Matt replied. "Hey man, is there a Bill Murphy in the place?" he yelled over the noise of the crowd gathered around the ping pong table in the patio and the blare of the juke box. After trying several times without success, he turned back to the receiver.

"Nah, he ain't here."

"Listen," the voice said, "this is Mitch from Deep Sea Diving. I'm looking for a tender to go out in the morning ..."

"You got one," Matt cut him off short.

He couldn't get the words out fast enough. This was it; just what he'd been waiting for. Hell, he was so excited he almost hung up before he found out where he had to go.

"Right," Mitch said, "be down in Venice at 5 o'clock in the morning to catch the crew boat Mary Ann. The diver's name is Jeff Morgan. Bye."

Click, the phone went dead in his hand. Jesus, Matt thought as he hung up the phone. Five o'clock in the morning? I'd have to leave here by 3 o'clock. Man, that's only four hours from now. I was hoping to catch Mary Ann alright, but not this one.

He emerged from the cold grey cloud of fog and exhaust fumes surrounding the crew boat and hollered over the noise of other boat's throbbing engines. "If you're Jeff Morgan, I'm your new tender, Matt Simms." Well, that was how we met.

Not only did he appear exhausted and suffering from the first stages of hangover, but he also looked frozen. Being new to south Louisiana, he figured it would be warm in February and was dressed accordingly - sneakers, t-shirt, and a windbreaker. At this time of the morning, it wasn't unusual to see a scattered ice patch here and there in the drainage ditches that lined the sides of the highway from Belle Chasse to Venice. It was cold alright, it was freezing-ass cold.

I told him to stow his gear, a set of matching luggage - two cardboard boxes - down below in the passengers' compartment. It was warm down there, a welcome change from the cold damp night. I suggested that he stretch out on one of the long vacant seats. It would take about four hours for the boat to get out on location; plenty of time to catch up on some badly needed rest. I didn't have to make the offer twice. He made a dive for nearest cushioned bench. With a life jacket for a pillow, it wasn't long before he was singing his favorite tune, if you want to call that music. 'Mattress Back' had joined the club.

That was the first of many jobs for us that year. We'd catch a few jobs out in the Gulf, then maybe hit one in the river. We weren't making a fortune, but we were doing OK. Making enough bread for the beer and the broads and to keep the bill collectors happy. Like most of the other divers, we free-lanced during the winter, taking whatever jobs we could get. In the summer, because of the milder weather, work in the Gulf would pick up and the season would get into high gear. Then we'd settle down and work for one company.

Matt was like most of the guys who ventured into offshore diving. He started out as a tender and would give me a hand in the water every now and then. That was a good way for him to get the experience he needed so he could 'break-out' diving.

The next few months we spent out in the Gulf working on a pipe lay barge, one of the huge new fleet of vessels that were becoming a familiar sight at sea as the industrial fleets started to expand. It was on this barge that Matt got his chance to 'break-out'.

We'd been working around the clock for a couple of days on an underwater flange connecting the pipeline to the riser, which is clamped to the leg of the platform. As is usually the case, when all the divers had used up all their bottom time, one more dive is needed to complete the job. That was Matt's chance and he took it. The old adage, "In the right place at the right time", paid off. He made the dive and I was left looking for a new tender.

My coffee had cooled off enough by now to allow me a few quick sips. I felt quite contented as I performed this morning ritual. Being one of those people who doesn't function too well until they've had at least two cups, I downed my first in short order. I was pouring my second cup when Pete's sleepy head poked out from behind the curtain. Pete was the inside tender on this trip. Rubbing the sleep out of his eyes and squinting in the unaccustomed light, he fumbled for a speaker.

"Hey, topside, what time is it? What depth are we at?"

"0930, 505 feet."

"How's the coffee?" he asked turning to me.

"Still warm, " I replied and grabbing the stainless steel pitcher, I poured him a cup.

"Hey, topside," he called, "what's the weather like?"

"Rough and getting rougher, I'll send you a copy of the latest weather report as soon as I get one."

"Who is this?" Pete demanded.

"This is Ralph, I'm the new Dog-house trainee. Don't worry, James is looking over my shoulder, watching every move I make. You guys are in good hands."

"Listen Ralph, what's the latest on the rig that's on fire?"

"The last thing I heard was that it was still burning and that a mini-sub was going to assist in some way. We received a batch of newspapers when the supply boat came out yesterday with the mail and stores. Let me see if I can get one of the tenders to round y'all up a couple of copies. There are a few interesting articles about the rig. They can tell the story better than I can."

As usual, we were the last to find out anything. They should have called this isolation instead of saturation.

I got to thinking about that rig. The first news we'd received had been three days ago. A rig had caught fire in the oil field, 80 miles north of us about 140 miles out of Aberdeen, Scotland. I knew there were several rigs in that field and a lot of activity in the area because of the urgent need to get the oil ashore.

The jet barge we were working on was burying a 30 inch pipeline that linked up the two fields. The pipeline wasn't hooked up to the northern field yet. It had been laid last year and was anchored on the bottom, waiting to be habitat-welded this summer. It was part of the main trunk line system which connected the two fields with the tank farm at Ennisburg, just north of Aberdeen.

"Is it OK to take up the lock? I've got some newspapers and several magazines," the Dog-house operator called down, bringing me back to the present.

"Yes, go ahead, take it up and send in another pot of coffee, five bowls and five spoons, two cartons of milk and some All Bran cereal."

"What's the matter, you guys getting stopped up?"

"Well, you've gotta be regular don't you and a person can only eat so many prunes, smartass."

We certainly didn't want to get constipated while we were coming up, need to let that gas escape, right?

Although a minor problem on the outside, constipation can become relatively serious on the inside and quite painful for the poor s.o.b. with the blocked plumbing.

The Pressure Zone by Mike Cooke

One time, Joe had been coming up from a depth of 210 feet and was in the final day of decompression before he experienced excruciating pain and swelling of the lower abdomen. As the pressure (depth) decreased, the pain increased. All Stop ... decompression problem .... immediate action.

The chamber was pressured back down to a point where Joe received relief. This was the first step taken to remedy the situation. The next was a matter of determining just how close you and your bell partner are. (It ain't everybody who will administer suppositories - in this case, half a dozen.) No problem, Joe and Bob were tight, especially Joe! Well, with the silver bullets in place, various laxatives and some steady stomach massaging, total relief finally came for Joe ... everyone else nearly passed out from asphyxiation ... talk about expanding gases ... Whew! Carry on decompressing. Thank God.

The cost of this little decompression incident - $11,000 for wages and gases (no pun intended). That's one hell of an expensive bowel movement. The boys in saturation had no complaints - more for them. And to show their appreciation for Joe's efforts and suffering he was presented with the 'Gold Turd Award'.

A quarter of an hour went by before the stuff we'd ordered got sent down to us. The lad's topside were looking after us, not only had they send down everything we'd asked for, but they'd also added a tin of Rover cookies, several slices of hot buttered toast and a jar of strawberry jam. I noticed that the lid had already been loosened on the jar, some on-the-ball tender was using the ol' noggin. At this depth, with that much pressure on the jar, if the lid wasn't cracked, or a hole punched in it allowing it to equalize, there was a good chance of it being crushed. The reverse would be the case on sending things out. If they were sealed tight, they'd explode on the way up.

I fixed myself a bowl of cereal and started to glance at the newspapers which were a few days old. The front pages of all of them were almost identical. A full page picture of a blazing rig standing out from a background of thick, billowing, black clouds of oil smoke darkening the sky. The only thing blacker were the 2 inch headlines. "IRA BLOWS UP RIG." "FANATIC ARAB SECT SET RIG ABLAZE." "SCOTTISH NATIONALS SAY IF THEY CAN'T HAVE IT, NO ONE CAN."

From the reading of the papers, it was apparent that some clown had finally gone off the deep end and blown up a rig, taking the lives of 22 innocent men. The blame, or credit, was being put on any number of subversive organizations depending on the paper you were reading and its political leanings. The articles went on to say that it was assumed the person responsible for blowing up the rig had been one of the victims ... poetic justice?

It was believed that the demented individual guilty of this insane act had been a specialist, an electronic technician, sent out to work on a faulty radio. He had been flown out by helicopter and was to have been taken back into the beach by the supply boat that was due out the next day. Due to the weather picking up, the supply boat was unable to get in close enough to the rig to pick up passengers. Fortunately, the supply boat had stayed in the area and along with the fishing trawler, which remained with the rig at all times, rescued the remainder of the crew that had jumped from the blazing inferno.

The story went on to say that two barges working in the field were moving into position to combat the blaze. They would set up across the rig from each other.

One of the barges was a sister vessel to the one we were working on. It had been burying the northern half of the 30 inch pipeline. This 'super jet' barge with two 20,000 hp jet pumps that could put out 20,000 gallons of water per minute, was ideal for throwing water on a fire. Water wouldn't put out this blaze, but it would help contain it. The other barge being used was a derrick barge. This barge was huge, larger than a football field, 400 feet long and 150 feet wide. It was outfitted with a 1,600 ton crane, one of the largest revolving cranes afloat. The advantage of such a long boom, 245 feet in length, would allow fire-fighting equipment to be directed over the fire. Due to the fierceness of the fire and the extreme heat, it was almost impossible to get within 150 feet of the rig.

The article continued, stressing the danger of oil pollution. There was no doubt about it, the chances of a large oil slick creating havoc weren't too remote. In the meantime, however, most of the oil was being burnt off. The oil company was being assisted by the Royal Navy in getting an oil boom set up to surround the area and trap any escaping oil. This loose oil would be sprayed with a chemical allowing it to dissolve and mix with the seawater, becoming harmless.

The oil company did admit that a few small slicks were in existence, but for the most part were being effectively taken care of by the speedily erected oil boom. Not all of the escaping oil had been corralled. But the small amount that was drifting wasn't expected to be of any problem. It was being tracked by aircraft and was reported to be breaking up, due to the rough seas, into small harmless patches.

The immediate problem, aside from the fire, was the weather. A gale Force 8 had been predicted for the area. I thought that must be the storm we were experiencing now. This was the first time an oil boom had been used in the North Sea. They were a tricky piece of equipment to work with in the best of conditions. Now, with the state of sea worsening, keeping the boom in tack would be a difficult job. In fact, the danger of the boom breaking up was becoming another major problem.

If the boom did break and the oil slick did increase, there was the likelihood of another disaster. I could understand the concern of every country that bordered the North Sea. It would only be the small matter of a change in wind direction and a beautiful, sandy beach would be turned into a mess of thick, oily, black, coagulated globs. What a mess it would create, turning shorelines into sticky tar masses, beaches ruined, wildlife destroyed, fishing grounds spoiled. If this thing did get out of hand it would make the Torrey Canyon disaster seem like spilt milk - and to think that the person that could be responsible for all of this happening would be considered a martyr by certain warped individuals.

I left Pete sitting on the shitter, reading one of the papers and headed to my bunk in the outer lock. Trying not to disturb the two silent, sleeping forms in the inner lock, I quietly moved down the aisle between the stacked bunks. Pushing aside the dark green, plastic curtain separating the two locks, I was greeted by Matt's voice coming from the still darkness.

"Hey, I'm awake. Go ahead and have topside turn on the overhead."

"Topside, turn on number one," I called into the speaker hanging by my bunk. I'd no sooner gotten the words out when our section, the outer lock of the chamber, was flooded by the soft light from the low wattage bulb at the forward end of the chamber.

Blinking and wiping the sleep out of his eyes, Matt went through the motions of getting up.

"Coffee, toast and cereal came in about a half an hour ago, if you want some," I told him. Stifling a yawn, he got up mumbling something about "coffee bladder racehorses"... something like that. Anyway, he was back in a few minutes with a cup in his hand.

Sitting on the edge of his bunk, he turned to me and asked how I was feeling. "Alright," I told him "how about you?"

"Great, but you don't look too good," he said. "You look down, man, like something's bugging you."

"Oh, I was just thinking of those stories in the paper about that rig on fire. Here, see for yourself," I said and handed him a copy of the Daily Mail.
He glanced at the front page picture and commented.

"Those guys fighting that sonofabitch have got their hands full. Remember that rig that caught on fire in the Gulf of Mexico a few years back? That damn thing raged out of control for more than a month before it was snuffed out."

"Well it's enough to piss a guy off. Those roughnecks have it hard enough trying to make a decent living on one of those things without some asshole coming along and pulling a stunt like that," I fumed.

"You're right, but I guess it was bound to happen sooner or later. No matter how safe the operation is, it only takes one irresponsible, hot head to create a catastrophe. Well, there's not much we can do about it now, and anyhow, in a few days we'll be out of here and heading home. Cheer up man, don't let it get to you" he said.

"It's easy for you to feel that way, you'll be leaving here and heading back to the States. I've got my family here and I live with these people. There's a good chance I know, or did know, someone on that rig," I said. I'd been living in Aberdeen for the past four years. In that time, we'd made a lot of friends, both American and Scottish. I like it here. Being from up north, I was accustomed to the climate and found it a good place to live (even if they did have lousy liquor laws). The oil community was close-knit, but we also had friends who were born and raised here.

Oh sure, every now and then we'd run into the 'Goddamn American' routine, but usually it was in jest or envy. What the hell, if we couldn't take it by now, we'd never be able to!

"Shit man, we been hated most of the best places around."

"Come on, Jeff," Matt consoled. "Snap out of it. It's one of those things. Everyone knows it can happen, but you must hope and pray that it doesn't. Oil is a precious commodity. It's the life blood of many nations, and this here oil patch ain't any different. Some people figure it's worth fighting for, and from the articles in the paper they figure the loss of a little blood - the red kind - is a small price to pay to get control of the life blood of a nation – oil. Not a very pleasant situation to be in, I confess, nevertheless, we are in it, if not directly, then at least in part and I don't like it any more than you."

"I know it doesn't affect us directly," I said, having no idea what the next few days would have in store, "but how long do you think it'll be before some jerk decides to sabotage a barge? This work is dangerous enough without having to worry about being blown to bits."

"Just look at the number of rigs that have been set adrift or gone down, and the number of lives that have been lost due to the extreme weather conditions. That sucker out there ain't no mill pond! Hell, right in this area where we're working winds have been recorded up to 100 mph and have furrowed the seas with waves of the same figure," I reminded him.

As though to add a little emphasis to what I was saying, the barge took another big one over the bow. The impact of the blunt, raked bow colliding into a massive wall of grey-green angry water was amplified for all of us as the chamber went through it's shake, rattle and roll act for the umpteenth time.

"Also, I continued, "apart from the weather, there are the normal occupational hazards. Even with the most stringent regulations, there's always the unknown factor. We've probably got one of the highest risk jobs going, and if insurance premiums are an indication, then it certainly is."

In the past 10 years in the North Sea area there had been 22 diving fatalities. Last year alone, six divers were killed because of one type of diving accident or other.

"One thing we certainly don't need is some mad fool juggling with the odds and turning us into a macabre statistic."

"Well, I'm glad you got that off your chest," Matt mockingly replied, "can I go back to sleep now?"

"Ah, fuck you," I retorted.

With that, he rolled over and went back to sleep.

"Turn out No. 1", I called up to the Dog-house through the speaker by my bunk. Almost immediately, the chamber was plunged into total darkness with the steady hum of the blower motors and the intermittent hissing and popping of the solenoid valves, the only reminder that this black, steel void was connected to the outside world. The perfect environment to think and ponder.

The Pressure Zone by Mike Cooke

As I lay there staring into nothingness, I thought about some of the things I'd mentioned to Matt.

There was no doubt about it, we are in one of the most dangerous rackets around. The list of occupational hazards reads like a physician's desk reference – let alone human error.

With the increasing demand for expansion and development of the oil and gas fields located in the North Sea, more and more companies were being attracted to the area. Naturally, competition increased and the demand for experienced personnel became greater. Well, with only a limited number of experienced offshore commercial divers available, the demand was being filled with inadequately trained, inexperienced divers taking what they could get and doing whatever was necessary to get a shot at the big apple. It wasn't long before the accidents started to happen. A few fatalities and the newspapers were starting to have a heyday. This type of publicity had a dull effect on the industry; not only was it putting us in the limelight, but also created an awareness that something had to be done, and soon.

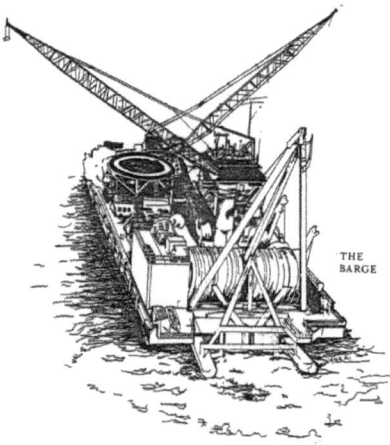
THE BARGE

The diving companies were being portrayed as perpetrators of some sort of mass murder. The hazards of diving were being expounded upon, that's for sure but, the articles seemed to generalize and failed to differentiate between the guilty and the innocent parties, reflecting adversely over the whole industry.

With everyone aware of just how dangerous diving could be, it wasn't long before individual governments started to issue and enforce basic diving regulations. So the publicity paid off in dividends for the guy was getting wet.

Yes, the industry has come a long way in the past 10 years, and it's getting bigger, going deeper and becoming more sophisticated all the time. But, most importantly (with the inevitable helping hand from Uncle Sam), it realized the potential hazards and is spending a lot of money, time and effort towards making diving safer.

THE RIG

Artwork by Diane R.
compliments of Paul Kalman

The Pressure Zone by Mike Cooke

Lament of a Saturation Tender

HELP! My name is 074 and I am being held prisoner on the M-280 somewhere in the North Sea. I am only 25 years old even though I was born in 1943. The reason is I was sick for five years. I am 5'11" and weigh 190 pounds and have 11 years of high school.

Out here on the Barge M-280 they just call me 074. All the slaves out here have serial numbers and sometimes we are referred to as tenders or something similar. All slaves live in one room below decks next to the engine room. I guess this is to ensure we don't get any sleep. They have six slaves on my watch that is from noon until midnight. All six of us sleep in the same room. The room has only one bed, so sometimes it takes quite a while before we are able to fall asleep.

When we are awakened, we are all sent to the stern of the barge. Here we work for 12 hours. Most of our work is done in the saturation house. In this house, they keep this huge white monster. Our slave driver, who calls himself Herb, makes us keep this monster well fed. So far, it has swallowed 4 divers and one slave. On the port side is located its mouth into which we are constantly shoving food, coffee, tea, newspapers, magazines, towels, sheets, and a seemingly endless supply of toilet paper.

Usually, after each feeding, Herb makes us bang on the starboard side of the monster and the monster always bangs back. This means the monster has to void his bowels. We tenders have to operate a handle connected to the monster's rectal grommet. As soon as you open it, you hear this loud swoosh. The discharge comes out so fast that the fire hose connected to the grommet jumps 6 or 7 feet in the air.

Every so often, the monster moves forward till its head is out over the water. Only then does the monster put its head under water. As soon as the head enters the water, the slaves have to slack off its neck. The neck is extremely long, often 900 feet.

Sometimes its head goes down 200 or more feet. All the slaves have to pull real hard when the monster wants its head up on deck again. Three slaves already have hernias from hauling on the monster's neck.

When the head is back in place and its neck is hung up, the monster moves back into its house. During this time, the slave master, Fred, is there to check on the slave driver, Herb, and the slaves.

Fred and Herb are the only ones allowed to talk to the monster while its head is under water. For this, they use a special radio. Once in a while the monster gets a headache and the slave master and slave driver get excited and make us take the top off the monster's head. They refer to this as "removing the dome."

After the monster's headache is relieved, the dome is put back on. The slaves are not allowed to look under the dome. Just Fred and Herb. There's a rumor among the slaves that under the dome is a note saying, "Left is port ...right is starboard."

I understand there are several monsters in the North Sea. I must go now. I hear the monster banging on its starboard side again.

LJC

Chapter 3

Sat Log – Day 33 – Decompression Schedule – 1,000 ft Dive

Vessel: Ocean Venture   Sat Unit: SDC/TL 12
Date: 31 Oct 77   Time: 0100   Shift: Midnight/Noon
Depth: 468 ft

Generally, the first few days in saturation pass by rather quickly. Being kept busy with the steady workload, setting up house and basically getting accustomed to the change of environment.

Because you usually plan on staying for a month, the very first thing to do is get your bunk, your back's best friend, your home for the next thirty days, all squared away. Just the way you like it. Reading light in the proper location and cassette recorder within easy reach. The shelf beside the bunk (if you're fortunate enough to have a shelf, that is) stuffed with an array of articles.

This would include reading and writing materials, several diving logs, which had to be filled in daily (part of the new regulations), and all the other little knick-knacks you might be into at the time. Of course, it is usually rounded out with a rainbow of assorted little bottles containing A's, B's, C's, D's, EFG's, everything to make the stay as healthy and comfortable as possible. Maybe something a little stronger? Nuh-uh. Uppers and downers are a no-no.

Of course, all of these things must be close at hand. I mean, heaven forbid that you should have to strain yourself by getting out of bed for one of life's necessities. Undoubtedly, the most important item in this lot is the cassette player. Equipped with a set of headphones, it allowed you to isolate yourself into your own private world. Being carried away by your favorite sounds or having 'sweet nothings' whispered in your ear by the latest tape from home. It is also great for giving the kids a charge. Just what little Billy always wanted - a cassette recording of his big bad deep-sea diver Dad sounding like Donald Duck.

If it's ever decided to give out Oscars in the diving profession, the first should go to the individual who developed the portable cassette player. It is this instrument that makes four weeks of confined, boring decompression bearable.

Let's see, where was I? Oh yeah. We've finally gotten settled in.

The bunks have been made, usually with the pillow end furthest away from the toilet (unless the guy's a masochist) and the Sat tender, being junior, ending up with the least comfortable rack. This could mean any number of inconveniences.

Being in a top bunk, there's the chance that he won't get to roll over and be comfortable, because the curved side of the chamber is about six inches above his nose when laying on his back. Of course, this is easily overcome once you get in the rack, you just don't move.

I remember one rack that was a beauty. Getting up and into it was easy, sleeping was the hard part. Due to the poor circulation and the layering effect of the atmosphere in the chamber, the bunk was a sweatbox, while the guy below had the blankets pulled over his head trying to keep warm. Every now and then, though, it would cool off. The inlet for the makeup gas was protruding into your backside and you could regularly expect a refreshing blast of gas in the ass as cold helium makeup gas was added. But you really weren't settled in until you got your feet jammed in between the oral/nasal masks with their twin hoses and associated valving. As I said, the first few days were a new experience. It was after that things got boring, somewhere around the fifth day. From then on, it was just a matter of putting your mind in neutral and your body in overdrive, which isn't an exaggeration by any means. After two or three 12 to 14 hour bell runs, the ol' bod is ready for the rack.

No matter how hard you work, eventually the confinement gets to you. Oh, I don't mean you're stark raving mad, but you'd sure like to do something different, just as long as it doesn't take up too much time. That's another one of the peculiarities about saturation and confinement. You have all the time in the world to read and study, but you don't want to because it takes too long and too much effort.

Let me give you a classic example of this indolent feeling. Two good friends had been in saturation for several weeks when one, just out of curiosity, asked the other for the time. Now his friend, not being a man of many words in the first place, turned very slowly toward him with a pained look on his face, and with a tremendous amount of effort, raised two fingers. Hell, it was no effort to tell him the time; however, if he had turned around with a pleasant look on his face and cheerfully replied, "Hey man, it's two o' clock" then he might have gotten trapped into a conversation, and that would have been an effort having to carry out a conversation.

However, sometimes one does get his ass into gear and does stay busy. For instance, this story was conceived at 300 feet, written at 500 feet, and edited at 1,200 feet. In other words, started and finished during saturation.

Anyhow, it does get very tedious in saturation and the most boring time of all is coming up when the pressure decreases but your anxieties and cabin fever increase in inverse proportion with the gradual approach to the surface.

We were in our third day of ascent and were ready to get out here. Oh, to get out, have a cigarette, walk, walk, and walk. Then to get on the boat, hit the beach and wink at the one-eyed bear.

Well, I'd been laying down for the past month becoming quite attached to my mattress, so I guess another two days shouldn't be too difficult.

Let's see ... if I can sleep at least 20 hours out of the next 48 and watch a movie or two through the porthole, I should have it knocked. Jesus, I hope no one gets bent.

On the last Sat, a guy got hit on both knees at eight feet. Just two hours to freedom and this guy gets bent. The whole crew had to go back down, thirty feet deeper, before he got relief. It took them another twelve hours to get out. When you're that close to the surface, it's terrible to have to go back down, but it's the only cure for the bends - recompression.

"Hey, everyone OK down there?" Charlie inquired, bringing me back to the present. "Nobody feeling any pain?" Talk about ESP.

"How about any cash advances or hotel reservations? I need to know as soon as possible, so I can call the office and get it taken care of."

That Charlie, he had it together. One of the best supervisors in the business. Even though he'd never been in saturation he understood what it was like and how some of the smallest things, like making reservations, for instance, were appreciated by the crew. (While most of the time you were treated like a mushroom and kept in the dark and shat on.)

"Hey Charlie," Al called from his bunk, "Buddy and I would like $2,000 each and reservations at the Imperial Hotel in Aberdeen. The suite, if possible, if not, then two doubles with a shower."

They were dreaming ... a bath, maybe, but a shower ... no way.

"Got you covered Al, anyone else need anything ... no? OK, see you guys in two days."

Lying there, I couldn't help smiling as I thought about the two of them. It sounded like they were getting ready for another one of their famous runs.

They usually started out as a proper pair of gents with nothing but the best of intentions. This strict regimen usually lasted through two bottles of champagne, but by the time the third cork popped, well ... the best laid plans of mice and men ... but you had to admit their intentions were generally good, usually spiced with a pinch of genius and always loaded with laughs.

Al and Buddy went back a long way and had been through a lot of rough water together. Naturally, they had their ups and downs, but as friends, they were tight. Anyway, I didn't know anybody who didn't like Al or could stay mad at him for any length of time. His charm was irresistible.

He had a line as smooth as black velvet (Scotch, that is) and the saddest looking watery blue eyes, that would come to life and sparkle as you were being had. He was beautiful people.

Al was one of those rare people that once you'd met him you could never quite forget him. He was right out of the pages of Cannery Row.

His face had so many red and blue lines it looked like a road map. He had short cut steely-grey hair and a nose that had either stopped too many punches or was the by-product of too much Thunderbird.

He had a habit of always blowing the drooping ends of a beautiful bushy red moustache away from his mouth, or with a red bandana handkerchief, wiping away the remnants of his last meal.

The Pebble Beach golf shirt he always wore went through sheer torture trying to cover a massive stomach that protruded out over the top of a pair of faded blue Levis. He wore his jeans in such a fashion that revealed several inches of posterior cleavage and only stayed up by the grace of God. This ensemble was rounded out with a pair of well-shined, size twelve, brogans.

At times, when the season was slack and he was 'tap city' you might find him living on the beach in Puerto Vallarta washing elephants for his bread. At other times, he'd be rolling high. All decked out in a white sport coat and charcoal gray slacks. His right knee covered with black shoe polish to hide a hole he'd burnt in the pants. Then there'd be the occasion when he'd want to borrow ten bucks off you so he could buy the next round and not have to lose face.

Al had entered diving through the back door, so to speak. He had a run in with the law several years ago. It was a side of Al very few people knew about.

He didn't talk about his past much unless you happened to catch him in the right place ... the Seven Seas, at the right time ... about three in the morning, in the right mood ... busted flat and feeling sorry for himself.

He'd been fishing out of San Francisco at the time and had come home unexpectedly to find his old lady between the sheets with someone else. He laid out his old lady and broke the guy's jaw and had most of the apartment re-arranged on the street below before a couple of cops were able to contain him. The judge decided a short spell in jail would calm him down.

Torn up pretty bad inside by the incident, he just wanted to burn the bridge behind him when he got out. He decided to get lost in the oil fields. Working the Gulf of Mexico as a roughneck, he drifted from rig to rig. From the rigs, he moved on to a pipe lay barge where he worked as a welder's helper. With welding being the best paying job on the barge, it didn't take him long to master the art. But pushing rods 12 hours a day for a living in 100°C heat isn't any joy. Especially when he could see those divers, not 40 feet away, hitting that cool refreshing water and making about the same amount of bread. Al made his move and he couldn't have picked a better time.

There was a demand for experienced divers who wanted to weld and experienced welders who wanted to dive. Of course, the majority of divers knew the basic fundamentals of welding and could tack a patch on underwater, no sweat. So why the big need for trained welders?

Several diving companies, by this time, had developed a technique for dry hyperbaric welding.

A new method for more positive and safer underwater tie-ins. Most underwater tie-ins (the connecting of two pieces of pipe) were being done using several different methods; bolted flanges, hydraulic couplings, and welded sleeves, or any combination of these.

These various methods had two major drawbacks in common. They were assembled in the wet and were prone to leaks.

Now with the advent of dry hyperbaric welding, it was possible to join two pieces of pipe together with a weld that would meet the rigid standards set up by the regulating agencies. This weld was made possible by the use of a habitat, a large box-shaped affair that was placed over the two pieces of pipe to be welded together.

It was then blown dry and made habitable for two men to enter and perform the weld. Thereby allowing the customer many restful nights by alleviating the worry of a leaking flange.

One company, in particular, had become so proficient in the technique of dry hyperbaric welding, it had found it necessary to institute its own diving and welding programs.

Al quickly got on the list and found that he was right. This is where it was at! Being able to hit that cool refreshing water and still keep on welding. He was one of the first of a new breed of divers, the dry hyperbaric welder/diver (or diver/welder, depending on your specialty).

That had been some time ago and he'd been with us ever since, except for off-season jaunts and Lord knows where he went then. It would take a melancholy evening in the Seven Seas to find that out.

The chamber slowly came back to life as the lights were turned on and caught all of us in various stages of waking and getting up. Buddy, a fresh steaming hot cup of coffee in his hand, was standing by the shitter, looking into the metal mirror admiring the four weeks of growth on his face. The telltale gray in his beard seemed to add another five years, belying his forty-four. Now, thinking back, I can't remember when I didn't know him as "the old man". He wasn't the oldest diver working for us, but he was getting close to it and in a few more years he'd be ready for a nice cushy job as a consultant on the beach. That is, if he'd been wise enough to put a little away for that rainy day and the inevitable time when it came time to 'hang it up'. But, like most of us, he'd probably been a little foolish and had been living beyond his means for most of his life.

"Hey, topside," Buddy called into the speaker just below the mirror, "will you get the shower ready, please?"

"OK, but it'll be a few minutes before it's hot enough," came the reply from the Dog-house.

In an environment as closely confined as saturation, one becomes acutely aware of the other fellow's odor. What? Me? My farts don't stink. Taking a shower not only eliminated b.o. problems, it was also one of the few luxuries available to us.

Making a shower possible was no big thing; it was simply a matter of heating some water in a tank topside, pressurizing the tank over the pressure in the bell, piping it to the bell, opening a few valves and voila, hot running water. However, it would take about fifteen minutes for the water to heat up so this would be an appropriate time to tell you a little bit about Buddy.

Buddy had been in this racket a long time and there weren't many jobs in the water that he hadn't tried.

He'd caught langouste off the Florida Keys, tried lumbering (breaking up log jams with explosives) up in New Brunswick, did a stint on the locks in the St Lawrence Seaway, worked the slips in a dockyard on the west coast and done 101 other things. I'm sure the list could go on and on and if I figured his age out for the number of jobs he's had and the stories he's told, he'd be pushing 105, instead of the 50 he was coming up on.

Not having any formal civilian or military training, he was one of the few guys around who had always been a commercial diver. I think he mentioned one time that he got his start by clearing a fouled screw on a tug in the St John's River just outside of Daytona. He started with a set of tanks (SCUBA) and from there went on to bigger and better things as he'd hot-shot across the country gaining more experience and confidence with each different job. Finally, he ended up in New Orleans, and from then on it was the big green of the ol' oil patch.

Missing out on formal training, he'd learned about the hazards of diving from the school of hard knocks and had the scars to prove it. He was one of several divers that I know who can only give half a 'peace-sign' because he had only three fingers on the one hand. This type of affliction is most often accredited to one of two causes; one, the menacing jaws of a submerged pipeline flange springing open and snapping shut in rough water with no visibility, or two, because someone on deck wasn't paying attention - "I said come up on the davit, not down, up on it, goddamn it. Shit ..." another member to the club.

I think, however, Buddy's most harrowing experience, and the one that gave him religion, was the first time he got bent and didn't know how to treat it. Fortunately, one of the crew he was working with had enough sense to get in touch with the Navy. The Navy, as do most diving companies, has a list of all the hyperbaric facilities and recompression/decompression chambers and their locations in the country.

It's said that the Lord protects saints and sinners and He must have had Buddy's name on the list. The nearest chamber was five miles away. Some quick action and smart thinking on the part of the crew enabled him to receive immediate treatment and walk away with no crippling side effects.

The Pressure Zone by Mike Cooke

He was one lucky fellow. This incident had taught him a very valuable lesson - it made him realize that there are hazards associated with diving and that it wasn't just a matter of getting wet. Some basic education was needed and fast. Probably the best source of detailed information on diving is the US Navy Diving Manual, which can be purchased from the Navy. Problem solved.

Basically, yes ... however, it still couldn't compare with a formal diving course, either military or civilian, coupled with the experience gained by supervised on-the-job training.

It was a close call for Buddy at the time, but to hear him talk about it now, he'd just shrug his shoulders and come out with the typical saying, "Some you win, some you lose and some get called on account of rain". He had a devil-may-care attitude about life. His size probably had a lot to do with that. He was one of the biggest guys I knew in the business, about 6' 4", weighing in at about 215 pounds. Played a little semi-pro ball at one time and from the looks of his helmet maybe a little too much. But this rugged appearance added character to his looks. This along with his impressive size and audacious manner was his passport to success. He was able to get away with pulling some of the funniest stunts.

Chapter 4

Sat Log - Day 34 – Decompression Schedule – 1,000 ft Dive

Vessel:	Ocean Venture	Sat Unit:	SDC/TL 12
Date:	1 Nov 77	Time: 0100	Shift: Midnight/Noon
Depth:	372 ft		

> *Put your mind in neutral and your body in overdrive.*
> *"The days don't count 'til ya count the days."*

Another day: A carbon copy of yesterday! Well, at least nobody was going to suffer from a heart attack due to the excitement.

With everyone showered and smelling like the inside of a French whorehouse, we settled in for another day of exciting decompression. Those who could, would pass the time sleeping. Those who couldn't, would while away the hours reading or just staring out at nothing or fantasize with one of the nude pin-ups strategically taped around the chamber and think about getting out.

It is said you can tell about a man by the books he reads.

That being the case, then we must all be a little "schiz". It wasn't unusual to have four different books going at the same time. One for each personality! Due to the confinement and the same monotonous routine, even reading gets to be a drag after a while. You become bored with the book you're reading and look for something else to do. Eventually you pick up another book hoping to find some escape between the covers. If not - well, there's always another book.

And just what type of personality do we have? From the array of literature scattered about the chamber, I'd say It was Intellectualized, science-fictionized, historicalized, dramatized and sex magazinized. Quite frankly, we're just an average bunch of horny bastards.

As for me, this was a good time to write home. Having explained that we were coming up and I'd be home soon, I was now caught staring off into space. I didn't have any daring exploits to write about or any deep-sea tales to tell.

Whatever I had to say had been said in the previous letter and then again in the one before that. How many ways can you say "I love you"?

With letters being the link to the outside world and it taking letters to beget letters, I had become a master of the one page special.

Even a one-pager can hang you up. It's the only thing you have to do all day and yet it seems such a chore. After taking several hours to get up enough momentum to write, you feel so relieved once it's over, but you also feel a little let down because now you don't have anything else to do.

Then again there's the other end of the scale where an individual will derive a great deal of satisfaction and pleasure from churning out letters. Not a full page letter by any means, but an envelope containing an ad from a recent magazine. Invariably it would have to be for something that was free and at no cost whatsoever to the sender.

There was one industrious fellow who had acquired 'A Whole Earth Catalogue' and over a period of several months systematically sent away for every free thing in it. At the time, I thought this a little extreme until he started receiving bags of mail at which time my skepticism turned to envy. Hey, it was killing time, right?

While the rest of us were seeking our individual escapes from boredom and reality, Pete, the sat tender, was taking care of the daily chores. Now that we were on our way up he was able to relax and settle into a daily routine which wouldn't be nearly as hectic and demanding as that of a few days ago when we were diving back-to-back, one team after another.

No sooner had he checked the bell, had it ready to go with one team of divers on their way, when it seemed that they were coming back up and it was time to go through the whole routine again: dry diving gear sent in, wet sent out, underclothing changed, diving mask free-flowing, needs to be changed out, having communication problems with the primary rig, scrubber motor making a racket, "Take up on the lock, Topside". "What happened to the hot water and coffee?" "Send in a change of sheets and pillow cases." "You sent in Matt's boots instead of Al's" and so it went, dive after dive. A few days at this pace and it wasn't long before you were hoping for a spell of rough weather to be able to catch up on some badly needed sleep. Today, however, the weather was foul and we were coming up. The routine wasn't nearly as rigorous and there would be plenty of time for rest.

With everyone settled back in their bunks and out of the way, Pete began sweeping down, cleaning up the dirt and lint which had accumulated around the blower motor intakes since yesterday. Once this had been done, he would then scrub the deck and toilet area with a mild disinfectant solution. This routine was performed daily, in an effort to keep the chamber as hygenically clean as possible.

The CO_2 in the chamber had started to climb and the Dog-house Man had said it would be necessary to change out the CO_2 cannisters. This was another job Pete would take care of. Even though the CO_2 is being constantly monitored up in the Dog-house, there are telltale visual signs that warn of the need for a cannister change-out.

The granular particles of CO_2 absorbent had changed from a normal off-white color to a dark shade of mauve - a good indication that they had absorbed their fill of CO_2. Now that we were on our way up and all of us in the chamber, the cannisters would be changed out every other day instead of the customary three or four days when diving operations were being performed.

The cannister change out is a quick five minute operation. The used cannister is sent out in the Med-Lock and a fresh one is sent in. At the same time, the Purafil would be replaced. Purafil, another granular substance, helps eliminate (debatable) some of the odor building up inside the chamber. Let your imagination run wild here as you try to imagine what the chamber must smell like after a 30 day Sat. It could hold it's own with the best (worst) locker rooms.

Pete was probably the most efficient and conscientious Sat Tender I've had the pleasure of working with. He kept the chamber clean and orderly and well stocked with supplies. There was a place for everything and everything was kept in its place. A well organized and comfortable quarters area made for a better Sat all the way around. He was quickly gaining a reputation as a good man to have on the job. He'd been with the company for two years, but this Sat was the first opportunity we'd had to work together.

Because the offshore diving industry is so spread out - the Gulf of Mexico, North Sea, off the coast of Newfoundland, South America, Alaska, the Arabian Gulf, Singapore and West Africa - it was common for two guys to be working for the same outfit for several years before their paths would cross. However, when you got locked inside an 8'x 23' piece of pipe with an individual, it didn't take long to find out about a person.

About three years ago, Pete, being an avid skin diver, was attracted by one of the flashy ads touting the big money that could be made in commercial diving. Pumping gas and fixing cars in upstate New York wasn't getting him rich quick, so he begged, borrowed and stole to get the two grand it would cost to get through diving school. He threw everything he owned in the back of a beat up old VW and headed for sunny Florida. What a beautiful place to learn how to dive. It's a shame there's no oil there - at least offshore.

One or two well established commercial diving schools have been in operation for many years. However, with a sudden increase in demand for experienced, well-trained divers by the diving industry several years ago, a whole slew of schools came on the scene. These schools varied in size and curriculum, from the fly-by-night outfit to the industry-oriented school, to a two year college course with Associate Degree. There was one ingenious entrepreneur who offered a correspondence course (a diving course through the mail and no water - come on!).

Certain schools became VA approved and with this approval naturally came the rewards associated with an unbiased organization - no discrimination.

Though they had various shortcomings, the one thing these schools did promise was a letter of introduction and a list of the major diving companies. It wasn't long before reception areas were flooded with daring young men, full of drive and eager to prove themselves. But, after a week or two of waiting for an interview, playing reception musical chairs and hearing the now familiar line "Come back in a few months" or "Try another company", it didn't take long to realize that the end of the rainbow was starting to lose it's lustre and was drifting out of sight. The supply was exceeding the demand and fast.

Certainly there was work, but not as much as had been forecast or anticipated. The seasonal work that was available was being performed by the established, experienced, qualified divers in the company. The fact that a man had a diving diploma didn't make him an experienced diver, at least not to the diving companies - not by a long shot. There were disappointed looking faces when they were told that, if hired, they would be required to complete the company training program. "Back to school again". It could long as four years to 'break-out'.

Diving companies weren't deliberately trying to discourage anyone from becoming a diver. They were just trying to tell the eager young aspirant that the picture wasn't as glossy as the ads portrayed.

And to make a safer workplace for all, the diving organizations were setting and implementing new and very rigid qualifications for all future employees. These included a certificate of previous diving training (military or civilian), and thorough physical examinations which include long bone x-rays to determine any predisposition or evidence of aseptic bone necrosis - a painful, crippling disease of the bone indigenous to men working under pressure. This was just the pre-hire qualifications. Saying you were a diver was one thing, but qualifying to break-out and proving it was another. Gone were the days of the midnight phone call to the Seven Seas.

Eventually, Pete got hired and, like the several hundred others before him, he went through apprenticeship training: marrying hoses (umbilicals), painting chambers, sweeping floors, maintaining compressors, stripping down hot water boilers, learning about various diving equipment, how it works and how to use it safely. Then came the in-house diving programs: learning the basic fundamentals of diving again and how they were applied offshore, terminology, safe practices and equipment familiarization. Yep, when you got off that crew boat you were expected to do more than stand there getting a sunburn on your tongue and your finger up your ass. Once through the basics, it was back to the shop marrying hoses and fighting a paint brush and scheming to be in the right place at the right time. Pete spent the rest of his first year tending in the Gulf of Mexico, making the rounds to the different barges, gaining valuable experience and also getting the odd chance to get in the water. Nothing very deep, but at least he was getting wet. These dives would be recorded in his log-book (another regulation).

Oh yes, as I mentioned earlier, you had to prove your worth. He was proving himself alright and that winter he got sent overseas to the Arabian Gulf. The job over there ended a little sooner than expected, so on his way back to the States, he stopped by the company's UK office gambling on picking up some work in the North Sea. This area still being very active, there was always the chance that someone might be looking for a relief. Sure enough, within three days he was on a boat heading out to the barge.

I first caught sight of him pacing the upper deck, anxiously waiting for the supply boat to come alongside.

The brisk sea wind blowing sun-bleached blonde hair away from a young, lean and tanned face, shoulders hunched, hands pushed deep into pockets of a new Navy blue parka, the coat zipped all the way up barely exposing the top of a white wool turtle neck, the boat secured alongside and he straddled the guard rail onto the barge.

"Holy snapping assholes, this place is cold", he greeted.

Yes, Pete had arrived in the North Sea.

Looking up from the letter I was struggling to finish, I glanced over into the inner lock to see how Pete was coming along with the final cannister change. I noticed that his hair had turned a dirty, light brown and the Middle East tan had faded to a dull anemic color. The price one pays while in saturation - along with pimples, bedsores, water boils and a host of assorted fungi, viral and bacterial disease - a really friendly environment, ain't it?

I finished the one-page masterpiece, eased out of my rack and with five or six short steps made my way through the inner lock and placed it in the make-shift Ritz Cracker mailbox located by the Medical Lock. It would be sent out on the next lock run, maybe. I then relieved my bladder of its pressing burden. (Christ, in Sat you have to pee at least 50 times a day, so it seemed). I retraced my steps back to my bunk and observed that everyone was settled in.

The immediate chores taken care of, Pete finally got a chance to shower. Having crawled up into his top bunk in the inner lock, he was attempting to block out the 'now' with a set of headphones perched on his head. He was tripping out to better times and places. In Sat, a good set of headphones could cure just about anything. In the bunk below, Al, resembling a gnarled old walrus, was wrestling with his mattress for a more comfortable position and was slowly conceding defeat. Across the narrow aisle in the opposite bunk Buddy was embroidering a brilliantly colored tropic fish on his favorite pair of blue jeans. He'd been working on them for over a year. At least three or four hundred hours of stitching had been put into them. Hmm...let's see, 400 x $500 an hour...at the going Sat rate, he had the most valuable jeans in the world.

And in the outer lock across from me, Matt was making Z's. How does he do it? That shit-eatin' grin on his face: What could he possibly be dreaming about? There was one sure thing, whatever it was, he was dreaming in vivid color. In Sat you experience the most life-like dreams and always in color. Erotic movies couldn't hold a candle to this trip. What he was dreaming didn't really matter. What counted was the fact he was killing time. And time ... well, time is what diving is all about.

From the diver's first introduction to diving, he becomes aware of how important time is - a miscalculation in bottom time can be harmful, if not disastrous. Time means money and money means time. With a barge that rents from $100,000-$150,000 a day, hours and minutes become expensive. Time is of the essence. The company that can perform the fastest and safest is the one that can give the customer the bang for his buck.

For a diver to earn a living, he's got to do his time. How hungry the individual is will dictate the amount of time he'll spend offshore away from home and family. There are a few long-ball hitters who have been on the books for almost a full year. Giving them a fair piece of change, the good side of $100,000 and a good edge in attaining one's goals. At least until the old IRS gets it's cut. It is an awfully long time to be away from home and puts a tremendous strain on a marriage. Yes, I know the odd guy who's gone to the alter for the second and third time.

Generally, most offshore diving is usually seasonal. At least the majority of it is done during clement weather. For one reason or another, most divers call it a season when they accumulate enough bread. The time required to acquire this amount of money averages out to be about eight months of the year, which is still no picnic and one helluva long time to be away from home. Time away from home is dead time. It's the longest drawn-out time of all, but it doesn't count. It just takes its toll. Heck, I've been married ten years and I'm still on my honeymoon. When time does count, it's for the number of days left to complete a contract, to finish a job, the amount of decompression remaining, or "when will the next mail boat arrive?". It's strictly a waiting game with the winner being the one who can kill time best. Working is killing time; sleeping is killing time; reading is killing time; writing is killing time; and decompressing is time to kill. With $4^1/_2$ days to kill, sleeping is sacrosanct (decompression from 1,000 feet is 10-11 days).

During saturation, and especially decompression, three major events take place to help pass the time. They are the 3 M's: Meals - the most common; Mail - the most looked forward to (receiving, not sending); and Movies - a rare luxury.

In an area as confined as the saturation chamber, it doesn't take long for the mundane, boring existence to set into a routine pattern with very few highlights. Work, consisting of the several daily bell runs, has top billing because that's why we're here, to work, right? Oh, by all means.

This excitement over, you are confronted with the next big attention getter - eating. Eating: Nourishment, calorie intake to be burned off during the gruelling bell runs. Four meals a day and all the snacks and goodies (groan) your little heart desires. From my bunk, I can see shelves stocked with over two dozen jars, bottles and shakers of assorted condiments, jams, sauces, spreads, garnishes, dressings, all there to tease, tempt and tantalize the palate. Then there's fruit juices, cans of soda pop, heat treated milk, hot water and coffee to be consumed with the cakes, crackers and cookies, chocolate, assorted and plain. All this to make one's stay a little more pleasant and fatter. But wait, this is not all; there's still the main course to come and that's where the surprise comes in, the topping on the cake. Each meal is a different experience.

The menu for a particular meal is sent in, filled out (X), sent back up post haste to the topside tenders, who then rush down to the galley with great speed, so the food won't get cold, taking great pains in preparing an appetizing tray.

On a barge where the cook could be European, the tenders British, the appetites American, the menu might read like this:

EKOFISK MENU

ENTRÉE:	SHRIMB SALARD
	TUNER FISHES ON BUNTS
	LETUS, TUMATO, QCUMBER SALADE CELRY
	CHEASES
	SOUPS ASPARIGOOSE
	OKSTALE,
	NUDL TOMESTOE
MAIN-COURSE:	T-BORN STEAK
	PURKSHOPS + GRAVE
	EGS + FR. FRIDS CHELLY + RISE
	PITZA PIE
VEGETABLES:	COLLIE FLOUR SOWSCRAWT CARRIOTS
	BAKET BEENS GREAN PEACE LIMEY BEENS
DESSERT:	DORNUTS
	YOGUARD
	CUSTERS PIE
	LAMONMERANK PIE
	BANNARNA PUNNINCK
	FRUTE SALARS w. RAISON
DRINKS:	COFFIE EYSED TEA

What you ordered was not always what you got. A typical confrontation with the steam tray might go something like this:

'Corn' - easy to serve - 3 heaping spoonfulls.
'Rice' - the same.
'Potatoes' - the same.
'Steak - well done' - 5 minutes extra for a well done.

"Shit, give him rare. I'll be off shift by the time he gets it."

"Hey, you forgot the T-Bone on this one."

"Tell him they ran out. There's no way he'll know."

"This guy ordered 7 things. I don't have enough room on the tray. What do I do with the salad? Put it in a bowl?"

"Hell, No! Just dump it on top of the corn."

"Hey, Buddy, you got that guy's spaghetti sauce running into the section that has the lemon meringue pie."

"So?"

And so it went. Don't ever make an enemy of a tender ... there's always a way to get you back.

Finally, everything is ready to be rushed up to the chamber and sent in before it gets cold.

The half dozen foil-wrapped metal trays, bowls, plastic cups, pitchers of ice, tea, water, coffee, cartons of milk and cutlery are meticulously placed in the Medical Lock.

"Ah, that's the lot, send it down."

"Hold it a minute, here're two more bowls of fruit cocktail."

"They won't fit."

"Sure they will. Squeeze them in on top of the trays. See, told you they would. Lock going down."

Food. When did I last eat? Two hours ago? Never mind. It's something to do - a highlight of the day. Here comes my tray. God, it's dripping all over the place. The whole tray's only one-half inch thick. Whoever heard of meringue pie being that thin. Oh, my tray was on the bottom. I see. Gingerly, I remove the aluminum foil. My God, everything's tomatoey looking and it's only half here. Ah, the other half is stuck to the foil along with the top of the meringue pie. Appetizing? Yuck.

You weren't hungry anyhow, right? So you lose a little weight. You could stand to lose a few pounds. Everyone loses weight in Sat. It's been proven and documented in most of the test dives. "Oh yeah". Bullshit: If that's the case, then what's this Goddamn mound sticking up between my sternum and pelvis lolling from side to side emphasizing every movement of the barge as an ugly reminder that tomorrow I start my diet.

A few people might lose weight in Sat, but on the average, I think most guys put on a pound or two. Right now, I think I've gained ten.

Let's see ... it's now 2 o'clock, another three hours 'til the next meal. Ah, time for a nice cup of tea and a couple of cookies and...

Well, it was something to do. It was killing time. In the battle to kill time, there comes a moment when your efforts are rewarded.

"Hey you guys, the supply boat is coming alongside."

"Can we come up on the lock so we can send in the mail and newspapers?"

"Get up on it."

"Anybody down there know a One Long Dong?"

"Yeah, topside, he's down here. Just send in the mail."

I looked over at Matt and cracked up "One Long Dong? You're putting me on."

"That's Won Long Dong, Dummy, a Chinese gentleman from Singapore," he replied.

"Sure, Matt, Sure," I said. Won Long Dong, that was his best yet. Matt had a hang-up for collecting plain wrapped literature which he pursued under the guise of several amusing and ingenious aliases such as VD Burns, IP Daily and CS Poole just to mention a few. Whatever your thing.

The much-awaited bag of mail has finally arrived with it's sky blue reward of love, news, mishaps and misunderstandings.

There's the Air Mail letter saying, "Johnny broke his arm while flying his kite ...but don't worry, he's alright and everyone sends their love" ... Shit, that was 10 days ago. There's the official brown envelope with the yellow slip informing you that your checking account is overdrawn ... when you left home four months ago, there was 10 grand in it. There's a card with a picture of the saddest looking basset stuck in a basket with the inscription, "Time sure flies when you're having fun. That goes for me too, miss you, Hon". That's it, that's all until the next boat comes. But for the guy that didn't get any mail, that next boat's a long way off.

Receiving mail offshore can also become a frustrating experience. With a letter normally taking 10 days to reach you, news from home is old and events have already happened. Here I am in the present, living a week or two in the past, planning for the future. Any important decision you made in your reply inevitably gets overruled because, by the time your answer has arrived, 20 days have passed and it's too late and it isn't until another 20 days go by until you receive a reply and wonder what the fuck you were talking about. By now so much time has passed - hell, you don't even remember, but at least it's getting a letter and knowing someone cares.

For the guy that didn't hear from home, the time game is all too real, minutes become hours, hours become days and each day is an eternity. Fears worsen, anxieties increase, suspicions arise, nerves get on edge and the full impact of just how restricted one becomes when confined in saturation is only too real. Where is she? What has happened? Why doesn't she write? You need to call, but you can't. You feel so helpless, trapped and the situation only worsens. At least until the next boat. And then ... laying there with a stack of mail and nothing but time to kill and getting paid for it. Well, it's almost like stealin', ain't it?

The rare luxury. The gorgeous nurse slowly reaches behind her back and gently pulls the zipper down. The uniform slips off a smooth shoulder and slides down her naked body to end up in a neat pile at her feet. Nimbly she steps out from the center of this white nylon halo and moves toward the bed. Her pendulant breasts quivering temptingly, the magenta nipples already erect. Reaching down, she pulls back a corner of the sheet and in a heavy voice whispers to the patient, "a cop should never be horny." Fade. Cut. The End.

"Hey, topside, it's over, turn on 1, 2, 3 and 4," Al called out.

With a flood of light, we were back to reality.

The projector had been set up outside the port in the outer lock and the opposite bulkhead was used as a screen. The sound was piped over the PA system. If a Sat unit wasn't set up for movies then it was quite possible that video recordings were shown. Watching a video flick was a kick. One almost had to be a contortionist. Visualize this if you can. Seven or eight hairy bodies crammed around a 6-inch diameter port checking out Linda Lovelace. It was more congested than a three-man rush on a one-hole shit house. Loewe's it wasn't, but it sure beat talking to the walls.

"Yo, Jeff, would you pass me a beer please," Al asked. "All that salty popcorn's given me a powerful thirst."

"Sure thing, one cool one coming up. Anyone else need one?" I answered reaching into the portable ice chest. What, booze in Sat? Consuming alcohol while under pressure? That's right. It was a strict rule. No alcohol beverages in Sat. Well, I'd be lying to you if I said we lived strictly by the book - what fun is there in that?

Shit, if Cousteau can go to sea with a 1,000 gallon stainless steel wine vat, a few 10-ounce beer cans shouldn't cause any problem.

Nursing my Carlsberg, I nestled back against the pillows and pondered about the other guys in here with me. A good bunch to work with.

They knew what was expected of them and did it. Cooped up in a confined area such as this for a month at a time required teamwork and individual whims and hang-ups were left outside the entrance lock. All in all, one Hell of a fine Sat crew. Were we all great and good? No, not by any stretch of the imagination. We all had our little quirks that irritated the other guy: Matt was forever dropping bombs (whew, salt your food); Al always had a bitch about his meals (who didn't); Buddy kept weird hours and always has the lights on; Pete - he was still a tender. He'd better not develop any bad habits. Me - somebody has to be perfect. (Alright, you guys, I know the list is as long as your arm. Write your own story.)

These were trivial things and generally overlooked. For by the time you were ready for saturation diving, you'd better have your shit together. This was no place for assholes.

You only get one life, try and have the best people around you.

Chapter 5

Sat Log - Day 35 – Decompression Schedule – 1,000 ft Dive

Vessel: Ocean Venture   Sat Unit: SDC/TL 12

Date: 2 Nov 77   Time: 0100   Shift: Midnight/Noon

Depth: 276 ft

Drifting in and out of sleep, I woke with a start. There was no hissing of gas or popping off of solenoid valves. We were all stopped.

"Hey Topside. We can't be at our stop yet. That's not until we get to 198 feet. What's going on?"

"Well, if you'd read the newspapers we'd sent in, you'd know that the rig that is on fire has been damaged by an explosion that wasn't caused by the new guy on board. He was a decoy. The actual explosion was caused by an explosive device attached to the rig by a diver from a lockout sub."

"Apparently, a sub tender had approached the rig at night during that rough weather we had and without any lights on it was virtually undetectable. The rig's radar system had been compromised by the technician that had come on board. After the explosion and the start of the fire, he had been discovered communicating with the sub support tender and was quizzed by the Rig Superintendent. He admitted that the intention had been for the tender to release the sub so a diver could attach an explosive device to a leg of the rig. There must have been some problem and the device went off early. Realising that there must have been a malfunction, the sub support vessel got out of there as quickly as possible and had told him they had been unable to make contact with the sub."

"So right now, we are one of the few Sat units nearby that is under pressure and not working and the Ocean Venture is now headed for the UK sector of the North Sea. The Rig itself is in 460 ft of water. We're holding you guys at depth as we proceed to the location as you might be making a dive to see if you can locate the sub and any survivors and give an assessment of the damage to the platform."

"We should be there within the next six hours. You guys get some sleep. We're pressurizing the unit again."

That's all we needed – more sleep! All of a sudden, all the lights were turned on in the chamber as we started to discuss this turn of events.

The lockout sub as described in the paper wouldn't be all that unfamiliar to some of us as the company had just purchased a similar one about 5 years ago. It would have a control area, and a pressurized dive compartment.

Six hours later we were on site.

Looking out through one of the ports in the bell, we could see the rig and the water around it on fire and the derrick on the rig had buckled over, with the top protruding into the water. The barge was already starting to spray foam over the surface to contain the fire so the bell could be lowered into the water.

The thought went through my mind – what is going to stop that derrick from peeling away from the rig right on top of us once we'd been lowered down to the work site? Discussing this with Topside, Charlie told me they were making arrangements to try and get us as close to where they believed the sub was.

With the fire continuing to rage and the derrick hanging over the side, the barge could only get us so close – maybe about 50 - 60 ft from where they thought the sub lay.

Topside reported "It's understood that underwater the viz is pretty good so you shouldn't have too much trouble locating the sub. I think that about covers it. Can you guys think of anything else?"

With communications going silent, Topside made a final comment:

"I guess I don't have to tell you guys to be careful down there and don't do anything foolish. Just keep in mind we are fighting against time. According to the latest weather forecast, there's a deep depression moving this way from Iceland and it's expected to hit within the next 24 hours. So you guys might be down there for a long bell run. Just remember, if you need me, I'm just a phone call away".

With that, Charlie left the Dog-house and headed for the Dive Station where he would be in complete control of all operations for the rest of his shift.

This was turning into being one heck of a diving show in which we had the leading role and there'd only be room for one director and that would be the Diving Supervisor – the man running the Dive Station.

This wasn't play acting, this was for real and men's lives were stake.

Sitting there nursing my coffee and thinking about that derrick hanging over my head, I could hear Pete in the bell going through the pre-dive check. This in turn was repeated by the man on the radio at the Dive Station.

"CO_2 canister change out."

"CO_2 canister changed out."

"O_2 2000"

"O_2 2000"

"H_e 2100"

"H_e 2100"

"Donut emergency gas 2250"

"Donut 2250"

"Ready for a comm check"

"Roger – go ahead"

"Primary rig – 1234 how do you read me?"

"Loud and clear"

"How me?"

"The same"

"Standby rig – 1234 how do you read me?"

"Loud and clear"

"How me?"

"Loud and clear"

"OK Topside, check complete".

"OK Pete, tell the divers to get dressed and in the bell".

Almost at the same time, Charlie called down "Matt and Jeff, get dressed and in the bell".

"OK OK" we answered back as the tension started to mount.

Matt looked at me, well ol' buddy, "Let's give her hell".

We both put on our hot water suits and went slipping through the tunnel into the bell. Once inside the bell, we got our gear ready for our descent to the bottom.

The tunnel hatch was closed and against the hiss of escaping gas, the bell was pressurized to 470 feet, ten feet over bottom pressure. This was done as a safety measure in the event there was a malfunction in the winch and the bell was dropped sending it shooting down to the bottom where the hatch could fly open due to the greater external pressure.

Pete had the hatch inside the chamber sealed and the tunnel was now ready to bleed off. Once this was done, the hydraulic clamps holding the chamber and bell together would be released, allowing the bell to be separated from the chamber and lowered into the water.

While standing by in the bell waiting for all this to take place, I was drawn to the port like a moth to the flame by the yellow and orange light of the fire dancing on the surface waves, 15 feet below us.

Staring in disbelief out of the port, I got a good look at the bizarre scene spread out in front of me. What was once a majestic looking pyramid of the seas, was now a charred hulk of twisted steel resembling some grotesque monster from the past. A mortally wounded warrior, fire and smoke billowing from its massive body, black blood spilling on the surface, dying.

"Close inside skin valves" came the call from Topside.

"Skin valves closed".

I felt the bell shudder in the A frame as the strain was taken on the bell wire, jerking the bell off its retaining stops. With a slight bang, the stops were released and the bell started sliding down towards the water.

"Hang on" Topside warned over the speaker. "It might be a little rough getting through the chop on the surface".

We both automatically grabbed onto something secure to hold onto, to brace ourselves against the bucking action of the bell as it was tossed about by the waves. Our Liberty ride was short-lived, as we were quickly swallowed up by the emerald liquid and descended to the bottom.

The firey light dancing off the waves was gone from the ports. Now in its place was the light green of rushing effervescent air bubbles escaping to the surface as we approached the 50 ft level.

"Open your skin valves" Topside broke the silence.

Deeper and deeper we went. Eliminating all trace of light. The ports were pitch black as the bell came closer to the bottom.

Inside the bell, was the faint smell of cement caused by the jostling of the Soda-sorb cannister as we prepared for the coming dive: faceplate on the diving mask wiped with a light coating of soap – this was to eliminate fogging of the faceplate; bailout bottle secured to the diver's harness; ladder untied ready for hanging on the hooks in the lower bell tunnel once the bottom hatch was opened; gloves on; hand light OK, that's about it. We were ready.

I looked out a port – complete darkness. Must be getting close. The bell was getting colder and small beads of condensation were collecting to eventually sneak down the side of the bell in little rivulets. As the chill enveloped the bell like a silent mist, my hands were getting damp and I could feel a slight film of sweat as I anticipated not knowing what lay ahead.

The bell came to a stop with a bouncing jolt.

"440 ft. Unlock your hatch" Topside called.

Reaching down, Matt unscrewed the dog on the lower bottom hatch.

"Hatch undogged" he called out.

"Bleeding the bell" replied Topside.

The excess gas pressurized for safety purposes was now being bled off until the bell became ambient with the outside pressure. Care had to be taken here to ensure the bell wasn't flooded by bleeding off too much gas. The hissing of escaping gas was interrupted by a sudden pop as the lower hatch broke its seal, allowing the ice-cold sea water to flow in over the lower tunnel rim and pour into the bottom of the bell.

"Hatch open" Matt called.

And immediately the hissing stopped as an operator Topside closed the appropriate valve.

All of the breathing gas and life support system for the bell was controlled by Topside. However, the bell was equipped with a backup system which would be used in the event of an emergency.

I lifted the hatch open and secured it in position, exposing a dark shimmer about 3 feet in diameter. This was the entrance leading to the liquid silent world beyond. We went through the final phase of getting ready: double check on pressure gauges; main supply valve open; emergency supply valve closed; hot water valve open; pneumo valve open; exhaust valve open and so it went on. The bell had 34 valves – a bloody plumber's nightmare.

Most of the valves however, were normally kept in either the open or closed position, so it this final check only took a few seconds.

While Matt was tying the ladder in position, I slipped on my weight belt and bailout bottle, flipped a loop of my umbilical hose from the primary rig over the saddle and let several feet of it snake down into the water.

Clipping the umbilical hose onto my belt, taking the load of the mask in my hand, I slipped the black rubber hood over my head and adjusted my mask to fit. Mask on, gloves on, hand light hanging from the clip on my belt, final comm check, "Topside how do you read me?"

"Loud and clear".

I gave Matt a final nod to connect the hot water hose to my suit. I gave a sigh of relief as I let my bladder have its way as I stepped down the ladder into the waiting silent world.

I swam over to the platform and utilizing my hand held light I made a sweep of the area. As expected, the water was very clear. There below me, crushed between one of the jacket legs and a mangled horizontal beam was the sub. The front observation dome had been smashed in which would mean that that compartment would be flooded. As I approached the sub, I saw a diver's umbilical extending out from the bottom hatch. As I followed the umbilical, I found it had been severed and there was no sign of the diver.

I pulled myself towards the sub using the diver's umbilical, to check if there was a second diver in the pressurized compartment.

Once inside I could see the compartment was still pressurized and not flooded but I could see the other diver lay lifeless on the deck. He had obviously exhausted his supply of breathing gas. I informed Topside I would bring the diver's body back to the bell and to let Matt know what I was doing.

Once outside the sub, I had Matt take up my slack and pull me and the other diver's body back to the bell.

I then returned to the sub to see if there were any other crew. When I checked the observation compartment, I could see it was flooded and the sub pilot was face-down on the deck, obviously having drowned. I retrieved his body as well and returned to the bell. With both bodies back in the bell it was starting to get very crowded.

We closed the hatch, sealed the bell and were brought back up to the surface and mated to the Sat chamber. We passed the bodies through to Pete on the inside.

The two deceased bodies were placed into the entrance lock of the chamber so they could be decompressed and brought back to the surface.

As for us, we would have an extended bout of decompression. Just what we needed. By the time we reached the surface we would have been under pressure for 40+ days.

Terrorism had arrived offshore.

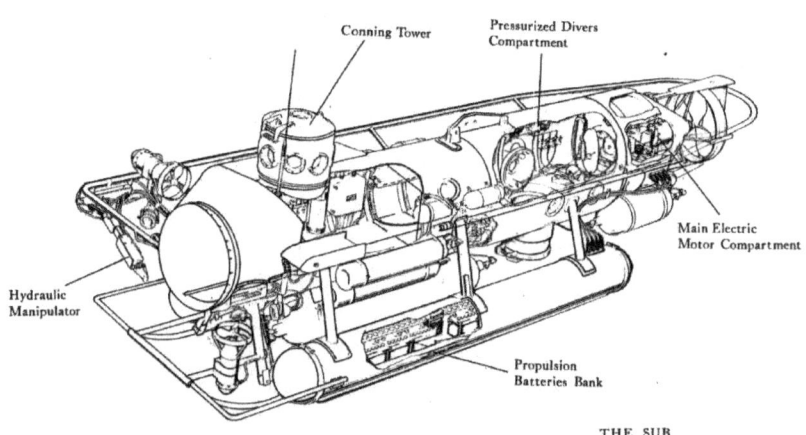

THE SUB

The End

1973

Back to my blossoming career.

By now I was starting to get a reputation as a 'can do' type of guy. At least according to George Morrissey. I was seconded by Roy Jenkins of Brown & Root in London to write the diving installation procedures for the Forties Field, NS project.

I first met Roy during my initial tour (1966-68) in the NS. He was in charge of B&R's Marine Division which consisted mainly of derrick barges, *Atlas, Hercules and Global Adventure.* One of these barges was having a bit of trouble underwater. Although the divers onboard weren't from Taylor, I got sent over to lend a hand. It was late December and the seas were picking up. There was pressure on to try and get the job completed and be able to send everyone home for Christmas. I got the job done and Roy was one happy chappy. Once we got talking, I found out his family was from Newfoundland - we had something in common. Best of all, Taylor took over as the diving crew on the marine barges in the NS.

Forties jacket leaving Nigg Bay and being towed to location in 1974.
The diving involved would be saturation and one of the tasks would be to burn off the two flotation tanks. This was the first jacket installed in the Forties field.

While I was in London working for Roy, Lee came into town. We got to spend a weekend together. And what better way to start off an evening than to get stuck into a couple of pineapple punches at Trader Vic's in the basement of the Hilton Hotel. It's got to have the best Polynesian food on that side of the pond. Having been fed and watered, it was now time to get down to some serious pub crawling. The closest one I could think of was the Red Lion, which was only a few blocks away.

I can't remember how many places we visited, but it ended all too soon. It seemed we'd just gotten started when we heard the only too familiar, "Drink up, gentlemen, closing time". Our only option was to give the private clubs a whirl. Lee suggested the Playboy Club, but I had heard Churchill's was the place to be seen. After a couple of 'right gov's" from our cabbie, we were on our way.

Pulling up in front of the club I had the distinct feeling we'd made a bad call. With Lee in a sport coat and open neck shirt and me in a leisure suit and turtle-neck we just didn't seem to be in accord with the guy at the door, who was decked out for either a wedding or a funeral. I hopped out of the cab and checked with the guy dressed like a penguin, to see if we would be allowed in, while Lee took care of the tab. He politely informed me that 'gentlemen', emphasis on the 'gentlemen', were required to wear a coat and tie. He reluctantly added that they were able to supply a tie if necessary. Upon scrutinizing my attire, he disdainfully informed me that it was not the club's custom to supply a shirt with the tie. This didn't please me one bit.

I was back at the cab in a flash, looked the driver straight in the eye.

"I'll give you £2, for it."

"For what?" the driver asked.

"For your shirt."

"For me shirt?"

"Yeah, I'll give you £2 for your shirt."

It took the cabbie about five seconds to go for it on the condition that I throw in my turtleneck.

"I mean, Mate, 'oe can't go round driving me cab in me suspenders now, can 'oe?"

"You're on," I replied and the cabbie handed me his shirt.

I'll never forget the look of astonishment on the cabbie's face when I handed him the turtleneck. With one swift move I slipped it over my head and handed it to the driver who quizzically asked:

"What the bloody 'ell is this, then 'eh?"

To which I replied in my best Cockney imitation, "A bleeding dickey, mate."

The Pressure Zone by Mike Cooke

My side was killing me and tears were rolling down my cheeks as I desperately tried to stop laughing at the sight of the departing cabbie, shaking his head and mumbling, his two bleached arms protruding from purple floral suspenders and the short flapping loose ends of a woolly collar, as he pulled away from the curb and disappeared into the foggy night.

And with that, Churchill's was able to add two more distinguished visitors to their notable guest list.

[Extracted from my original story]

1974 & 75

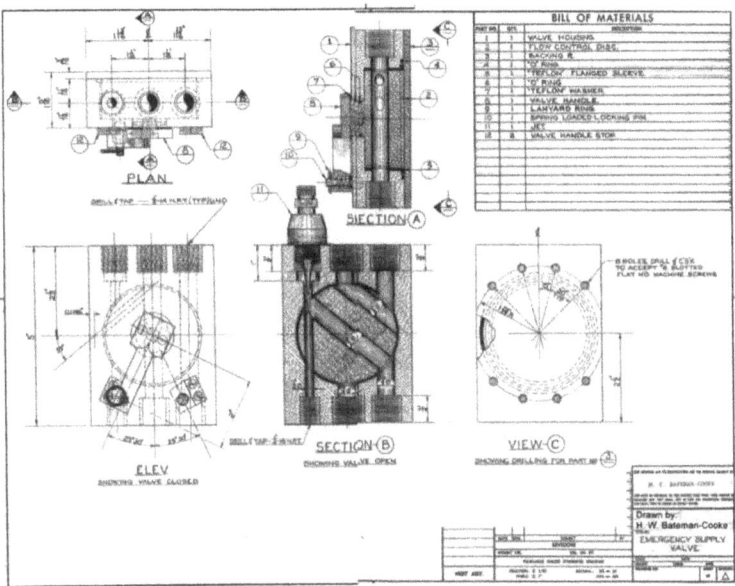

Emergency supply valve I designed and had built by Armac (Melvin Arroyo) for Taylor's push/pull system which re-circulated breathing gas to the diver. The drawing was done by my Dad, master draftsman.

In August 1975, George Morrissey and I attended the Port Ocean and Engineering Conference under Arctic Conditions in Fairbanks Alaska, as representatives of Taylor.

Then in November, I acted as Technical Adviser to legal counsel at the Hearings before the Department of Labour on OSHA's proposed Commercial Diving Standards in Washington DC.

During this period, I also wrote the diving procedures for Elf Frigg Field in the NS.

When not ashore, I was offshore Sat diving as usual.

1976

Early in the year, I had a short stay in La Defence in Paris. I was seconded to Elf / Total to assist in the writing of the dive procedures for Brown & Root who were designing the Frigg Field Development. Because I was needed back in Belle Chasse, Bob Grantz took over the supervision of the procedures.

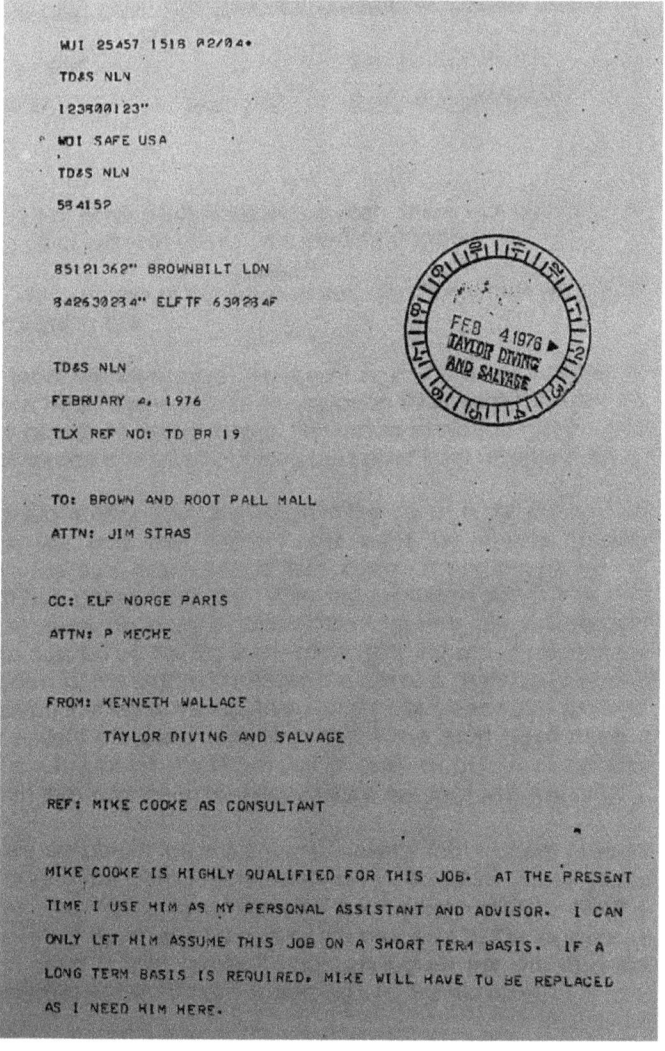

Telex from Ken Wallace confirming my secondment to Elf / Total

This was the big one - the year I went deeper than 1,000 ft (305m). Actually, it was a research saturation dive to 1,200 FSW (365m) in support of Shell Oil Company's Cognac Project and was accomplished at the hyperbaric complex at Taylor Diving's Belle Chasse headquarters. The following is a brief summary of that dive.

SHELL COGNAC INSTALLATION - RESEARCH DIVE
03 December – 20 December

General Description

An HeO^2 saturation dive to 1,200 ft will be conducted in the hyperbaric research complex between 03 and 20 December for the purpose of testing oxy-arc cutting, wet welding, dry welding, helmet and system functions, U/W hydraulic unit and impact wrenches, He (Helium) speech unscrambler and communications systems, diver's helmet - mounted TV, RCV and controls, and related diver work tasks.

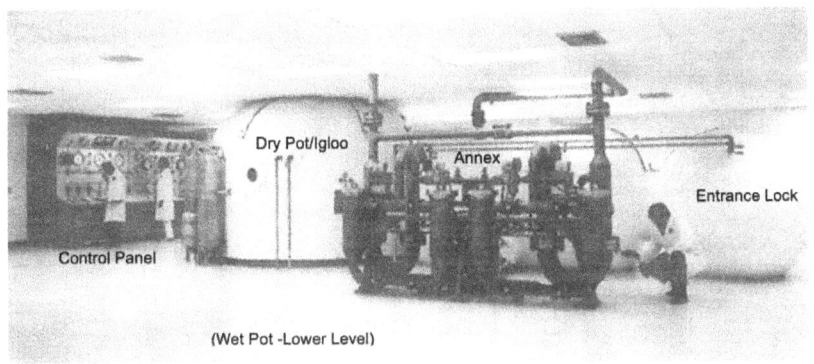

TDS Hyperbaric Research Complex

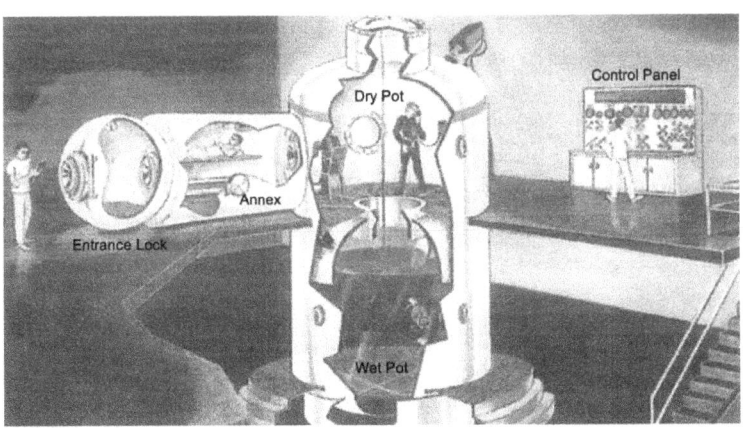

This dive is in preparation for an open-water test of U/W work tasks integral to the installation of the Shell "Cognac" Platform scheduled to begin in April 1977.

The total dive time of 16 $1/2$ days includes one day of compression, 4 days at depth for the scheduled tests, and 11 $1/2$ days of decompression.

Compression of the annex and igloo section of the complex will commence on 03 December.

Following the completion of 4 test days, decompression will be carried out according to the decompression profile.

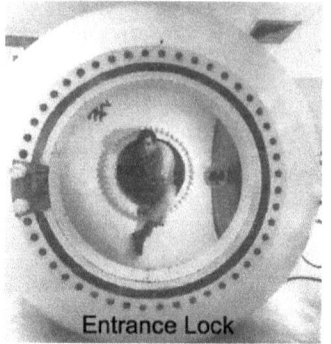

Diver exiting Annex entering Entrance Lock

GENERAL TEST SCHEDULE

Day 1 Acclimatize to depth – get accustomed to the pressure change
Day 2 Oxy-arc cutting at 1200 ft. (This was my dive – the deepest underwater burning/cutting to date).

Day 3 Hyperbaric pipeline weld at 1200' (diver/welders)
Day 4 C/D (Compressor/Depressor Rebreather System) dive and test 1200 ft (divers)
Monitor:
- Pressure flow in the hat, temperature in the C/D unit, CO_2 in the hat, diver's activity and tasks, log.
- Duration of come-home bottle supply.
- Helium speech, 4-wire communication, unscrambler, remote controlled vehicle.
- Helmet-mounted TV.

Day 5 C/D tests 1,050 ft (divers & diver/welders)
Monitor: As above also:
- Sub-tek hydraulic wrenches, unbolting task.
- ET tests; record He speech; RCV.
- Helmet - mounted TV.

During all stages of decompression, divers should be encouraged to move about in the chamber to help maintain circulation in their extremities as a precaution in preventing bends. Active exercise such as deep knee bends and push ups should be avoided.

I exercised daily using a rubber workout band – stretching.

Underwater burning/cutting pictured above is similar to the set up I performed on that dive.

Photo of John Roat (Ex-Navy SEAL / TDS Diver)
holding a typical burned-off section of 36'' steel pipe.

Following is my written report of that dive.

OFFICE MEMO
TAYLOR DIVING & SALVAGE CO., INC.

TO: Bob McArdle
FROM: Mike Cooke
SUBJECT: Report On 1200 Ft. Saturation Dive
DATE: December 14, 1976

GENERAL

The dive commenced at 0300, December 2, 1976. Though very early in the morning, I feel this is an ideal time to start a dive; everyone is tired and ready to sleep.

The rate of descent was at a good speed, making it quite comfortable for sleeping or resting. I had no trouble sleeping; in fact, I slept through the whole descent.

Once at depth, I had a feeling of complete exhaustion and a sense of being light headed and sluggish. The feeling persisted on into the second day. The excursion dive, from 1050 feet to 1200 feet, neither added to or relieved this condition.

Intra-chamber communication at this depth is very difficult. The speech is so badly distorted, that it is easier to keep quiet about a certain point, than to expend the time and effort trying to make ones self understood.

On December 3rd, we spent the day doing underwater burns on 1 3/4" and 3" plates, using several different types of rods. The test proved that burning at this depth shouldn't present any problem.

At one point during the test, air was substituted for oxygen. It was not possible to achieve any penetration using this media.

I did notice that even though the work (burning) wasn't all that strenuous, it was taxing enough to cause noticeable fatigue after 4-6 hours.

No trouble sleeping the second night.

The morning of the third day was spent doing more burning. This was very short and only lasted about 1½ hours. The rest of the day was set aside for welding.

Even though I feel hungry, I lack the desire to eat and only consume a small portion of what I've ordered. It wasn't until the third day at depth that my appetite returned to normal and my system had become fully adjusted to the pressure change. The sluggish feeling had disappeared and I now feel back to standard.

Office Memo
December 14, 1976
Page 2

Now that my craving for nourishment had returned, I wished it would disappear. The majority of the food being served is very bland, lacking spices and appeal. The dessert, on the other hand, has been consistant and what it might lack in nourishment, certainly makes up for in taste. Enough said -- the food is only fair.

EQUIPMENT

C/D HAT

We started diving the C/D hat on December 6th. The stress test resembling moderate work, proved satisfactory. It showed that it was certainly easier to breathe and required less effort, respiratory wise, using the C/D hat than it would to do the same task using the KMB-Mask.

This is where the praise for the C/D system should end.

SEVERAL OF THE MAJOR BAD POINTS ARE AS FOLLOWS: (C/D HAT)

1. The umbilical is far too big and cumbersome to have to work with. I can see many excuses arising for not wanting to use the hat, because of the umbilical.

2. The hat is still uncomfortable in the water. This was noticeable by the frequent adjusting of helmet and jockstrap. When the exercise rate was increased to one (1) rep. every three (3) seconds, the hat would shift around the divers head. In turn, obstructing 1/3 of the divers' visibility and also forcing the diver to jam his chin against the side of the hat to stop it from banging against his mouth.

3. The jockstrap - a derivative of the rack. The harder and faster one has to work, the more uncomfortable it gets. At one point during the dive, it left the realm of uncomfortability and approached the point of becoming painful.

Office Memo
December 14, 1976
Page 3

MAJOR BAD POINTS FOR C/D HAT (CONTINUED)

4. The hat is an abortion to try and put on. Not only is it too heavy and bulky, but also difficult. The mechanism for attaching the hat to the neck ring is too intricate and restricted for the simple function of securing the helmet over the divers' head. After two or three attempts of trying to line up four moving parts controlled by two different sources, it is understandable how ones patience with the system can be tried.

Combining all of these inherent points and enclosing them in the confined space of the S.D.C., can only lead to frustration and aggrevation.

I trust that once the divers confidence in the system has been restored, the next step to be taken will concern his comfort (i.e.) a diving system that is not only economical and functional, but one that has the dexterity and comfort to allow the diver to perform his task as efficiently and effectively as possible, without undue restraint.

KIRBY 17

The hat is very light and tries to ride up over the divers head. This increases the pressure, caused by the bulky hat liner, against the divers jaw, making it very uncomfortable and hard to speak. The hat liner has several drawbacks. The adjustment strap across front, gets in between the divers face and the oral/nasal mask, restricting a proper seal and thereby defeating the purpose of the liner. It is also too bulky, keeping the earphones away from the divers ears. Communication is extremely poor. Though very pretty and a step in the right direction, this hat is still not the answer.

BAILOUT BOTTLES (A.G.A.)

Very neat, light and compact. Should be in use offshore now; especially for diving out of the S.D.C. They are less restricting for access to and from the bell than the bailout bottles presently in use.

Office Memo
December 14, 1976
Page 4

CHAMBER COMFORTS

PILLOWS

Should be of a synthetic material. Foam rubber pillows hold their shape better than fiber or feather filled ones. Loosely filled pillows add to the contamination of the chamber atmosphere. This being very evident to anyone allergic to down or feather filled pillows.

BLANKETS

The use of wool blankets should be avoided whenever possible. 90% of the material cleared from fan screens is lint or loose fibers from wool blankets. These particles also contaminate the atmosphere.

CURTAINS

An inexpensive item finding a lot of use in saturation units offshore. They afford privacy and block out disturbing light.

BUNK LIGHTS

Of all the data being sought and compiled by the different departments, the most beneficial aspect, though not the most important, was the warranted proof that a 6 volt reading light is usable, safe and capable of withstanding pressure to 1200 feet. Also, very economical - a total investment of $6.37.

CONCLUSION

I feel that the dive was a success and proved that on a man/work ratio, we should have very little difficulty working at 1200 feet.

Once at depth, it would be necessary to have a 12 hour period (minimum) for the diver to become acclimated to his new environment. It should be understood that the divers actions will be sluggish for the first few days and will probably not reach his full potential until the third day.

Office Memo
December 14, 1976
Page 5

CONCLUSION .. (continued)

Of the three (3) types (KMB-Mask, C/D Hat, Kirby 17), the C/D hat offered the least breathing resistance and best communication. Where this is definitely to the divers advantage, the rest of the system is a hindrance and very cumbersome, only adding to increased discomfort and diver fatigue. In its present state, the system is sound and economical, but not practical to work with.

M.C. Bateman-Cooke

OFFICE MEMO
TAYLOR DIVING & SALVAGE CO., INC.

TO: Mike Cooke
FROM: Bob McArdle
SUBJECT: Your Report on 1200 Ft. Saturation Dive
DATE: December 15, 1976

1. I have just completed reading your memo, which I must say is very well written and informative.

2. I will take necessary action on some of the things that you have suggested.

3. In the meantime, it will be distributed to everyone for other comments and possibly after the dive is completed, we can all sit down for a critique of your comments.

4. I don't know whether John Propeck is in the process of writing anything similar to yours, but if he hasn't, would you mention the fact to him so we can possibly have a comparison of your comments.

Robert F. McArdle

RFM/cc

Cover of Taylor magazine 1976 – North Sea

1977
Shell Cognac:
The World's Deepest Construction Job

The following is reproduced with the kind permission of Christopher Swann: Chapter 44 of his book *The History of Oil Field Diving - An Industrial Adventure* - a must for any comprehensive diving library [pages 541 – 546].

In early 1977 Taylor Diving & Salvage selected a team of their most experienced divers for what was then the world's deepest construction project: the installation near the Mississippi Delta of Shell Oil's Cognac platform. Assembling the three-piece steel jacket would take two seasons. Comparable in height to the Empire State Building, Cognac was to stand in 1,025 feet of water, 175 feet deeper than Exxon's platform Hondo in the Santa Barbara Channel.

The original plan was to set the platform without divers. However, Shell's diving consultant George Cundiff, an underwater cutting expert who had previously worked for Taylor, reminded the engineers that if anything went wrong there would be a considerable delay before divers could be brought to the scene. Better to have divers who were thoroughly familiar with the operation standing by on site in saturation.

Cognac was a huge leap for Taylor. Hitherto, the deepest they had worked was 350 feet, in 1969. This contract was also unusual in that they were working directly for Shell, and that the construction contractor was not Brown & Root but J Ray McDermott - whose diving division could certainly have handled the job. Nevertheless, Taylor had dived to over 1,000 feet in their hyperbaric complex and they were supremely confident. All the major diving companies had bid on the contract. "Our numbers were better, our capabilities were better, and they selected us"' said Bob McArdle.

As part of the preparation, the team burned 2-inch and $2^{3}/_{4}$ inch steel plate at 1,100 feet in the wet chamber. Underwater cutting was important as a backup measure. The platform was to be anchored by the usual method of driving piles through guides on the bottom section of the jacket, but if the mechanism that held the seals at the tops of the pile guides did not open automatically, divers would have to unbolt the locks. If that failed, they were to cut them open.

Taylor used modified torches, with enlarged valve porting to increase the oxygen flow, and very large electrodes. Because the oxy-arc process liberates tremendous quantities of oxygen, and flame from the oxidized metal burns in the bubbles, the chamber runs were carried out with a large funnel over the divers' heads. No one had ever done oxy-arc cutting so deep before.

To familiarize themselves with the platform, the divers went to McDermott's yard in Morgan City, where the bottom section was nearing completion. Three hundred and eighty feet by 400 feet at the base and about 190 feet high, it dominated the landscape. Fred Miller, at 47 the oldest member of the team and one of the most experienced, remembered taking the elevator to the top and looking down at helicopters flying about below. Anthony Gaudiano, no stranger to large-scale engineering, was in awe:

"It was staggering to go up underneath the thing and see this huge structure extending in every direction. It was bigger than any warehouse or blimp hangar I'd ever been in. I've been around heavy machinery all my life and I'm not easily impressed, but I was impressed that day."

McDermott used two barges for the installation. The main barge was moored to 12 huge buoys attached to 12 anchor pilings, driven without the assistance of divers by a third barge. A three-inch diameter wire went out and back to each buoy. In an emergency, the barge could instantly release all 12 moorings. Taylor put two 1,000-foot saturation systems, manned the first season by two teams made up of six divers and an inside tender, on the main barge. One man on each team doubled as a medic.

*The Taylor saturation systems on the main barge.
An RCV-225 can be seen next to the bell*

The diving equipment consisted of hot water suits, 'fine tuned' Kirby Morgan Band Masks and 5,000 psi bail-out bottles though the divers doubted they would do much good if they lost their main gas supply at 1,000 feet. Taylor also briefly used their push-pull gas-reclaim system. The first saturation lasted 39 days. Since it took ten days to decompress, the team in the first system did not start decompressing until the other team had arrived at saturation depth in the second. Thus, during the transition, there were divers in both complexes. Although Taylor clocked up 20,000 man-hours of saturation on the project, with 28 divers, most of that time was spent in the chambers. Diving accounted for only a small proportion of the work.

The base section and the main barge

One of the pile guides on the base section

(Collection of Drew Michel)

Building and installing the platform cost $275 million. Taylor were involved in the planning from the start, but the Shell engineers were evidently uncertain how much work divers could accomplish at 1,100 feet in the sea, as opposed to in a chamber, given the sums involved, it was therefore not surprising that before the installation began the divers had to demonstrate, on a small jacket built for the purpose, that they could carry out oxy-arc cutting and other routine procedures on the bottom at 1,025 feet. At the successful conclusion of the demonstration, the small jacket was pulled up and the first section of the Cognac jacket was brought out. By then the divers had been in saturation for ten days.

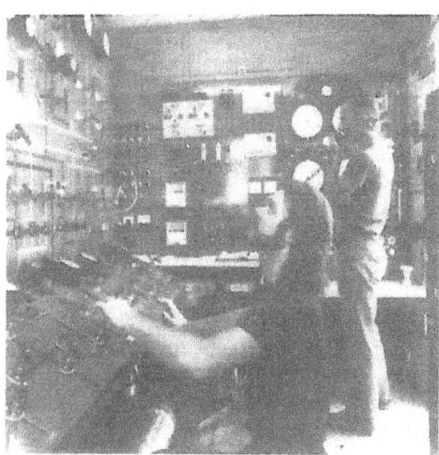 

The 'doghouse': the control van for the saturation system

A surface diver on one of the barges

(Collection of Drew Michel)

McDermott launched each jacket section in the usual way, by flooding one end of the barge and sliding it off. Once it was floating in the water, tugs towed it between the two installation barges and construction hands ran a double purchase of three-inch wire to the corners.

Divers from the two barges then opened valves on the legs, about 150 feet down, to start the remote-controlled flooding process. During the descent, the engineers maintained buoyancy in the skirt pile sleeves, which doubled as floatation chambers (metal seals at bottoms prevented the air escaping until the pilings were driven). Without a buoyancy system to control the descent, the weight of the structure would have carried away the rigging.

The seabed where Cognac was set down – as determined beforehand by Taylor's RCV-225s – was 12 – 15 feet higher on one side than on the other. Remote-controlled hydraulic mats on the corners of the jacket compensated for the difference. Although sensors told the engineers the structure was level, the divers were asked to check it anyway.

With the first jacket section in place, the principal diving job was removing the seals at the top of the 24 skirt-pile sleeves- six on each comer (either they did not open as planned, or Shell decided against releasing them automatically). The seals were a little over seven feet in diameter and some 100 feet above the bottom: in other words at about the 925-foot mark. The divers undid the lock bolts with an impact wrench and attached a crane wire to the seals for lifting to the surface. Tugs then towed out the piles.

The piles were 600 feet long and seven feet in diameter. Fabricated from two-inch steel plate, they weighed close to 500 tons and were buoyant. Each tug could handle only one pile. Since the top of the jacket was 850 feet beneath the surface, McDermott contracted Victoria Marine Works to build a gigantic elevator, somewhat similar to a casing elevator on a drilling rig, that fitted around the piles.

One of the two saturation teams at the end of the project
(Collection of Drew Michel)

Once the 300-ton elevator was around the pile, crew men in Zodiac inflatable boats flooded the far end to put it into the vertical position, and elevator and pile were lowered on wires from the main barge.

The stabbing process, orchestrated from the main control room, went off like clockwork. Inside the bottom of the pile, looking straight down and mounted on four wheels to keep it centred, was a television camera with lights; hovering above the skirt-pile sleeve, was an RCV-225.

With the television cameras for eyes, the control team instructed the computers which controlled the anchor winches to move the barge, in increments of as little as an inch, until it was exactly in position, then guided the pile into the yoke above the inserting ring and dropped it into the sleeve. An enormous underwater hammer, built for the job by the German firm Delmac, then slid down the wires to the elevator and drove the pile. Once the hammer had been retrieved, the elevator was released from the pile with an acoustic signal. (All signals were acoustic. The elevator could be reconnected to a piling without the help of a diver.) The piles were then grouted in place with the divers taking grout samples.

The second season saw the installation of the second section at 850 feet and the third and final section at 500 feet. Assembled, the jacket weighted 46,000 tons. According to Shell, the sections mated to within a maximum deviation of $1^{1}/_{4}$ inches; most measurements were less than an inch out.

Throughout, the water was astonishingly clear. Opening the flood valves on the legs, the surface divers could see each other almost 400 feet apart. From the 850-foot level, the saturation divers were able to see all 350 feet of the middle section; from the center, they could look out to the corners.

"At that depth" Miller said, "you had to have some light because it was fairly dark. At 1,000 feet you couldn't see your hand in front of your face, but when you turned on a light it was crystal clear."

The Cognac project was significant, not only because of the depth but also because it made extensive use of ROVs, a technology that was still relatively new to the offshore industry. Although the divers initially looked on the vehicles as spies, they soon came to welcome them. Alone in the darkness at 1,000 feet, it was comforting to have a robot companion to light the way. They also made for much greater efficiency.

"The diver and the ROV were basically one tool" said McArdle. "The diver would get out of the bell and go over to the leg he was working on, and they'd put the ROV above and behind him. The engineers on deck could see what the diver was doing and they could help him by communicating with him. It got to be that one depended on the other." The little vehicles proved so effective that John Harter used the videotapes to demonstrate the advantages of combining divers and ROVs.

The Cognac installation went off faster than expected, and without a hitch. Over two seasons, Taylor worked at 1,025 feet and 925 feet, then at 850 feet and 500 feet. Prolonged deep diving had become a routine procedure. As Gaudiano put it, with slight tongue in cheek, it was almost like going out and jumping in the family swimming pool.

Bibliography

<u>Taped Interviews</u>
Anthony Gaudiano: July 18 1991 (telephone)
John Harter: Kenner, Louisiana, July 7, 1989
Paul Heckert: August 29 1991 (telephone)
Bob McArdle: July 6 1991 (telephone)
Fred Miller: August 25 1991 (telephone)

<u>Published Material</u>
Weeden, Scott L., 'Shell's Problems with Production Drilling'. Cognac platform. Ocean Industry (November 1979)

As Christopher Swann indicated, Shell required Taylor to prove they could carry out oxy-arc cutting and other routine procedures on the bottom at 1,025 feet. This they did. My report on that 1,200 ft Shell Cognac Research dive in December 1976 is on page 183.

Part of the Taylor Diving Sat crews for Shell Cognac.
Crew members from left to right:
(1) Norm Heater, (2) unknown, (3) me, (4) Alan 'Doc' Helvey,
(5) Alan 'Crazy Al' Anderson, (6) Mark 'Bear' Wallace, (7) Jeff Sherry,
wearing thermal underwear - standard dress inside the chamber

Sadly, two of our crew would not be with us much longer. Crazy Al would die in a diving accident on Ixtoc blowout in 1979 and later that year, Jeff was shot during a domestic dispute.

An extract of the article on the Cognac installation from Popular Mechanics Magazine – April 1978 by Dan Fales follows:

Just how deep is 1,000 ft/305m? The above picture shows the platform next to the Empire State Building. Actual depth for surface to seabed – 1,025 ft / 312 m. I was a member of the 'Famous Cognac 6' Sat Crew and made the first dive – becoming the first person to walk on the bottom at that depth in the Gulf of Mexico.

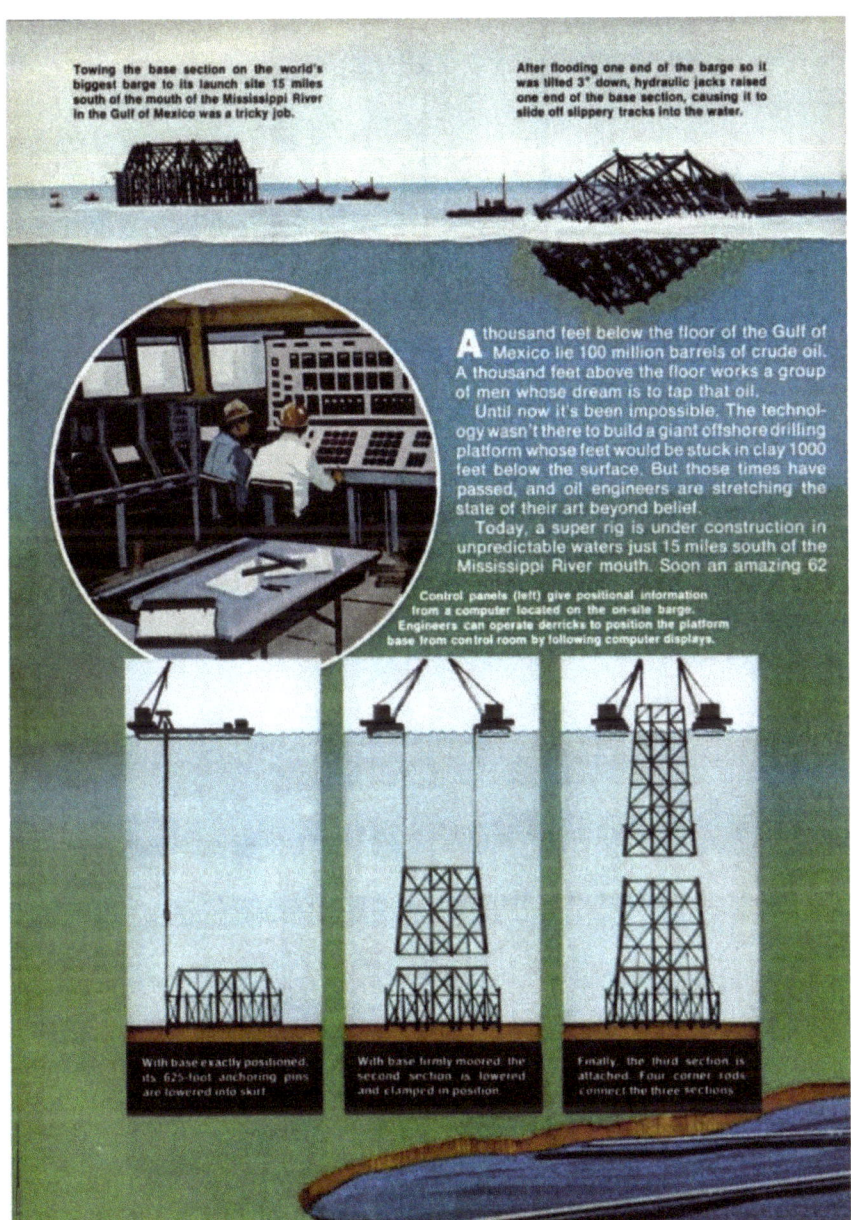

The Pressure Zone by Mike Cooke

Cognac platform bare section is loaded on mammoth barge that's 450 feet long by 150 feet wide. Note: 825-toot anchoring pins lying on ground (upper left). Pins weigh a total of 450 tons.

Base section on site, rigged in a lowering harness between two 500-ton derrick barges. Computer control center is on main barge No.16 in the foreground. Note: white cowcatchers (pipe guides) on the skirt.

[continued from article on previous page]

separate wells will fan out from under one platform like a blossoming flower - and strike oil.

But before that happens a lot of men must do a lot of strange things. Among the strangest is the fact that diving teams must stay cooped up for 89 days, most of them beneath the surface, in small, pressurized chambers and even stranger - they love every minute of it.

"Nine hundred dollars a day is what each diver gets," explains Bob Ferris, a Shell Oil Company vice-president in charge of seeing to it that an army of scientists, engineers, divers and roustabouts find and tap fields in the oil-rich gulf.

As we stand on Derrick Barge No.16 anchored on site, I realize the surprising $900-a-day pay is only one of hundreds of incredible facts that surround the oilmen's latest and most adventuresome offshore construction project. Actually, Shell is sinking the world's tallest oil rig into water that's deeper than any to be found beneath other surface-platform rigs.

Troubled waters
Though the gulf waters may seem docile compared to those of the North Sea or off Alaska - they are not. Only six days apart, two hurricanes forced postponement of my trip to Cognac - Shell's code name for this massive project that will take nine years from start to finish.

When complete, the Cognac tower will sit in 1,025 feet of water and rise off the gulf bottom 1,265 feet—some 15 feet taller than New York City's Empire State Building. The structure will also be the heaviest of its kind in the world - weighing 46,000 tons - about the weight of the famous steamliner Titanic.

Most platforms for undersea drilling are built erect and then towed complete to the launch site. Not Cognac, it is the first rig to be built in three sections, each separately towed to the site and launched. Shell engineers are literally putting together a giant Erector Set project of three sections.

Derrick Barge No.16 (right) is the central campaign headquarters for project Cognac. The barge had to be released from its sophisticated anchoring system twice last fall as two hurricanes approached the site, endangering the operation. Each time the barge was towed to protected waters.

Sinking a city block

The first section is the size of a city block. This base unit sits on the gulf bottom. Actually, it's spiked to the bottom by 24 steel pins that are 7 feet in diameter, 625 feet long and have a wall thickness of a whopping three inches.

Just to plant the base section took new techniques and special designs that have stretched the state of the art farther than anyone ever believed possible. To me, just getting the platform located in the general vicinity of the oil field is making engineering into a higher art form. But to Sam Paine, Shell's project chief, planting the base section is an exact science. I never realized how exact it is until he told me.

Even before you tow out the first equipment barge, a plan is developed. Shell's plan is to tap the oil that's spotted at various levels below the seafloor over an area covering 36 square miles. To do this, oil engineers decided the economics of an above-sea drilling platform would be best. Deeper water would force them into the more expensive submerge-drilling techniques.

They also decided that with modern drilling technology they needed to construct only one giant platform from which to drill 62 wells.

Cognac base section slides off launch barge into the water at a maximum angle of 300. Greased tracts aided the launching. Base section floats level and free immediately after the launch.

The final lowering preparations required about 36 hours.

This number is a record-breaker in itself, yet there's more. Drilling 62 wells straight down does nothing to bring oil from the far corners of a field as large as the one planned.

Blossoming wells
To get all the oil - about 106 million barrels (a barrel is 42 gallons) - drilling experts will drive drilling bits straight down 1,000 feet and then angle 58 of them up 70° from the vertical to within 20° of the horizontal and continue drilling for two more miles.

When completed, the 58 wells will surround the Cognac platform like the petaled flower of a dandelion. The "flower" will be four miles in diameter.

But before the flower can grow, seeds must first be planted. In this case, the seeds are transponders planted by divers in the mud of the gulf bottom after surveyors pinpoint the center of the site and its parameters. Once placed, these beepers will continue their pulsating signals throughout the life of the construction phase.

So - suddenly - Cognac has a heart. Orienting on the heartbeats, 12 temporary pilings are driven at selected spots around the site.

Workman lowers TV camera and lights into center of 7 foot diameter steel anchor pin. Camera helps locate pipe guides (cowcatchers).

These are the footings for the anchoring buoys that float on the surface and hold barges and derricks in exact locations. This includes the main construction barge that I am on - Derrick Barge No.16.

But unlike ordinary construction barges, Derrick No.16 has a brain. Three sophisticated computers receive, monitor, digest and reel off an amazing volume of information. Monitoring devices continually tell the computer how wind, wave and subsurface currents at varying depths are affecting the barge. Comparing this information with the steady beep of a sea-bottom transponder, the computer tells engineers not only if the barge is off station, but exactly how to relocate it.

By now the bottom section has been built and must be barged to the site. Towing a base section over open water that's 1,000 feet deep is one thing. But what do you do when you have a structure that's 380 by 400 feet in plan, is 175 feet high, weighs 14,000 tons - and you want to tow it down a Louisiana bayou that's only 14 feet deep?

Answer: Spread the load.

Get yourself a barge that's wide and long enough to permit a calculated draft of just under 14 feet.

But because a barge that big doesn't exist, it must be created by extending an existing barge to 450 feet in length - a length that will give enough flotation when the gigantic base section is slid onto the barge ...

At precisely 2:15 on a bright and quiet afternoon last July 25th one end of the launch barge was flooded, putting it down by the head 3º.

At 2:53 hydraulic pushers nudged the base section. It slid into the water at 3:00 o'clock with little splash and came to rest suspended from the derrick cables with 30 feet above the water and 145 beneath...

Diving breakthroughs

One of the other astonishing aspects of this operation involves the diving teams. When it's time to place the grout, divers using saturation breathing techniques supervise the underwater part of the job ...

As of September, 280-plus manhours had been recorded for Cognac divers working at depths of 900 to 1,000 feet of water. These men, who work for Taylor Diving, are also using other breakthrough devices. The divers work in an atmosphere that's composed largely of costly helium. Because of its high cost, they are using newly designed helmets capable of "scrubbing" the helium, thus making it reusable.

Cage for a remote TV camera and light is lowered to divers who work on the rig at 900 feet below the surface

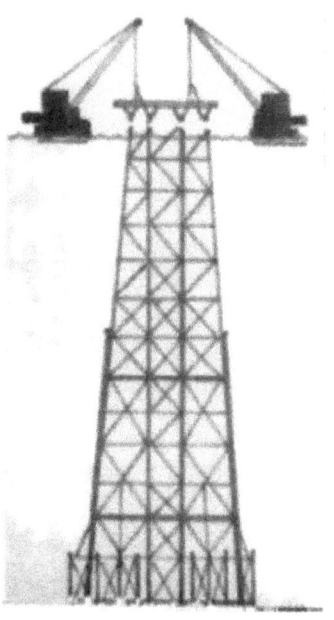

The actual working surface will be 1,025 feet on the floor of the Gulf. Two drilling rigs will be erected on this platform

The men also use a voice decoder, since the human voice becomes very squeaky after protracted breathing of helium. For those outside their world to understand them, the divers must speak through these electronic aids.

Decompression takes 9 days.

The divers stay in a state of saturation for 39 days. It takes a day and a half to get the body equalized to the proper pressure. The men are then available for work for 29 days, and it takes 9 days more just to decompress.

All this time, the men are either in a small, pressurized tank aboard the derrick barge or they are working from a diving bell with their partners hundreds of feet below the surface where the water pressure on their bodies runs about 400 pounds per square inch.

The water temperature is 50°F and the fishing's fine. Surface crews monitor diver action through TV cameras mounted on the divers' helmets. Cognac is really stretching the state of many arts.

Before the first drop of oil surfaces at Cognac, $700 million will have been spent by Shell, with lot leasing, planning, exploring, construction and drilling taking almost a decade. Part of that cost was to engineer and build the $275 million platform that will live for 50 years and be able to withstand hurricane winds of 150 mph as well as 70-foot waves. The platform is designed to take the worst storm nature could throw at it in 100 years.

With the base down, the 315-foot midsection will come next, followed by the 530-foot top capped with the platform and two drilling towers. The first oil will be piped ashore sometime in the 1980s.

This will probably be the last giant drill rig built in waters of this depth. New technology has pushed engineers on into submersible drilling. This technique will be used in future wells in water thousands of feet deep.

[Author: Dan Fales - Popular Mechanics]

Cognac base section being towed from Morgan City to location.

Caption: Presented to M Bateman-Cooke (Me) for your significant contribution to the successful installation of the Cognac Jacket Base Section by Shell Oil Company, October 1977

Fred Miller and I made the first bell run on Cognac. It was my turn to be first diver out of the bell. As a result, I was the first person to walk on the bottom in the Gulf of Mexico at a depth greater than 1,000 feet. A new depth record had been set - 1,025 ft / 312m. Neil Armstrong eat your heart out.

Talk about dark, I couldn't see my hand when I touched the mask faceplate. The only light I had was a standard handheld 6-volt Ike Light. With the light on, the water was crystal clear and visibility was as far as the beam would permit. The silence was deafening – there was no sound except for my breathing.

In 1977, a 1,000 ft Sat dive paid $1,000 / day at depth. $1,000 in 1997 is worth $5,750.96 today - not bad for a kid from the home.

1,000ft Club – Norm Heater and I at the Sat unit entrance lock
Getting ready to go down into the pressure zone

TAYLOR DIVING & SALVAGE CO., INC.

ROBERT F. McARDLE
SENIOR VICE-PRESIDENT

795 ENGINEERS ROAD
BELLE CHASSE, LOUISIANA 70037
PHONE (504) 394-6000 · TELEX 058-4192

October 4, 1978

Mr. Michael Bateman-Cooke
Taylor Diving & Salvage
"Norwhal"
B.O.C. Base
Keith Inch
Peterhead, Aberdeenshire
Scotland

Dear Mike,

    We received the enclosed letter from Shell in reference to the Cognac Project. The letter speaks for itself and the only thing that I can add is my personal congratulations and appreciation from Taylor.

                  Sincerely,

                  TAYLOR DIVING & SALVAGE CO., INC.

                  R. F. McArdle
                  Senior Vice-President

RFM:jmp

Enclosure

Coincidentally, Shell's diving consultant was Oceans Technology Inc and my longtime friend and dive buddy, Linden Leask, was one of the principals of that firm.

SHELL OIL COMPANY

ONE SHELL SQUARE
P. O. BOX 60124
NEW ORLEANS, LOUISIANA 70160

OFFSHORE DIVISION

September 29, 1978

RECEIVED OCT 2 1978 TAYLOR DIVING & SALVAGE CO.

Taylor Diving & Salvage Co.
795 Engineers Road
Belle Chasse, Louisiana 70037

Attention Mr. K. Wallace

Gentlemen:

      The critical phases of the Cognac platform engineering, fabrication and installation have been successfully completed. This involved many new and, until now, untried concepts. These new concepts were conceived and implemented by the Cognac Project Team of which your Company was a member. The team was challenged to advance the state-of-the-art of offshore technology and responded with an effort which, I believe, will go down in history.

      The professional skills, dedication and cooperation of the members on the Cognac Team were the key ingredients which resulted in successfully meeting all the challenges. It is obvious that the right companies and the right individuals from each company were chosen to make up the team.

      Shell Oil Company wishes to express its appreciation for the significant contributions of Taylor Diving & Salvage Co., as a member of the team in the success of Cognac.

      I would also like to express my personal thanks to you and to each of your people that were involved. I feel the challenges of Cognac were so great that no one on our team was willing to give anything less than his very best, and in many instances the effort was well beyond the call of duty.

      I would greatly appreciate it if you would copy this letter to the various members of your staff to let each and everyone of them know that their efforts have led to this success.

Yours very truly,

A. O. P. Casbarian
Project Manager

Prior to the Cognac dive, I testified as a representative for the Association of Diving Contractors (ADC) in relation to diving procedures before the Ad Hoc Select Committee on the Outer Continental Shelf in Washington. I received the following letter of commendation from the US House Representative John M Murphy later that year.

NINETY-FIFTH CONGRESS

JOHN M. MURPHY, N.Y., CHAIRMAN

MORRIS K. UDALL, ARIZ.
JOSHUA EILBERG, PA.
ABRAHAM KAZEN, JR., TEX.
JOHN B. BREAUX, LA.
GERRY E. STUDDS, MASS.
CHRISTOPHER J. DODD, CONN.
WILLIAM J. HUGHES, N.J.
MARTIN A. RUSSO, ILL.
GEORGE MILLER, CALIF.
JOHN F. SEIBERLING, OHIO
BO GINN, GA.
LEO C. ZEFERETTI, N.Y.

HAMILTON FISH, JR., N.Y.
EDWIN B. FORSYTHE, N.J.
DON YOUNG, ALASKA
ROBERT E. BAUMAN, MD.
CHARLES E. WIGGINS, CALIF.
DAVID C. TREEN, LA.

TIA GREGORY, CHIEF CLERK

STAFF DIRECTOR
CARL PERIAN
MERCHANT MARINE AND FISHERIES

CHIEF COUNSEL
MARTIN H. BELSKY
JUDICIARY

COUNSEL
STANLEY E. SCOVILLE
INTERIOR AND INSULAR AFFAIRS

MINORITY COUNSEL
CHARLES A. BEDELL
MERCHANT MARINE AND FISHERIES

U.S. House of Representatives
Ad Hoc Select Committee on
Outer Continental Shelf
Washington, D.C. 20515

November 28, 1977

Mr. Michael C. Bateman-Cooke
Taylor Diving & Salvage Company
795 Engineers Road
Belle Chase, LA 70037

Dear Mr. Bateman-Cooke:

As Chairman of the Ad Hoc Select Committee on the Outer Continental Shelf, I thank you on the Committee's behalf for your participation in the hearings held this year on H.R. 1614, the Outer Continental Shelf Lands Act Amendments of 1977.

Your time and efforts have helped the OCS Committee to compile a thoroughly comprehensive hearing record on the issues surrounding oil and gas development on the outer Continental Shelf.

The legislative mark-up process took many weeks and the Committee relied heavily on the hearing record which had been compiled. The Members of the OCS Committee fully debated each of the complex issues raised during the hearings-- over one hundred amendments were considered during mark-up. H.R. 1614 was reported to the House on August 29, 1977.

I am very hopeful that passage of the OCS bill will occur early in the second session of the 95th Congress. It is my belief that expeditious passage of this legislation to modernize the Outer Continental Shelf Lands Act of 1953 is essential to insure exploitation of our OCS resources in a manner consonant with assuring a fair return to the U.S. Treasury and with protecting our precious coastal environment.

Enclosed, please find Parts I & II of the hearings on the OCS bill; you will find your testimony printed therein. Also enclosed, find one copy of House Report 95-590 by the OCS Committee on the OCS Lands Act Amendment of 1977. Additional copies of the hearings and the report can be obtained by contacting the Committee. Again, thank you for your gracious cooperation.

With kind personal regards, I remain,

Sincerely,

John M. Murphy

JOHN M. MURPHY
Chairman

JMM:tg

Enclosures

> *'Whatever precautions are taken, there will always be a disaster in the North Sea, sooner or later'*
>
> [Texan oilwell firefighter Paul 'Red' Adair]

1978

Cognac would soon be followed by another world record. This time in the Norwegian North Sea area.

The **Norwegian trench** or **Norwegian channel** is an elongated depression in the sea floor off the southern coast of Norway. It reaches from the Stad peninsula in Sogn og Fjordane in the northwest to the Oslo fjord in the southeast. The trench is between 50 and 95 kilometres wide and up to 700 metres deep. Off the Rogaland coast it is 250 – 300 metres deep, and its deepest point is off Arendal where it reaches 700 metres deep – an abyss compared to the average depth of the North Sea, which is about 100 metres.

Extracts from the writings of three authors set the scene for this record dive better than I could.

In "TRILLION DOLLAR BABY - How Norway beat the oil giants and won a lasting fortune" Paul Cleary wrote:

Pipe Dreams

Norway's plan to build pipelines linked to onshore processing plants also shows the power of education, as it was strongly influenced by Arve Johnsen's studies in the US more than a decade earlier on the Fulbright scholarship. One of the courses he took was called advanced American Economic Development', which in part covered American petroleum history, including the rise of JD Rockefeller and Standard Oil.

The key insight that Johnsen gained was that Rockefeller's control of the rail networks and pipelines from the Pennsylvania oilfields - rather than primary production alone - had been the source of his immense wealth.

At the time he took this course in 1960, there was no prospect of Norway's discovering oil, but a decade later Johnsen remembered what he had learned and was determined to apply the same principle in the North Sea - at the expense of American oil companies.

Applying the Rockefeller approach to Norway would involve creating state-owned businesses that could own the pipelines and the plants.

A major obstacle in the way of realising this ambition was the Norwegian trench, which dropped down to 360 metres between the Ekofisk field and the Norwegian coast. When the Norwegians had first raised the plan of piping Ekofisk oil and gas to Norway, the Phillips Petroleum executives cited the depth and ruggedness of the trench as a key obstacle. The Ministry of Industry set up the Ekofisk committee, which eventually agreed with Phillips to land the gas at Emden, West Germany, and the oil, UK. These pipelines went down to depths of just sixty to seventy metres.

Johnsen could see that Phillips looked set to do a Rockefeller on Norway, because its pipeline could become the trunk line for future oil developments, so he proposed that a dedicated company be established to operate the pipelines, with Statoil having a 50 per cent share ownership. Jens Christian Hauge, who had created a state-owned pipeline company, Norpipe, put the proposal to William Martin, Phillips vice president, who later became the chief executive of the company. Martin was visibly shocked by such an audacious move and shouted, 'This is immoral!' Evidently, the company was unaccustomed to such boldness from other countries. Hauge remained calm and measured as Martin fulminated, and simply asked him to provide a legal basis for this assertion. Martin was unable to do so. The demand was at odds with the provisional agreement negotiated between Phillips and senior industry department officials, who believed that a modest 10 per cent share of the pipeline business after two years would be a fair arrangement. Phillips caved in because it realised it could not afford a lengthy delay, and the Ekofisk field was so big that it was going to be very profitable even without control of the pipeline. As a result, Norway got a foot in the door of the pipeline business even though it had failed to secure onshore development with its first big field. This was an important first step towards achieving much grander designs down the track.

The following is an extract from a paper by HO Knagenhjelm published in 'Underwater Technology Offshore Petroleum' Bergen 1980:

Norsk Hydro, as Operator on behalf of the Petronord Group and Statoil, submitted in April 1976 a report to the Norwegian Department of Industry on the technical feasibility of landing gas from the Frigg Area to Norway.

This report indicated a number of critical operations in connection with a pipeline project in such deep waters. Among these operations were pipeline repair as this had not been carried out at the depths found in the Norwegian Trench. The report therefore concluded that deep water pipeline repair is crucial for the landing of oil and gas in Norway and that a 'full scale' repair test would be desirable. The undertaking of such a full-scale test was thereupon taken up within the Petronord Group.

Of the various alternative techniques which could be developed, the method considered most promising was welding under pressure by divers (hyperbaric welding). This method had so far been successfully employed at depths down to 150 MW. Analyses carried out by both groups, with the assistance of experts from companies experienced in this field, showed that there was great probability that this method would also be feasible in the depths found in the Norwegian Trench.

On this background the hyperbaric welding method was chosen for the Deepwater Hyperbaric Welding Test (DHWT). The aim of the DHWP was to demonstrate that it is possible to repair pipelines under the depth and bottom conditions present in the Norwegian Trench, by modifying the methods which have been used extensively in the North Sea.

In the Deepwater Hyperbaric Welding Program (DHWP), Norsk Hydro acted as operator on behalf of the Statoil/Mobil Group and the Petronord Group (incl. Statoil). Main Contractor for the DHWP has been Brown & Root Offshore NV (B&R NV) with Taylor Diving & Salvage Co Inc. (TD&S) as responsible for all the underwater operations. (End)

In "ON THE EDGE, UNDERWATER, offshore diving in Norway", historians Kristin Oye Gjerde & Helge Ryggvik set the scene:

Norwegian newspapers were full of reports in early February 1978 about what was seen as a technological and human achievement. A dive was to be conducted in the Skanevik Fjord north of Stavanger with the goal of welding two pipes together in 320 metres of water. If this succeeded, it would be a world record.

Nobody had previously carried out extensive work at corresponding depths. Many newspapers conveyed the impression that Statoil and Hydro were behind the dive. In reality, a number of foreign oil companies accounted for the bulk of the financing. The budget was put at roughly NOK 40 million, with Hydro as the responsible operator. The actual dive would be conducted by America's Taylor Diving. It was compared on the front page of Stavanger daily Rogalands Avis with a space mission. According to the press, everything was in safe hands. The dive had been approved by the NLIA, which would have representatives present along with personnel from DNV and the NPD.

It was no accident that the contract for the experiment had gone to Taylor Diving. After the creation of its UK subsidiary 2W in 1976, where Taylor Diving owner Brown & Root had a controlling interest, the US company had cut back its direct presence in the North Sea. In the late 1970s, nevertheless, it was still regarded as the world's largest and most experienced saturation diving specialist. It was also the most expensive. The dive in the Skanevik Fjord was a prestige project. If the Trench were to be crossed with a pipeline, the ability to do complex jobs in depths down to 360 metres would be essential. The divers who were due to take part in the experiment had been trained by the US Navy. Many of them also had long experience from the North Sea. <u>Hiring Taylor Diving indicated that the choice had fallen on the toughest and the most experienced of them all.</u>

This is my account of that saturation dive. The Sat lasted 44 days from 31 January to 15 March 1978.

It was a typically cold early winter morning, several hours after midnight, when the diving bell was lowered into the frigid dark water of the Norwegian fjord for the first bell run. As the bell started the descent, the three divers inside made preparations for the upcoming venture into the unknown where no man had gone before. At reaching working depth, pressure in the bell was reduced, allowing the bottom hatch to open.

Fully booted and spurred, breathing gas provided by the compressor/depressor (push/pull) system housed in the dome on top of the bell, as the first diver, I entered the water. Standing on the bell anchor I adjusted the flow of mixed gas supply of oxygen and helium and regulated the hot water flow to my helmet. Peering out past the halo of light shining through the open bell hatch I could see absolutely nothing - complete total darkness in the void beyond.

Paying out some slack in my umbilical, I leaned forward and leaving the relative safety and comfort of the bell I gently lowered myself down to the bottom.

I knew that once I stepped off the anchor weight I was alone descending into the totally black abyss beyond.

Due to the total black out, not being able to see my hand in front of my face, I landed on the bottom - feeling more than seeing. The silence was deafening, only broken by my heavy breathing. Every move was measured and took additional effort.

At 04:25 hours on 3 February 1978, I became the first person to make a dive to 1,056 ft (320 m) in the North Sea area. One heck of a present - it was my 36th birthday.

After my first bell run, I made a further three bell runs on dives 2, 4 and 7. Four days later, during bell run #10, tragedy struck. A fatality occurred.

Page 4

```
0035    Old CD rig on the surface.
0118    Barge started down on the pipe section.
0130    Commo Check on rigs #1, #2, #3 (O.K.).
0135    PUTCO 2 Scrubber in SDC (Emergency).
0145    Isolated SDC/DDC.
0215    Tracking unit out.
0218    Unit tracked out. - pinned.
0225    Unit equalized.
0233    RCV deployed to find pipe (lowering cage).
0239    RCV deployed - out of cage.
0243    RCV located pipe.
0245    Lowering P/L W/Davits - RCV follow. (Stop)
0255    Cont. lowering P/L.
0258    RCV to #3 davit to lower all the way.
0304    P/L on bottom (out of sight).?
0306    Down on davits 5' - stop.


Sat #1   Sat Depth 1000'      SDC Press   0318
Run #1   SDC Depth 1030'      SDC Equal   0652
         WTR Depth 1051.5     TET         3:34
         Excursion   51'      TTCD         :35
                              CD On       0422
                              CD Off      1501

         Diver #1             Diver #2             Diver #3

         M. Cook              J. Spencer           J. Kohl
                                                   CD Tender
RB       0500
LB       0425
TWT       :35

0315    Divers M. Cook, J. Spencer, J. Kohl in SDC.
0318    Press for a seal to 1065'.
0320    Tunnel Bled.
0334    SDC - DDC Separating.
0335    Inside skin valves secured
0337    SDC leaving A-Fram
0341    Inside skin valves open 40'
0407    SDC O/B 1030'.
0411    SDC Hatch Open.
0412    Run #1.
0413    CD Off.
0415    Surface gas to SDC on.
0422    CD on.
0425    Diver #1 in water. looking for P/L.
0430    Diver on P/L.
0433    Bottom pneumo = 1051.5
0438    Diver to #3 Davit.
0448    Down # 3 Davit - Stop.
0449    Up on #3 Davit - clear.
0450    Diver to #5 Davit.
0453    Down #5 Davit - Stop.
0455    Up on #5 - Clear.
0500    Diver #1 RSDC
0501    CD Off.
```

Taylor Diving & Salvage Saturation Dive Log – 3 February 1978 - Bell Run #1

It was a standard three men bell run. Two diver/welders (John Kohl and Dave Hoover) exited the bell and entered the hyperbaric welding habitat. I remained in the bell to attend to the other divers' umbilicals, provide assistance, and do a diver change-out if needed.

Approximately four hours into the bell run communication was lost with Hoover. Kohl found Hoover unconscious outside the habitat. Inside the bell, I reacted immediately, pulling in the divers' umbilicals while outside, John was dragging Dave back to the bell.

We got Dave back inside the bell, got his mask off, cleared his mouth of blood and sputum and I started mouth to mouth and CPR.

It was no easy feat. To help get Dave back into the bell, it needed to be partially flooded, which was controlled by 'topside'. To say it was a difficult task is an understatement. While performing CPR and mouth to mouth, we had to keep Dave secured in the bell and stop him from sliding out the bottom hatch. We didn't wear a safety harness back then and there was no device in the bell to secure him to. Further, the exertion involved was equal to 32 times on the surface as a result of the pressure.

After the bottom hatch was sealed, the bell was brought back up to the surface and mated with the saturation chamber. Dave was passed into the chamber to the medic, John VanBerschot, and treatment attempts were continued as instructed by the onboard doctor from outside the chamber. After a thorough check, further treatment ceased at 23:52 hours, an hour and forty minutes after John found Dave unconscious. Everyone in the chamber was shocked and in disbelief by what had just happened.

Many years later, John VanBerschot paid me one of the best compliments a diver could ever receive: "You were so brave and strong in the bell that day".

Completion of the weld was aborted and we were on standby waiting for a decision to be made as to whether we would continue diving and complete the weld. Norsk Hydro abandoned the project. Over the next six days a decision was made by the powers that be in Norway to cancel the project, authorising only the retrieval of the equipment. On 13 February, Crawford, Kohl and I made the next bell run (#11) to retrieve the SPAR and habitat off the bottom.

Although operations had ceased, the job was not complete. We had performed the most difficult part of the tie-in operation prior to the accident; involving the removal of concrete, rough cutting of the pipe, aligning of the pipes, placing the SPAR, lowering the habitat, pigging of the pipes and retrieval of SPAR.

Despite the tragic event, everyone involved agreed the job had to be completed. The intention was to prove that a pipeline could be repaired/welded at that depth and that hadn't yet been achieved. Taylor decided to carry out the actual welding on their own off the coast of Scotland.

```
              SAT #1,                      RUN. #10
BELL CHECK Commo Spkr. - O.K.  Headset- O.K.  Rig #1 - O.K. Rig #2 - O.K.
           Rig #3 - O.K. Donut 1875   He Bottle - 1675   PPO2 - .374
           CO2 - .147  Cannister - 1  Spare - 1

    DIVER #1              DIVER #2                DIVER #3

   J. Kohl               D. Hoover                M. Cook
   RB - 2010             RB - 2010                RB -
   LB - 1855  2058       LB - 1934  2049          LB -
   TWT - 15              TWT - 46                 TWT -
```

```
1705    PPO2 .374     CO2 - .147
        Sat. Depth 1000'        SDC Equal -
        Bot Depth - 1051'       SDC Press - 1801
        SDC Depth - 1030'       TET       -
        EXC. Depth -  65'       TTKMB     -
                                Sub Total KMV

1801    Pressed SDC - 1065'.
1805    Units Separated.
1814    SDC leaving "A" frame - skin valves closed.
1818    Skin Valves open - 40'.
1841    SDC on bottom.
1843    Hatch open.
1855    Diver No. #1 J. Kohl Pig to VWH
1900    Diver No. #1 in VWH with pig.
1915    Diver No. #2 D. Hoover in the water; waiting on H/W
1920    Diver No. #1 removing broken P/L from pipe.
1925    Spar is 80 PSI over bottom.
1934    Diver No. #2 in the water.
1935    Lower SDC 10' more feet.
1936    No. #1 and No. #2 divers in UWH checking control panels.
1951    Down on A & B clamps; all Stop pipe in Place.
2000    Increasing pressure on Hyd. System.
2010    Both Divers back in SDC waiting H/W. P/O as tripped out.
2026    Press SDC for seal.
2027    Got a seal going to 1065'.
2029    Hot water restored to bell.
2031    Hatch undogged equalized bell.
2032    Hatch open.
2049    Diver No. #2 D. Hoover leaving the SDC. Working on UWH hyd. system.
2058    Diver No. #1 in the water ST/BY in UWH.
2102    Pig is out of the pipe.
2110    End to install pigs.
2120    Pig is in the pipe.
2147    Pressurizing the pig in steam pipe.
2203    Diver J. Kohl over breath his mask (pull off his kirby).
2205    Divers both back on Kirby.
2210    Lost commo to Hoover's rig. Divers going back to SDC.
2212    Kohl reports Hoover is unconscious.
2222    Has Diver in SDC.
2223    DV stuck in hatch, SDC tender giving mouth to mouth resuscitation.
2230    Diver in SDC. Not breathing. No heart beat.
2250    Pressed for seal.
2251    SDC L/B
2300    Dv's lips turning blue.
2304    SDC in A-Frame.
2305    SDC & DDC mated.
2308    SDC & DDC Equal - Doctor examining patient via sat tender - doctor
        giving resuscitation instructions to sat Tender (J. VanBerschot)
        and other divers in DDC. All instructions being carried out.
2324    Sat Tender continuing with treatment advised by doctor.
2342    Treatment still being applied - no change.
2350    Sat Tender going through - checking for signs of life . as per docto
2352    Doctor advises sat. tender to cease further treatment - doctor
        pronounces man dead.
0004    Pressing down entrance lock to 1000'.

        RELIEVED BY B. BAKER AT 2345.
                                          R. A. Driscoll
```

Taylor Diving & Salvage Saturation Dive Log - 7 February 1978 - Bell Run #10

The barge relocated to Scotland with the Sat crew remaining under pressure. Bell runs re-commenced there on 28 February. I undertook a number of further bell runs, including the final bell run #23 with Jerry Mehl and Ed Thomas on 4 March.

```
Barge 324                    0000-1200                 4 March 1978

     SDC Pre-Dive Check    Run #23
     Rig #1 OK,   Rig #2 OK,   Rig #3 OK,   Bell SPKR. OK
     HDST OK,   Donut psi - 2000,   HEO2 psi - 1700,   Cannister - New.

          SAT Depth    1000'              SDC Equal    0536
          SDC Depth    1010'              SDC Press    0308
          Water Depth  1036'              T.E.T.       2:28
          Exc. Depth   1036'              T.K.T.       2:25

                                     T.K.T. (Job) 138:39

Diver #1 - M. Cooke          Diver #2 - J. Mehl         Diver #3  E. Thomas

R/B   0455                   R/B   0453                 R/B
L/B   0338                   L/B   0345                 L/B
T.T.  1:17                   T.T   1:08                 T.T

0232   Pre-dive check compelte.
0235   D.B.G. and press to SDC secured - lines disconnected and bled.
0242   D.B.G. and press reconnected and on - divers in SDC: M. Cooke,
       J. Mehl, and E. Thomas.
0245   Waiting on press, till RCV deployed.
0308   Press SDC to 1050'.
0311   Tunnel on surface - RCV deployed.
0315   SDC - DDC seperating.
0316   Inside skin valves secured.
0318   SDC leaving A-frame.
0319   Inside skin valves open 50'.
0334   SDC O/B 1000'.
0336   Hatch open - blowing down SDC.
0338   Dv #1 (M. Cooke) in water.
0345   Dv #2 (J. Mehl) in water.
0346   Dv's holding for B clamp to open port relief valve.
0350   Port relief valve open.
0354   STBD side relief valve open.
0400   Coming up on #3 davit.
0407   Moving barge to STBD. All stop #3 davit.
0410   Moving barge aft.
0413   Coming up on #3 davit.
0414   Moving aft 5' all stop #3 davit.
0415   Divers moving aft to #4 davit.
0422   Down on #4 davit.
0424   All stop on #4.
0426   Moving barge aft.
0430   Down on #4
0431   #4 davit hooked.
0431   RCV back to cage.
0438   Coming up on haul back cable.
0447   All stop on haul back.
0452   All Davits and haul back cable has strain.
0453   Dv #2 in SDC.
0455   Dv #1 in SDC.
0501   Press SDC to 1050'.
0502   SDC L/B.
0515   Inside skin valves secure - 60'.
0518   SDC on dogs - inside skin valves open.
0519   SDC - DDC mating.
0522   Unit tracking in.
0529   Unit secure in SAT house.
0536   SDC - DDC equalized.
```

Taylor Diving & Salvage Saturation Dive Log - 4 March 1978 - Bell Run (Dive) #23

After a saturation dive of 44 days, Taylor announces:

Taylor Diving, Brown & Root Set New Record for Deep Water Hyperbaric Pipeline Welding

A team of diver/welders employed by Taylor Diving & Salvage Co. Inc has established a new world record by welding two sections of 36 inch diameter pipeline in 1,036-feet (316-meters) of water near the island of Raasay offshore western Scotland.

Final phases of the test program to prove the feasibility of deep-water pipeline tie-in and repair by hyperbaric welding were conducted by Taylor in association with Brown & Root, Inc.

Taylor president Ken W Wallace said the technique and equipment were essentially the same as those used in performing 63 hyperbaric production welds in the North Sea since 1975.

The field test was designed to duplicate conditions encountered in the Norwegian Trench, an extremely deep portion of the North Sea, which runs parallel to the Norwegian coast.

Initial stages of the exercise were conducted under the sponsorship of Norsk Hydro, a major Norwegian company, serving as project operator for the Petronord Group and the Statoil/Mobil Group. Statoil represented the Statoil/Mobil Group within the project.

Three years of planning and preparation preceded the field test, with a majority of the preliminary work conducted in Taylor's hyperbaric research and training complex at Belle Chasse, near New Orleans, Louisiana ...

Ken Wallace said: "Successful completion of the exercise under actual 'at sea' conditions in extremely deep water served to verify the effectiveness of hyperbaric welding technique in support of petroleum developments at depths exceeding 1000 +ft (320m)."

[Source: Extract from Taylor Diver Special Edition Welding at 1,036 Feet (316 Meters)]

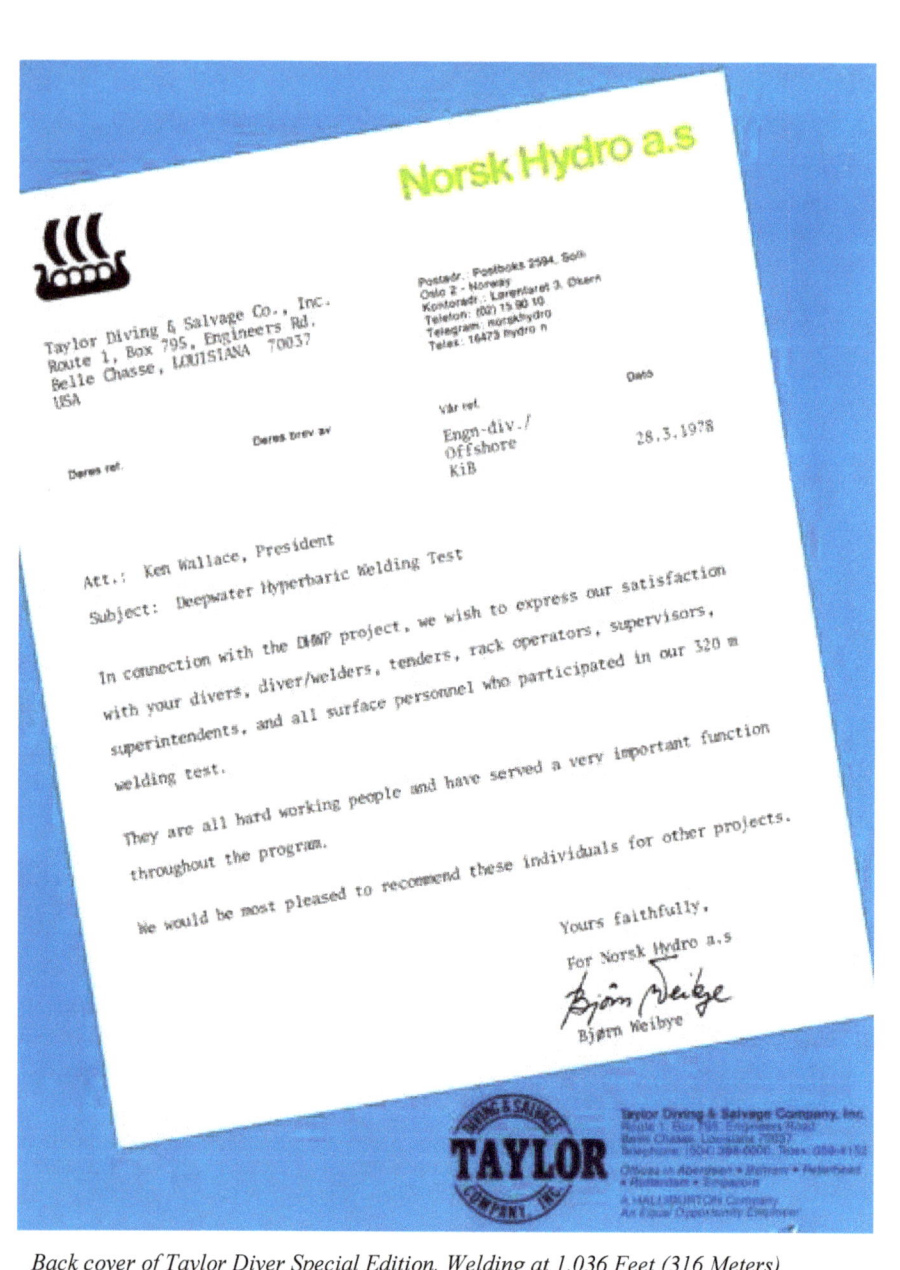

Back cover of Taylor Diver Special Edition, Welding at 1,036 Feet (316 Meters)

What followed …

10 June 1981 - As a result of the overall success of the Sat dive in proving our ability to repair pipelines in over 1,000 feet of water, three years later the Norwegian Parliament approved the development plans for the pipeline. Choosing to pipe the petroleum resources to the mainland made Norway one of the world's wealthiest countries.

5 February 2003 - A final report on Dave Hoover's death was released by The North Sea Divers Alliance.

30 August 2013 - 35 years later, the Norwegian movie **'PIONEER'** was released in Norway. The movie is based around the events and circumstances of the above. It incorporates several still shots of Taylor's crew, equipment and hyperbaric welding procedures.

13 Oct 2013 - **'PIONEER'** released in the USA.

Still shot from the movie of Jerry Mehl, my bell partner for the last bell run, entering the saturation chamber on the Norsk-Hydro dive.

12 February 2014 – From www.collider.com:

George Clooney and Grant Heslov to Produce Remake of Norwegian Thriller PIONEER for Sony

BY **DAVE TRUMBORE** FEBRUARY 12, 2014

11 April 2014 - From:
https://www.theguardian.com/film/2014/apr/10/pioneer-review-norway-oil-divers-film

The Guardian Newspaper – Peter Bradshaw, film critic – "**based on a true story that should surely have been told more directly in documentary form …**"

20 October 2015 - Norwegian television airs the documentary - '**THE DEEPEST DIVE**'.

This film is about that saturation dive and in particular Bell Run #10. Both John Kohl and Brian Pittari, another Sat crew diver, are extensively interviewed. I was mentioned but never interviewed.

The movie Pioneer appears to be *based* on that saturation dive and the documentary The Deepest Dive is actually *about* that dive.

Both films pay tribute to the fact that what was achieved back then was quite extraordinary and paved the way for further development in the North Sea.

Re: https://tv.nrk.no/program/MDDP11005115/the-deepest-dive

PRE-DIVE BRIEFING ON WELD PROCEDURES CONDUCTED BY M. TYSTAD

I am in the back row in the middle (head supported by left hand).

My last day in saturation – 3 October 1978

A Taylor advertisement

Chapter Five – 1979-85
(Commercial Diving Management)

Riding a desk, a plane, a boat - management!

1979

Reflecting on the difficulties we experienced in getting Dave Hoover back into the bell, early that year I undertook a study at Taylor with the assistance of Henry Hicks on the use of a diver's safety harness and bell securing method using a come-along lifting mechanism for rescuing a disabled bell diver. I recommended the installation of lifting devices in the bell, as well as the use of personal diving harnesses. The harness could also incorporate a bail out bottle, which had not previously been used.

During 1979, Taylor adopted these recommendations and modified diving bells and equipment. The full R&D report is attached as Appendix 6.

I was then seconded to Brown & Root (London) by Roy Jenkins, head of the installation team, as diving consultant for platform installation. I'd worked as a diver for Roy when he was in charge of the marine department working out of Great Yarmouth in the early years of the North Sea (1966-68).

In June 1979, following the breakout of a fire on a semi-submersible drilling rig on the Ixtoc 1 well in the Gulf of Mexico, Taylor Diving was brought in to assist in trying to bring the blowout under control.

Alan Anderson was one of the Taylor divers involved.

The following extract from Offshore Pioneers explains some of the work being carried out.

> *In late June, the shutoff effort almost succeeded. Operating out of a bell, divers managed to find their way to the BOP stack and hook in Choke- and- kill lines leading from a flat-top work barge called Able Turtle. The barge pumped seawater and 10-pound mud into the well through the lines to bring the pressure down. The BOP rams closed off the flow, the well showered down, and the fire went out. However, another break occurred in the wellhead. As pressure built, the rams were reopened to release the flow, and the fire was reignited to consume as much oil as possible.*
>
> *After this failure, crews tried a very unconventional method to control the blowout. PEMEX gathered up nearly 100,000 steel, iron, and lead balls and fed them into the well. They hoped that the balls would be heavy enough to form a bridge that would collapse the sides of the well, but the supercharged vent just spewed out the balls.*

Divers reported that the expelled balls were stacked like cannon balls all over the sea floor surrounding the well.

The idea sounds bizarre in retrospect, but PEMEX was desperate to find some way to snuff out the well. Professor Jerome Milgram, an oil spill expert from M.I.T. who monitored the blowout, said at the time that the plan "was motivated more by emotion or desperation than by reason, because straightforward engineering calculations show that the balls will be blown right out of the well.

This desperation led to tragedy. Taylor Diving lost a diver who had been sent down to tie in a device for feeding the balls into the wellhead. Diving around the stack was a difficult and dangerous job. Ken Wallace described the noise underwater near the well "like about 20 - 30 locomotives going down a railroad track all at the same time. It was such a roar. Communication was very difficult because of the roar that was coming over the communications to the diver."

One diver, Alan Anderson, swam underneath some wreckage near the vortex of the blowout. The tremendous force of the flow, intensified because its fluids were at a lower density than the surrounding water, swept him up into it. His lifeline air hose caught on a pipe and left him hanging in the vortex. When Anderson was finally pulled out, his wetsuit and equipment had been completely stripped off. This unfortunate incident revealed the awesome power of the blowout and the hazards of trying to deal with it on the seafloor.

[Source: Brown & Root *Offshore Pioneer Divers* pages 189 – 191]

Aerial view of Ixtoc blowout

Alan died mid August 1979. I lost a good friend and dive buddy. We made a lot of Sat dives together.

Diver preparing to descend with surface fire from Ixtoc blowout in the background

1980

I then presented a paper entitled "The Development of a Safe Diving Procedure: Rescuing a Disabled Bell Diver" which I presented at International Diving Symposium in New Orleans Louisiana in February 1980.

This paper must have had a positive effect as it was referenced in "Safety of Diving Operations", Commission of the European Communities, published 1986.

Since then, safety harnesses have become standard gear.

I then moved into Business Development and Sales working for John Harter and Ken Wallace.

My first successful contract was to provide diving services to Chouest Marine for the installation and maintenance of a Single Point Mooring (SPM) buoy for Louisiana Offshore Oil Port (LOOP).

Part of the contract was to place a Taylor Decompression chamber onboard Chouest's MV Loop Lifter.

A bit about LOOP. It is America's first and only deep-water port. LOOP provides tanker offloading and temporary storage services for crude oil transported on some of the largest tankers in the world.

SPM

1980

ECO's first highly specialized newbuild is delivered – the 200-foot dive support vessel M/V LOOP LIFTER.

Most tankers offloading at LOOP are too large for US inland ports. Tankers offload at LOOP by pumping crude oil through hoses connected to a SPM base. Some of these vessels require water depths of 85 feet - the water depth at each of LOOP's SPMs is 115 feet. Three SPMs are located 8,000 feet from the Marine Terminal.

The SPMs are designed to handle ships up to 700,000 deadweight tons. The SPMs are 21 feet in diameter, 46 feet high and are anchored to a seabed base with an anchor chain. Mooring lines connect the bow of a tanker to the buoy and flexible hoses are used to transport crude oil from the tanker to a submarine pipeline. The buoy and hoses can rotate a full 360 degrees allowing the tanker to maintain a heading of least resistance to wind and waves. The crude oil then moves to the Marine Terminal via 56-inch diameter submarine pipeline. Its offshore marine terminal facilities are located 18 miles south of Grand Isle.

I must have impressed them because Chouest asked me to form a joint venture and submit an independent bid. I told them sorry – no can do, I'm a Taylor diver – through and through. But it was good to be asked.

Later that year I went with John Harter to Caracas and Lake Maracaibo, Venezuela. I'd make this trip a couple of times to bid on diving services.

A major event that year was the forming of a joint venture between Taylor and Hydrospace Engineering of St Johns, Newfoundland. Bill Lukeman, my dive buddy from Navy days was one of Hydrospace's two founding partners. Another navy dive buddy made good.

1981 – 1984

Then in 1981, a major move. This time to Australia as General Manager, Taylor Diving Australia to provide ROV and hyperbaric weld services (Saturation Diving) to Woodside Offshore Petroleum (WA). We lived in Australia from August 1981 to September 1983. This is where I met my future wife, the lovely Miss Christine (Chrissie).

I returned to head office in Belle Chasse Louisiana as Operations Manager, responsible for all US domestic operations from October 1983 to December 1984.

In October 1983, Chrissie joined me in the States.

January 1985 – July 1985

For the last six months in the States, I was back in Business Development working with John Harter again as Marketing Manager - Maritime Inspection and Repair Services (USA).

I received one of the first long service pins Taylor issued - one diamond for every five years: 5 September 1964 to 30 June 1985 - just shy of 21 Years with Taylor.

Was this the end of my diving – not bloody likely!

In July 1985, I moved to Australia with Chrissie.

Chapter Six – 1985 - 2003 (Post Taylor)

1985 – 1995

Chrissie's Dad, John Napier, ran a ship agency and broking business out of Kwinana / Fremantle, Geraldton and Bunbury dealing primarily in the shipment of mineral sands to North America. He had had a bad car accident driving back from Bunbury to Perth and needed help - it was getting to be time for him to retire.

So, in 1985 I joined John at Marquisand and was introduced to ship agency and broking services. Having been in the navy and around ships all my life, it was an easy transition. I took over John's business a year later and ran Bimar (Maritime & Marine Services) for ten years. It also worked well, dealing so much with Americans, since we spoke the same language and enabled us to return to the States on a regular basis.

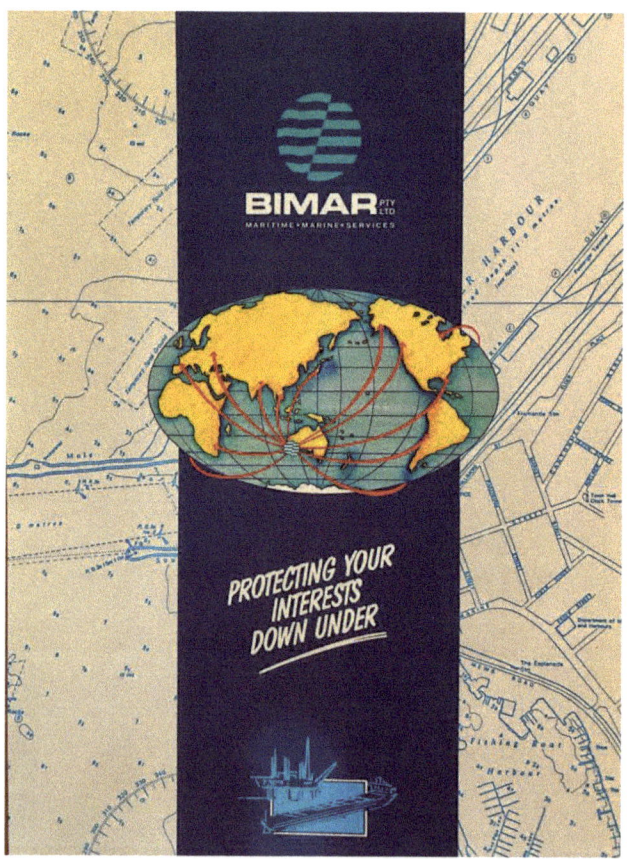

Bimar's information brochure

Chapter Seven - My Hockey Years

1975 – 1981 NOLA (New Orleans)

Although I spent a lot of time offshore, overseas and away from home, I was still able to be involved with my favourite sport - hockey. This was where I became great friends with Jeff Haskell, Joe Biderman and Paul Dion. In Australia, it's referred to as ice hockey, while the hockey they play is referred to as field hockey in Canada. Hey, I learned to play in Canada, eh!

The first men's hockey team in New Orleans (NOLA) - the N'Awlins Crawfish – naturally

The first NOLA youth team - 'Champagne Pirates' - late 1970s – I was Head Coach. My son Michael is front row second from right and my godson Brand first on the left, with Paul Dion Assistant Coach at right.

The Pressure Zone by Mike Cooke

1981 – 2014 Perth Australia

I was transferred to Perth in 1981. But how did I discover they played hockey there? I ran into Barry McKinnon, a WA Politician who later became State Leader of the Liberal Party in WA, at the 1981 Offshore Technology Conference (OTC) in Houston. We got to talking and I mentioned I was heading to WA for the Woodside project and regretted that I wouldn't be able to play any hockey there. He said "Why not? I know they have a rink there, I just don't know where."

So naturally, I brought my hockey gear with me.

I travelled to Australia via Singapore and touched base with our office there. Well, I very nearly got arrested on arrival in Singapore because my stick bag looked very suspicious on the baggage carousel and I was pulled aside by two armed guards for a baggage check. They must have thought I had a bazooka or something in there.

In fact, I got to play more hockey 'Downunder' than anywhere else.

1981 WA (Western Australian) State Team (me #17)

The first hockey team I skated with in Perth was the CIG Bombers. CIG just happened to be our supplier for diving gas. In other words, I was the first person to arrange sponsorship for a hockey team. This was soon followed by Guy Grant getting a sponsorship for the Wildcats from Budget Pest Control. Pretty soon we had a four team league – the Bombers, the Wildcats, the Pirates and the Flyers. Ex-pats - American, Canadian, Swiss, German – everyone needed somewhere to skate.

1985 Head Coach - WA State Team

1995 Head Coach - WA Women's State Team

It was during this period I taught Chrissie how to skate and play.

1998 Head Coach - National Women's Team

The guy on the right is the team manager. When we were in Concord, MA he was billeted in a local family home with one of our players. When it came time for us to leave and return to OZ he decided to stay - seems he got along real well with the lady of the house – that's hockey.

When we decided it was time for non-contact, the Ol' Stars was born. We also played in a few Masters tournaments - in Bendigo, Canberra and Perth. I still meet a number of the guys from our original team for lunch on a regular basis.

My last skate was in 2014, on my 72nd birthday.

2010 Ol' Stars Xmas skate

Chapter Eight – 2003 – present
(Back to basics – full circle)

The final chapter. I can't believe it; with the number of years I'd spent under pressure diving, I still needed a PADI card to do recreational diving. Guess that's what happens when you start diving before PADI or NAUI existed! Back to basics.

Hard Hat and Club diving

Chrissie got her card in 2004. Time to hit the pressure zone together. Diving for fun and not work is a whole different thing. It's the first time I had to pay to dive!

In 2006, we met a couple of members of the Dive Section of the Fremantle Sailing Club (FSC) on a cruise out to the Rowley Shoals. They encouraged us to join. We were members of the Dive Section from 2006 to 2018, during which time we had a lot of fun and met a lot of good people.

As a member of the FSC Dive section, I produced a number of dive calendars over the years, one being a tribute to Max Sheen. Max was a WWII hero in mini-subs, receiving medals from both Australia and the US. He was also a well-renowned solo sailor and long-time member of FSC. He and I trained with the same type of CDBA gear – he in the RN and me in the RCN.

Receiving a signed copy of Max Sheen's book: Corvette and Submarine.
I'm holding my bronze statue of a CDBA Diver.

A tribute to Max Sheen

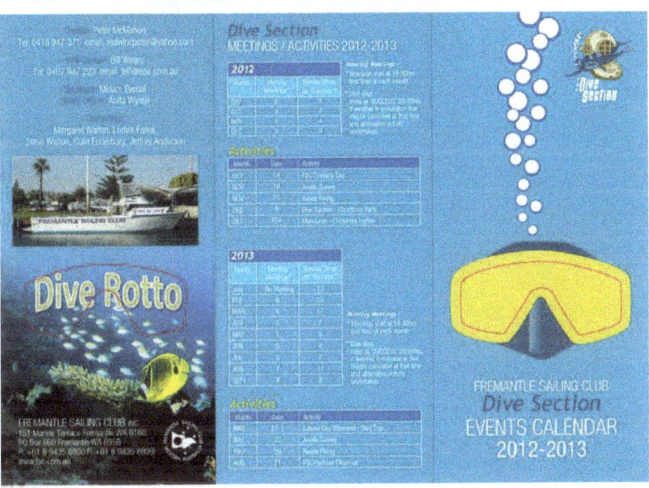

Dive calendar showing the dive sites on Rottnest Island, Western Australia

With Peter McMahon, a friend I met at FSC, I've done more hard hat diving than ever – I might have introduced him to it, but he has the gear.

In June 2010, Peter and I went to Portland, Victoria. It was the middle of winter on the southern tip of Australia, so it did get cool. But nothing like the North Sea. The Historical Diving Society Australia – Pacific arrange these dives each year in Portland.

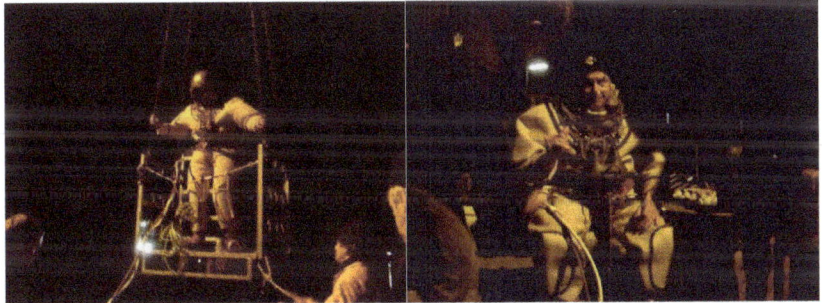

Hard Hat Dives, Portland Victoria - we finished up around 10 at night

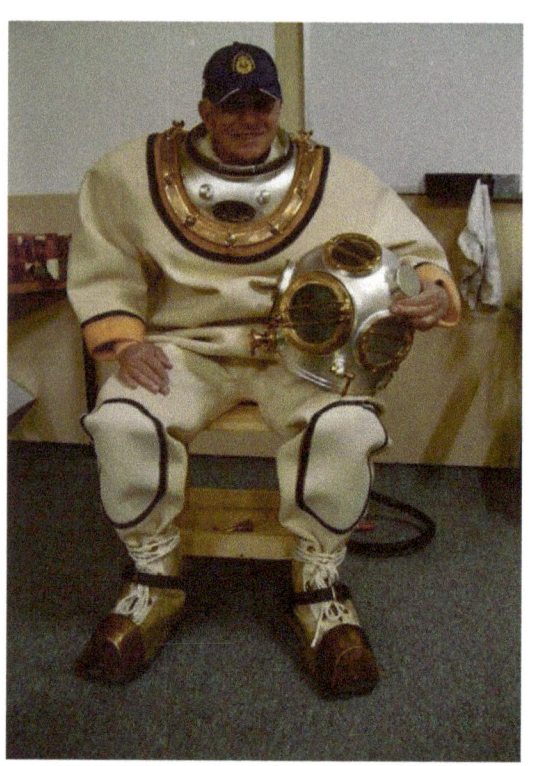

I am in the front row on the right in standard dress

In February 2011, Peter and I put on a Hard Hat Diving display at FSC.

One of many we put on over the years for the Open and Opening Days at the Club.

With my grandson, Lochlan

The following year, I introduced the *Creature from the Black Lagoon* to yet another Hard Hat demo at FSC. Also got to use my Desco mask which brought back fond memories of my earlier years at Taylor.

Shades of West End Boulevard on Taylor's back deck, where I married my first diving umbilical

Ready to go with my Desco mask

I got the idea to have my own Creature suit from Dick Long, who helped advance saturation and surface deep diving, especially in the North Sea, when he invented the hot water suit.

I first ran into Dick at an ADC symposium in New Orleans in the early 1970's where he had his marketing representative dressed out in a creature suit.

My youngest grandson, Aiden, decided he had to try out the creature suit himself!

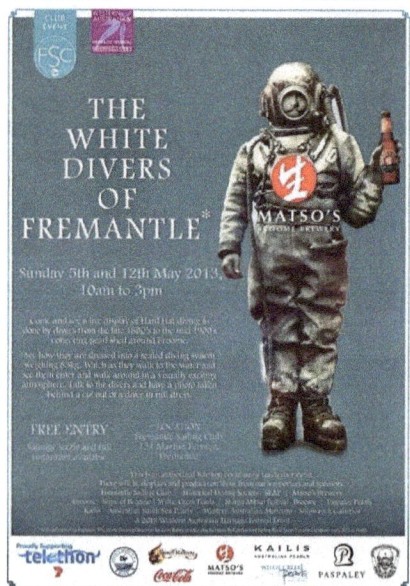

Another hard hat dive at FSC, this time sponsored by Matso's Brewery in Broome and Willie Creek Pearls

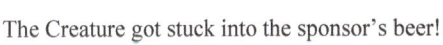

The Creature got stuck into the sponsor's beer!

Me with my grandsons

The Pressure Zone by Mike Cooke

Chrissie with the Dive Commodore & Harbour Master drawing the winner of a Hard Hat Statue

"The Shrine"

Bronze Statue of a navy CDBA

Presented to Fleet Diving Unit (Atlantic) by Mike Cooke* at Canadian Navy Divers Association Reunion 2012 to commemorate the 50th Anniversary of the 'Class of CD2/62 ODU (A)' Mike Bateman-Cooke*, Moe Coulombe, Keith Jamieson, Mike Kettle, Gilles Lariviere, Linden Leask, Bill Lukeman, Victor Vautor

Bill Lukeman and Gilles Lariviere (two members of my CD course in 1962) presenting the CDBA statue to FDU(A) on my behalf

We also did a hard hat demonstration at the Aquarium of WA. We organised some pearl shells which we picked up off the bottom to give the kids an idea of what the pearl divers did in Broome. We had a great audience and it must have been good – they asked us to come back again.

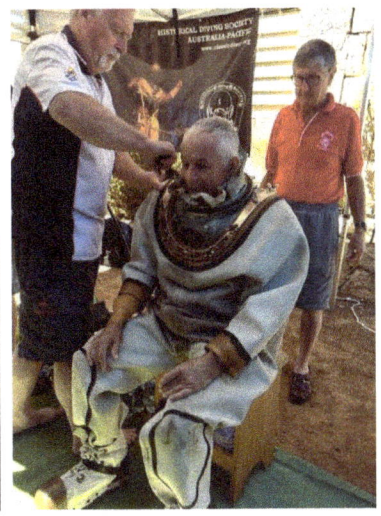

Apart from having fun with working dives – anode replacement, marker buoy setting and cleaning, harbour bottom cleaning (trash), hull cleaning and the like at the Club, I designed some dive benches with bottle racks which were built by Arthur Johns, Bosun and put on board the FSC dive boat, Success. At the end of every dive trip, they were removed, folded flat and returned to the dive locker.

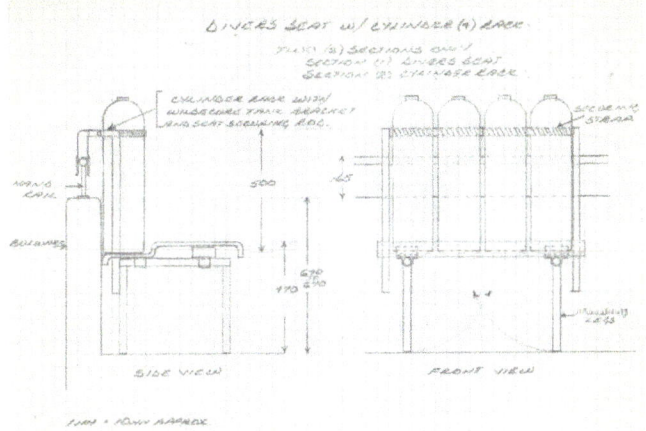

The Pressure Zone by Mike Cooke

Colleagues and friends

During the period 2009 to 2013, I was lucky enough to catch up with a former colleague from Taylor Diving and my good friend Linden, but sadly had to say goodbye to two special people who had a major impact on my life.

In January 2006, we received an invitation to my mentor and friend, Ken Wallace's 80th birthday celebration. Unfortunately, we couldn't make it and sadly he passed away three years later.

And then, on 31 May 2012, I got a message from John Valz's partner, Ethel (one of the first ladies I met in the French Quarter in 1964), with some very sad news. Mitch, my dear friend and mentor had gone.

When a friend is gone

What do you say when one of your closest friends passes away?

Does it hurt – you're damn right it hurts.

Is there a void? There's emptiness ... there is nothing ...

How do you describe someone who had such an impact on your life?

Can I think back and honestly count the ways? Not really – they're too numerous.

Mitch was the first person I met in New Orleans. I was 22 years old when I walked into Taylor Diving. I had five years of Navy diving experience, yet I still looked like a kid who was in High School. And the first guy I met was Mitch.

Back then, he was the 'go to' guy – that was 48 years ago – nothing much changed there. Who was this guy? As far as I knew, he ran Taylor Diving. He was the guy on the other end of the phone line sending you out on a job. He sent me on my first job offshore, which was out of Intracoastal City. I asked him how will I know when I'm there? Hell, I'd only been in Louisiana four days. His reply: when you run out of blacktop. No shit. It was true – at the end of the road was a field full of cows. My welcome to commercial diving.

When I got my leg crushed in my first diving accident, where did I go to? 509 Avenue F - it became my home and my family.

He was the big brother I never had. If it wasn't for Mitch, my life wouldn't have turned out the way it did.

After my accident in the winter of '64, I went back to Montreal, where I got stuck in knee deep snow, out of funds and needed a helping hand. I called Mitch and asked for $200 so I could fly back down to New Orleans. Ever the accountant, he sent me $50 with a note – "take a bus, leave the flying to us".

I arrived back in New Orleans in the Spring of '65. It was on a weekend and I only had a dime in my pocket and two phone numbers. One was for Taylor and the other was for Mitch. If I called the wrong number I had one hell of a long walk ahead of me. I called Mitch and he was home. He was there for me again. But it was only the start of a long-term friendship.

Some of the highlights ...

- *He taught me how to live life and introduced me to the French Quarter.*
- *He made me laugh.*
- *We joined a West Bank gym together – along with Eddie, Val and Bob Evans. I forget the owner's name, but he offered Mitch a sweetheart deal – don't tell anybody you work out here and I'll give you free membership.*
- *Scuba diving in the Florida caves and Keys and the Cayman Islands.*
- *He taught me a lot – in particular, how to enjoy life and live in the moment. If it wasn't fun then it wasn't worth doing.*
- *He loved to live on the edge – especially where bureaucracy was concerned. Chrissie and I can never thank him enough. He certainly helped us out. We wouldn't be where we are today without his help.*

Thanks again my friend.

Mitch was involved in my life in so many ways.

He was best man at my first wedding; hell, he even gave the bride away at my second wedding.

Distance didn't seem to be a problem for us. When he was living in Aberdeen, I stayed with him when I was able to get ashore and we even took off to tackle the Scottish Highlands. Introduced him to his first contact with some serious snow on the trip to Aviemore. He told me he was petrified driving in snow. I responded – you're not driving. He said – that doesn't help!

Back home, Mitch and Norma always made me welcome. I used to stop by without notice and sure enough, there'd always be a glass of Norma's beautiful ice tea or her special chicory coffee on the table.

It wouldn't be Mardi Gras without walking down the road from Mitch's house and checking out the Poseidon Parade (Pon-si-don).

I left New Orleans in 1985 and moved about as far away as you can. But that didn't present a barrier. We talked regularly and hell, I'm still turning on the computer expecting to see an email from him. I don't think there was a day that went by where I didn't hear from him.

When my first grandson was born, Norma sent a quilt. Hey – you guys were as close a family as I ever had.

He might not have been the biggest guy in the world, but to me he was larger than life. You might be gone my friend, but you can't get away. You're in our (mine and Chrissie's) hearts and memories forever.

We love you man.

Mike

Mitch doing what he loved best

In October 2012, my good friend and dive buddy Linden visited us in Perth for the first time. I hadn't seen him in many years, so it was great to catch up and take him on a sightseeing trip down south.

At Bunker Bay, Dunsborough

Busselton Jetty

Then, in February 2013, Winston Chee (ex-Taylor engineer) visited. He was in Perth installing a new hyperbaric treatment chamber locally at Fiona Stanley Hospital. Took him over to Rottnest to go snorkelling for the day.

Diving together: 2004 - 2019

Local diving – Western Australia

In the first couple of years after Chrissie got her Open Water card, we did a number of local dives – both shore dives at Woodman Point and boat dives out to Rottnest and Carnac Islands with the University Dive Club as well as some boat dives with the delightful Patrice on the Big Island of Hawaii – clear water but little colour. We also dived Busselton Jetty – the longest timber-piled jetty in the Southern Hemisphere.

After joining FSC in 2006, we had many dive trips over to Rottnest Island with the Club. Rottnest is about 21 kms from Fremantle and has some pretty diving – limestone overhangs, soft corals, temperate fish and the occasional wobbegong or reef shark. And only 40 minutes from home. More recently they have had a few great whites, but fortunately not while we've been diving, although they have been spotted where we've dived. There is also some good cray-fishing over there.

Our holidays from here on tended to revolve around dive trips.

Apart from local dives at Rottnest, in September 2007, we did our first overseas dive trip with members of FSC to Bandos Island in the Maldives.

We're also lucky to live near Ningaloo Marine Park - a World Heritage-listed site and the world's largest fringing reef, a 260 km (162 mile) long coral reef. It's located at Exmouth, which is about 14 hours drive north of Perth (Australians have an interesting interpretation of near!) Ningaloo offers turtles, tropical fish, manta rays and at certain times of the year, humpback whales and the elusive whale shark. And the beauty of it is you can snorkel right off the beach.

Turquoise Bay, Ningaloo Reef

One long weekend, we took a dive trip down to Bunbury – about 2 $^1/_2$ hours south of Perth. I used to drive there regularly to load ships when I ran Bimar. We dived the MV Lena which was a long line fishing boat scuttled in 2003. It's located about 3 nautical miles from the coast. We had fun on the way back - the charter boat started taking on water. We were ready to don our fins and swim back to shore but Sea Rescue came and towed as back to Port. But they refused to do anything until we all put on life jackets. Hell, my wetsuit was better protection than that life jacket!

Wreck Dive on MV Lena – Bunbury

There are a few really special places we've been lucky enough to dive together.

Rowley Shoals, Western Australia

The Rowley Shoals – a group of coral atolls about 160 nautical miles off the coast of Broome in Western Australia – is one of them. When we first visited in 2006, little more than 200 people would visit each year.

The diving was so easy - off the back of the boat into tenders and then at most a ten minute ride to the dive site. At the Cod Hole, it was just jump off the back straight into the water. Clear water, beautiful corals, loads of clams and fish - big and small. The fisher-folk onboard would return with Wahu which the chef cooked for dinner.

At Rowley Shoals, not only did we dive but also had some awesome express snorkels on the outgoing tide.

Told Mitch about the trip and the dives and he just happened to pass it on to Joe Schouest, one of my old Taylor buddies, who said:

> *"Snorkelling, the fucking guy used to dive to 1,000 feet and now he's snorkelling!?"*

Coming back to the vessel after a dive

Plenty of Dolphins

At the Cod Hole

One of our trips was crowded – a sailboat appeared in the distance.
Usually there's no one else in sight. Some of the slickest water ever.

Our third trip to the Rowley Shoals was with a group from the FSC Dive Club – an awesome trip. There were 14 of us on a boat that took 33 passengers. Although it was a bit early, the trip was a celebration for my 70th birthday, but who's counting.

Mantas - the Big Island, Hawaii

Some of our best dives ever have been the manta night dives off the Big Island of Hawaii. I'd done one in 2004 and it had been a hell of an experience. Something like 20 mantas performing an underwater ballet, swirling and dancing overhead while you just knelt on the bottom and enjoyed the show. You could be lucky or unlucky with seeing them, but we've never been disappointed. The mantas just come swooping down over you attracted to the lights and the krill. You almost had to duck to get out of their way.

The Big Island - Hawaii – Manta Night Dive: hair-raising!

During one dive, before we even jumped off the back of the boat, there was a manta coming up to greet us. The manta's name was Sam. The mantas are all named and recognised by their spots.

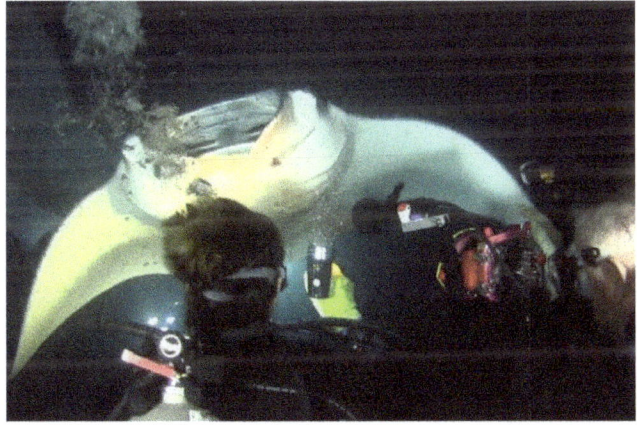

Wakatobi, Sulawesi

We first discovered Wakatobi Dive Resort in 2013 and loved it so much we've been five times. It's located in south-eastern Sulawesi, Indonesia. Easy diving with most sites within 20 minutes, good viz, warm water, lovely staff, gourmet food, comfortable dive boats, great dive guides and brilliant facilities. Peter McMahon has joined us on two trips there and we've been lucky enough to dive with our favourite guide, Ketut, three times.

You have to really look to find things in the coral - Wakatobi is famous for pygmy seahorses

Peter, Ketut and us

Had to take the Creature to Wakatobi one year

With Dive Guide Sylvia & Chrissie

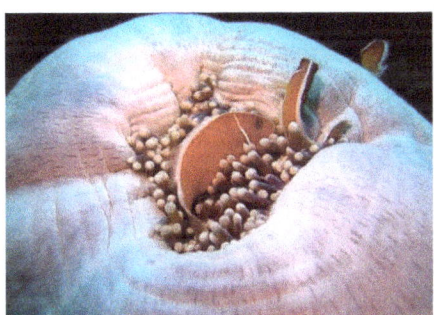

Wakatobi is great for photography

The Pressure Zone by Mike Cooke

Lembeh, Sulawesi

In May 2014, we figured it was time to try somewhere else in Indonesia. So we went to Lembeh Dive Resort in the north eastern part of Sulawesi. Another fantastic resort with great dive guides. It is known as the *Critter Capital of the World* – our first muck diving experience. It reminded me of working on the bottom in the Gulf of Mexico – you couldn't see your hand in front of your face because you were so knee deep in muck. Lembeh gets on the special list not so much for the diving as the people we met there and where it took us next.

We lucked out with great dive buddies in Ed and Elizabeth from the UK and met up with them again at another two Indonesian dive resorts. Ed is a wildlife photographer. One time he came in for a close up and a coconut octopus took a liking to his camera. If you were little slow taking photos you lost the group real easy due to the limited viz.

This is also where we first met Ana and Miguel, who were managing the resort. They later moved to Siladen in Bunaken Marine Park which became one of our favourites.

Lembeh is known for coconut octopus. Fascinating watching them collect a bunch of shells and hide in them.

Siladen, Sulawesi

Well having been to both the south-east and the north-east of Sulawesi, we figured it was time to check out where Ana and Miguel were at Siladen Dive Resort, Bunaken Marine Park. They are the best hosts you could ever meet. And we met Ed and Elizabeth there twice! Lots of fun, friendly staff and fantastic accommodation. Dives off the mainland were more like Lembeh – viz not great and not a lot to see other than little critters, but off both Bunaken and Montehage Islands there were lots of turtles, tropical fish, pretty corals and plenty of little stuff like nudibranchs. And the beach villas are a stunning spot to stay overlooking the volcano in the distance.

 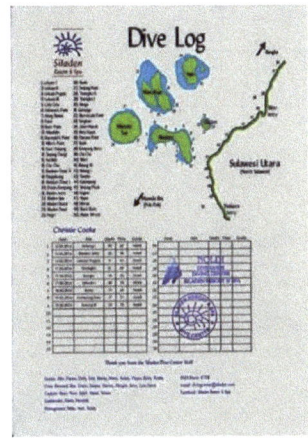

Siladen: Me with Ed and Elizabeth   Magic view from our beachfront villa

On our second trip I couldn't resist taking the Creature. And this time, instead of me wearing it, Miguel had some fun with it.

The children from the local village come one night a week and sing to the guests. Ana had them line up for a photo on the beach and Miguel came out of the ocean as The Creature. Scared the life out of them. Some ran all the way back to the village. Miguel got into strife with the village chief the next day for not warning the parents ahead of time!

Ana and I helping Miguel suit up

Kids on the beach ready to sing

The Creature aka Miguel

The reaction when they realised who it was

The end to another perfect day

Misool, Raja Ampat

In January 2018, we joined Ed and Elizabeth again – this time in Misool Eco Resort, Raja Ampat. Raja is supposed to be one of the best dive locations in the world. Unfortunately, the currents and viz were disappointing – coming off a super moon just before we arrived. We had one great manta dive and another was a nightmare.

A West Papua welcome at the airport

Dive sites

3 Feb 2018:
40th anniversary of my 1,000 ft dive

The good manta dive

(L-R): Elizabeth, Frank & Steffi and Pat & Jim in the background

Our overwater bungalow

Met some great people here – it was the best part of the trip. Shame we only got to know them at the end.

Looking down to our overwater bungalow in the bay

Back to basics

Well not actually diving this time. In September 2019, we joined the two couples we'd met in Raja Ampat, in Siladen. They were on a snorkel tour of Indonesia and we gate-crashed part of it. I couldn't believe it – this was my first ever total snorkel holiday. One big advantage - no problem with too much luggage – didn't have to bring my dive gear.

Even snorkeling you get to see plenty of reef life

The Perth soccer team gave us free balls for the village kids

Talk about going back to basics. I'd done a complete circle.

Back to basics with our snorkel buddies - Steffi, Jim, Pat and Frank

2020

We had made plans to meet again this year and introduce our friends to Rottnest Island. But COVID hit and put paid to that plan. Western Australian borders slammed shut. Just gonna have to do it another time.

We couldn't make it to Siladen, so Siladen came to us – well their masks did anyway.

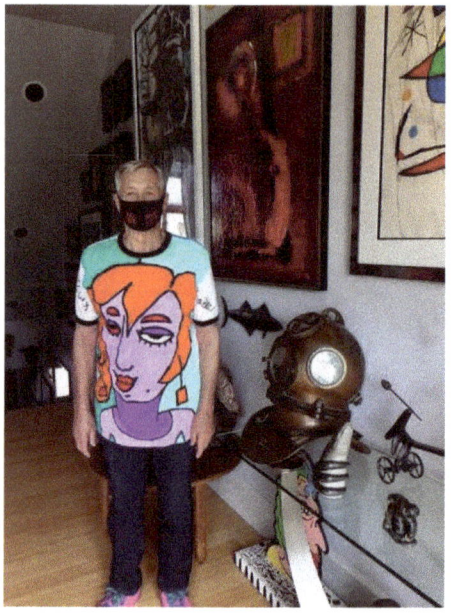

Even my ol' dive buddy Linden got to wear a mask from Siladen

Waiting for the next dive.

Sure, as shit, "aint gonna let the ol' man in" [6].

"See ya on the bottom" and laissez les bon temps rouler!

[6] Toby Keith *"Don't let the old man in"* Song in The Mule, Warner Bros 2018

Appendices

1. Acronyms
2. The Evolution of Diving – Diving History 101
3. The Challenge of Deep-Sea Diving - A paper presented by me at American Welding Society Conference November 1980, New Orleans, Louisiana
4. A Very Short History of Saturation Diving – by James Vorosmarti, Jr, MD
5. My 1200 ft. home – General Description of Operation and Purposes of Manned Hyperbaric Research Facility – A paper by George Morrissey, VP Taylor
6. Rescue and Recovery of Disabled Bell (SDC) Diver – A paper presented by me to the International Diving Symposium February 1980, New Orleans, Louisiana
7. Taylor Diving Hyperbaric Welding – Brochure
8. Taylor Diving Special Edition 'Diver' Magazine 1978

Appendix 1 - Acronyms

B&R	Brown & Root
BAR	barometric pressure
CABA	Compressed Air Breathing Apparatus
CD	Clearance Diver
CD(S)	Clearance Diver (Ships)
CDBA	Clearance Diving Breathing Apparatus
CPO -	Chief Petty Officer
DDC	Deck Decompression Chamber
EOD	Explosive Ordinance Demolition
FCW	French Cable Wharf
FDU(A)	Fleet Diving Unit (Atlantic)
fsw	feet of seawater
GoM	Gulf of Mexico
HMCS	Her Majesties Canadian Ship
HWG	Hugh W Gordon
LS	Leading Seaman
MCM	Mine Counter Measure
NAD	Naval Armament Dock
NAUI	National Association of Underwater Instructors
NEDU	Naval Experimental Diving Unit
NOLA	New Orleans, Louisiana
NRE	Naval Research Establishment
NS	North Sea
NSNS	Norwegian Sector North Sea
PADI	Professional Association of Diving Instructors
PSI	pounds per square inch
RCMP	Royal Canadian Military Police
RCN	Royal Canadian Navy
Sat	Saturation
S&R	search and recovery
SBM	Single Buoy Mooring
SCUBA	Self Contained Underwater Breathing Apparatus
SDC	Submersible Diving Chamber
SPAR	Submersible Pipe Alignment Rig
TAS	Torpedo Anti-Submarine
Taylor	Taylor Diving & Salvage Co
USN	United States Navy
UWH	underwater welding habitat
YMT	Yard Maintenance Tender

Appendix 2 - The Evolution of Diving - Diving History 101

Man first became acquainted with petroleum through natural seeps, or spots in the earth's surface where shallow deposits of crude oil oozed upward into pits, creeks, or sometimes along beaches and bays.

Petroleum, as the ancients called the 'rock oil', is referred to in the Bible and in early Greek history. These early discoverers used it to waterproof cloth, caulk boats, for fuel and in crude remedies for their illnesses.

No one knows for sure who was the first to drill instead of dig for water, brine, or oil. But the art of drilling did begin many centuries ago. By 600 BC the Chinese were using percussion tools, the forerunner of cable tools, to dig brine wells. By 1500 AD they were drilling to depths of 2000 feet.

900 BC	An Assyrian frieze shows men swimming with inflated animal skins strapped to their torsos for use as air tanks or flotation devices.

In the Iliad, Homer describes the military use of divers in the Trojan War.

360 BC	Aristotle, Greek philosopher, observes in *Problemata* that ancient sponge divers used containers of trapped air to extend diving time.
332 BC	Alexander the Great is said to have descended in a diving bell to observe his diving warriors destroy the underwater defences of the besieged island of Tyre.
300 BC	Greek laws are passed regulating those who dive for sunken treasure.
AD 77	Pliny the Elder, Roman naturalist refers to a breathing tube in his encyclopedia of natural science, *Historia Naturalis*. Ancient warriors drew air through a tube inserted in their mouths while the other end floated on the surface, an early version of the snorkel.
500	Japanese and Korean women, the ama divers, are trained from early adolescence to dive for pearls without apparatus or diving dress. (In the twentieth century, the ama dive mainly for food.)
1240	Roger Bacon alludes to "instruments whereby men can walk on sea or riverbeds without danger to themselves."
1511	Leonardo da Vinci sketches an underwater breathing apparatus that encases a diver's head in a leather bag with a breathing tube to the surface.

1662	*Robert Boyle, British physicist and chemist, invents the vacuum pump and uses it in the discovery of Boyle's law, which states that the pressure and volume of a gas is inversely proportional to one another.*
	Thus, bubbles of gas dissolved in human body tissues become smaller under pressure at depth and expand as the diver returns to sea level.
1680s	Capt. William Phipps, American adventurer, locates and retrieves 52,000 pounds of gold and silver from a sunken galleon in a salvage operation backed in part by British royalty. Phipps is knighted and later appointed governor of Massachusetts.
	Dr. Denis Papin, French physicist and pioneer in the development of the steam engine, suggests pumping a continuous supply of fresh air to a diving bell to extend the duration of a dive. This revolutionary concept evolves into standard equipment for the deep-sea diver: a helmet (hard hat) connected by a hose to an air pump on the surface.
1690	Edmund Halley, the English astronomer, invents one of the most famous diving bells. A weighted barrel is hauled down by ropes to supply fresh air to the diving bell. Halley and four others remain at 60 feet under the River Thames for almost $1 \ ^1/_2$ hours. Twenty-six years later, Halley spends more than 4 hours at a depth of 64 feet.
1715	John Lethbridge develops a completely enclosed one-man diving dress: a reinforced, covered barrel of air equipped with a glass porthole for viewing and having two armholes with watertight sleeves. It was intended only for depths shallower than 10 feet.
1776	David Bushnell designs *Turtle*, a small, wooden submarine manually operated by cranks attached to screw-type propellers. During the American Revolution, Turtle's crew planted explosives beneath the British fleet.
1809	Frederic Von Drieberg devises a system in which air is pumped from the surface to a large cannister on a diver's back. Air is delivered to a mouthpiece by the continual nodding of the diver's head.
1819	*Augustus Siebe devises an open-dress diving suit in which a metal helmet has an extension in the form of a shoulder plate that attaches to a leather jacket. The helmet, acting as a miniature diving bell, is fitted with an air inlet valve connected to a flexible hose that leads to an air pump. The air is expelled at the bottom of the diver's jacket. Many improvements, including closed suits and telephone connections to the helmets, are made to this dress over the years, but <u>the basic design remains in universal use.</u>*

1828	John and Charles Deane market Deane's Patent Diving Dress- a helmet and heavy suit for shallow water. Eight years later they publish the first diving manual.
1859	Col. Edwin Drake proves that oil could be obtained by drilling through rock. August 27 is noted as the birthday of the oil industry.
1864	Benoit Rouquayrol and Auguste Denayrouze design a self-contained breathing apparatus using compressed air in an *open circuit (the spent air is forced out)*. The system stores a small amount of compressed air on a diver's back, so that the diver can disconnect the air hose to the surface and move freely on the ocean floor for a short time. A regulator controls the flow of air to the diver's mouth. This equipment is immortalized by Jules Verne in his classic tale, Twenty Thousand Leagues Under the Sea.
1867	Commercial production of air cylinders with regulators begins.
1870s	Paul Bert, French physiologist, discovers the cause of decompression sickness (bends) in tunnel workers and deep-sea divers. Bert attributes this painful and sometimes fatal disease to the sudden change in gas volume when the human body goes from high pressure at depth to sea-level pressure on the surface without giving the body time to eliminate excess gases. Bert advocates recompression (return to the working depth or lower) for victims of the bends.
1878	Henry Fleuss develops a high-pressure bottle of oxygen with a demand regulator. Exhaled oxygen is recirculated through rope soaked in caustic soda, which absorbs the carbon dioxide and purifies the gas to be rebreathed (closed circuit).
1893	The first recompression chamber to simulate rise and fall in air pressure is installed on site to treat laborers stricken with the bends while working on the Hudson River Tube in New York City, at a depth of about 90 feet.
1903	Robert H. Davis assembles the original submarine escape apparatus, consisting of a breathing bag, relief valve, carbon dioxide absorbent canister, emergency oxygen capsule, main oxygen cylinder and valve, non-return valve and flexible tube for charging the breathing bag, and a tube leading to the mouthpiece.
1905	John Scott Haldane, British scientist, expands the understanding of the action of gases under pressure. He devises a staged decompression technique that requires the diver to stop rising every 10 feet for a period of time determined by the depth and length of the dive. The length of time required for each stop, or stage, is listed in predetermined decompression tables for safe ascent.

1915	The U.S. Navy Mark V heavyweight diving outfit features a telephone and improved exhaust valve. Both the Mark V and the British Admiralty six-bolt pattern diving dress are used in commercial projects. Robert H. Davis develops the concept of using diving bell chambers to rescue crew from disabled submarines.
1917	In the United States, Elihu Thomson proposes that helium, an inert and extremely light gas, be used instead of nitrogen in underwater breathing mixtures.
1920	Joseph Peress builds a diving suit of stainless steel, the Iron Man, which weighs about 800 pounds and functions as a personal submarine. The suit is used in 1935 to help locate the Lusitania, sunk off Ireland.
1924	The U.S. Navy's Bureau of Construction and Repair, responsible for Navy diving operations, tries to solve problems caused by compressed air diving by joining with the U.S. Bureau of Mines to conduct experiments with helium as the main gas in artificial breathing mixtures.
1927	U.S. Navy divers descend to 150 feet using a breathing mixture of helium and oxygen. The first U.S. Navy diving manual is published, with decompression tables to 250 feet.
1928	Robert H. Davis develops a decompression chamber that is lowered to the bottom from a surface support ship. The diver exits to work on the ocean bottom and reenters the chamber through a lower hatch. An attendant assists in removing the diver's helmet. The chamber is raised to the deck of the support ship, and the diver breathes oxygen from special apparatus during the long decompression stages. This technique is used to construct the harbor at Dover, England, and in laying bridge foundations.
1929	U.S. Navy divers go to a depth of 364 feet using a breathing mixture of helium and oxygen (heliox). From the 1930s through the early 1950s, the petroleum industry adapts onshore technology and equipment for use in shallow waters.
1930	Jack Browne develops a lightweight, air supplied mask for shallow-water diving. The full-face mask has an air supply valve and an exhaust valve. *(Widely used in the commercial diving industry mainly for air diving but also for mixed gas during the early stages of deep diving, circa 1960).*

1933   Yves Le Prieur markets a commercial type of self-contained, underwater breathing apparatus (scuba) with a manual control valve that provides up to 10 minutes of air at 40 feet and up to 30 minutes at 20 feet.

1937   Auguste Piccard constructs the first bathyscaphe, a marine application of his free stratospheric balloon with a tightly sealed cabin.

1939   The U.S. submarine Squalus sinks at 239 feet off New England. Thirty-three crewmen are rescued in the McCann submarine rescue chamber, a diving bell constructed to lock with the submarine.

Although the first of 640 salvage dives are made with compressed air, most of the dives are made with helium-oxygen mixes. The technique of helium-oxygen diving proves to be far superior to compressed air breathing for deep diving operations. The Navy establishes 380 feet as the new operational limit for 30 minutes of hard-hat diving on the bottom.

1943   Capt. Jacques Cousteau and Emile Gagnan develop the Aqualung and provides the breakthrough for open-circuit scuba by using a fully automatic compressed-air regulator.

The U.S. Navy's Experimental Diving Unit and School for Deep Sea Divers work out a continuous progression of decompression tables.

Although dives to 561 feet are successful, the decompression penalty reaches a ratio of 2 hours decompression for 1 minute on the bottom.

Brown & Root, a Houston based engineering and construction firm, built the platform from which Kerr-McGee Oil Industries drilled the first producing well beyond the sight of land in the Gulf of Mexico. The well came in on 14 November 1947, a date that marks the birth of the modern offshore oil and gas industry.

Before 1947, companies had extracted oil from underwater fields, but these deposits were located primarily in protected inland waters. Oil had been produced in the Gulf of Mexico before 1947, but always in sight of land. Kerr-McGee's well, in 18 feet of water, ten and a half miles from the Louisiana shore, went a step beyond previous developments.

The Kermac 16 stood in the open waters of the Gulf, exposed to the forces of waves, winds, and hurricanes. The success of this platform in producing oil from beyond the horizon heralded a new era of technological innovation that subsequently spread to offshore provinces throughout the world.

1955	***I win underwater swimming competition at summer camp in the Laurentian Mountains, Quebec. Receives first swim mask with 2 snorkels attached to mask – the seed was sown).***
1957	Taylor Diving & Salvage Company (TDS) is formed in New Orleans, Louisiana by Edward Lee Taylor and Mark Banjavich, two ex-US Navy divers, along with French diver/musician Jean Valz.
1959	Commander George F. Bond, USN, in conducting research in individual submarine escape, establishes a record for buoyant ascent (no breathing apparatus) in the open sea from a submarine bottomed at 322 feet.
	I enlist in the Royal Canadian Navy (RCN). The following was during my active diving career.
1957-1963	U.S. Navy diving scientists George F. Bond, Robert D. Workman, and Walter F. Mazzone begin the experiments called Genesis in the Naval Medical Research Laboratory in New London, Connecticut. Bond tests the saturation theory, which proposes that after 24 hours under pressure at a given depth, the tissues of the diver's body will have a gas saturation equal to the surrounding atmosphere. Once saturated, the diver's decompression can be based on depth rather than duration of the dive. Thus, a diver saturated to 300 feet would need the same decompression time (about two and a half days) whether the stay was one day or one month.
	By the early 1960s oil and gas was being delivered from water depths of 200 feet.
1960	Jacques Piccard, son of the inventor Auguste Piccard, and Lt. Don Walsh, USN, dive in the bathyscaphe Trieste to 35,800 feet in the Marianas Trench, deepest point known in the ocean.
	Hannes Keller, Swiss mathematician, dives to 700 feet in the Navy Experimental Diving Unit chamber breathing a mixture of inert gases. Two years later, Keller descends to 1,000 feet in the open ocean off Catalina Island, California. Although two lives are lost in the dive, Keller accomplishes his goal, proving that humans can dive to incredible depths in the open ocean.
	I qualify as Clearance Diver – Ships CD(S) – RCN.
1961	Taylor divers provide underwater services for laying 20-inch subsea pipeline by Brown & Root in Tierra del Fuego, Argentina. (Taylor becomes first American contractor to undertake international diving job).
	I qualify as Clearance Diver II (CD) Deep Sea Diver – RCN.

1962	Edwin Link's experiment in saturated diving begins with Belgian diver Robert Stenuit breathing helium-oxygen in a small recompression chamber for 25 hours at 200 feet in the Bay of Villefranche. Using a breathing tube, Stenuit exits the capsule for a short time. His decompression is completed successfully.
	Jacques Cousteau launches Conshelf I with Albert Falco and Claude Wesley breathing nitrogen-oxygen for seven days at 35 feet of depth off Marseilles. The divers work a few hours a day at 85 feet, demonstrating that tasks can be accomplished at depth.
1963	The USS Thresher sinks with all hands lost in deep water far beyond the reach of the Navy's salvage capability. The Deep Submergence Systems Review Group is appointed to determine the Navy's capability to rescue sailors from disabled submarines and to locate and retrieve large objects lost in the deep ocean.

I receive emergency recall to base – RCN Diving Unit placed on standby in case it can be of any assistance in Thresher incident.

Jacques Cousteau expands his underwater experiments with Conshelf II and puts seven men in the Red Sea. Five divers live at 32 feet in the main unit, Starfish House, for a month, and two divers live in Deep Cabin at 82 feet for a week, making excursion dives to depths below 330 feet. A prime goal is to test a diver's efficiency when working extended hours from a pressurized habitat. The French oceanauts also demonstrate that a saturated diver can descend to a lower depth for a reasonable period and return without difficulty.

1964	Edwin Link and Dr. Christian Lambertsen send Robert Stenuit and Jon Lindbergh down for two days at 432 feet off the Bahamas.

After the divers complete their assigned tasks, they surface in their submersible decompression chamber, which couples to a large recompression chamber on the deck of the support ship. The divers transfer to the deck unit, where they decompress safely for nearly four days.

The U.S. Navy approves a five year program to achieve deep ocean capability. Capt. George Bond and his co-investigator, Capt. Walter E Mazzone, coordinate Sealab I and send four Navy divers down for eleven days at around 193 feet off Bermuda. The aquanauts breathe a heliox mixture and demonstrate that no short-term physiological damage occurs from the extended dive and short decompression.

I leave KD Marine and join Taylor in September 1964. While working hand in glove with the US Navy, Taylor undertakes a program to develop saturation diving techniques and equipment for use in the offshore oil & gas commercial diving industry.

1965	Prior to June 1965, efficient decompression tables were not available for helium mixtures in scuba diving. Under the supervision of Capt. Robert D. Workman, MC, USN, tables are developed over a period of years and tested in open-sea trials. Prior to the trials, the Navy's Atlantic and Pacific diving fleets make sixty indoctrination dives.

The introduction of new diving tables is completely successful.

Capt. George Bond, principal investigator, and Capt. Walter Mazzone divide twenty-eight divers into three teams that spend fifteen to thirty days at 205 feet in Sealab II off La Jolla, California. Astronaut aquanaut Scott Carpenter serves as team leader for two shifts, and Master Diver Robert C. Sheats leads the third shift. Extensive physiological data are collected from the aquanauts, and complex job assignments are performed on the bottom.

Simultaneously, in Conshelf III, Jacques Cousteau puts six divers for twenty-two days at 328 feet off Monaco in the Mediterranean. The goal is to prove that divers can perform difficult maintenance tasks over a period of time at that depth.

Marine Contractors, Inc and Westinghouse, Inc. use saturation diving for the first time commercially at Smith Mountain Dam in Virginia.

I had the pleasure of working with Dr (Capt) Workman after he retired from the Navy and joined TDS in 1970. I still have a US Navy Diving Manual with his name on it.

1967	That summer, Taylor makes first total saturation dives to install risers for Shell Oil's Marlin System at 320 feet in the Gulf of Mexico.
1970s	Tektite I (1969) is sponsored by the U.S. Navy, Department of the Interior, and National Aeronautics and Space Agency (NASA). Four divers submerge for sixty days in 40 feet of water off St. John, U.S. Virgin Islands. Extensive biological studies produce a wealth of scientific data, and behavioral studies prepare for future journeys into space. After sixty days' submergence, the aquanauts decompress for 19 hours on a support barge.

In Tektite II, eleven successive five-person teams spend fourteen to twenty days at 50 feet off St. John. One all-female team of scientists, led by Dr. Sylvia A. Earle, prepares the way for women in space.

In 1971, a habitat called AEGIR hosted six aquanauts for six days at 520 feet off Hawai'i.

The US Navy employs Taylor saturation personnel and equipment as back-up support. I along with Neil Landry make saturation excursion dives to habitat.

In the early 1970s, Taylor was one of the major diving companies in the world and the pioneer for oil patch saturation diving.

Saturation diving progressed dramatically through the 1960s and 70s. New diving records were set and broken, including the first 600 fsw dive in 1964, the first 1000 fsw dive in 1968 with the U.S. Navy and Duke University, and a 1,600 fsw dive in 1973 at Taylor in Belle Chasse, Louisiana, which was then the world's largest hyperbaric facility.

1969 –1978 *I made many saturation dives, accumulating well over 600 days confined, living and working, under pressure. With at least 100 days involving saturation dives between 1,000 – 1,200 feet (305 - 366m).*

This chronology is based on:

- an outline provided in the book Siiteri, HA (Ed.) (1993) *Papa Topside: The Sealab Chronicles of Capt. George F. Bond, USN.* Naval Institute Press
- the chapter, *Inner Space Pioneer: Taylor* from the book: Pratt, JA, Priest, T, Castaneda, CJ (1997) *Offshore Pioneers: Brown & Root and the History of Offshore Oil and Gas.* Gulf Publishing Company
- and my own experiences.

Appendix 3 - The Challenge of Deep-Sea Diving

A paper presented by me at the American Welding Society Conference
5-6 November 1980
New Orleans Louisiana

The Challenge of Deep Sea Diving
By Mike Cooke
Taylor Diving & Salvage Company Inc.

Down through the centuries, technology has decreased step by step the limitations of diving, but probably more in the past decade than ever before. The original limitations were very basic things, such as how long could one hold one's breath, how deep could one breathe with a snorkel, and how long could one survive on the air contained in a diving bell.

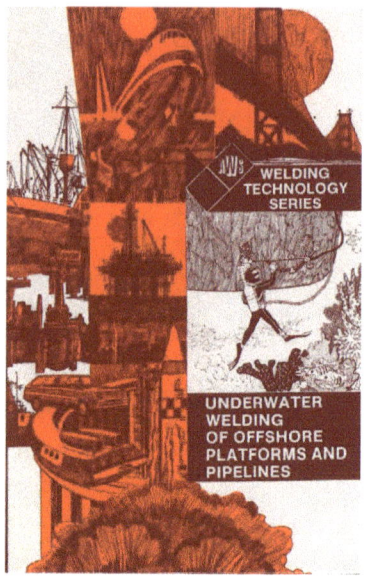

The first real breakthrough occurred around the turn of the 19th century with the invention of the air pump and the closed deep sea diving rig by August Siebe in 1837. Today, however, there are many methods of diving employed in offshore oil fields, depending upon the nature of work, the depth of water, and the required bottom time. This paper will deal basically with the rather recent and rapid progression of deep diving over the past decade and a half and its relationship to the advancement of hyperbaric welding.

General

Anyone who has participated in the performance of a deep water hyperbaric weld will certainly agree that the successful welded connection, repair, and attachment of two (2) pieces of steel in a dry environment is still one of the most ambitious and challenging projects with which the diving industry is confronted with today.

It is not the intention of this paper to elaborate on the history of diving and its progression from shallow air diving through surface mixed gas and eventually to that mode known as saturation. However, the majority of hyperbaric welding being performed is by saturated diver/welders, and, for the benefit of those who are not familiar with the expression "saturation diving" a brief explanation is in order.

In conventional diving (that is, surface-to-surface without the use of a bell), the diver is decompressed during the ascent. This is accomplished by following a precalculated schedule that consists of a prescribed rate of ascent plus a number of stages or stops. This provides for the elimination of gases that have been forced into solution in the various body tissues by escaping without forming bubbles in the blood stream and thus causing decompression sickness or bends.

The time of the dive is limited by what is considered a reasonable amount of decompression. In deep water, the dive must be relatively brief in order to avoid an unbearable decompression schedule. Employing the saturation diving technique, the divers are sealed in a deck-board chamber and pressurized close to the depth pressure at which they intend to work. A diving bell at the same pressure may be attached to or detached from the deck chamber so the divers can be lowered away under pressure to the job site and, upon completion of their mission, be returned to the deck board chamber still under pressure. After 12 hours at a given pressure the body is said to be saturated; that is, it has absorbed or taken into solution the maximum amount of gas it is capable of containing at that pressure level. The main object of saturation diving is to eliminate decompression after each and every dive; thus, the length of time the diver may spend working at depth is limited only by his physical endurance.

Finally, when the project is completed after a matter of days or weeks, the divers are then decompressed in the deck board chamber by very slowly lowering the pressure while observing certain stops at predetermined levels as part of the schedule. This method necessarily requires that an artificial atmosphere be maintained in the bell and chamber and that a somewhat complicated environmental control system be employed. Temperature and humidity levels must be maintained. Carbon dioxide and other harmful gases must be removed, while oxygen has to be maintained at a constant level.

While all helium and oxygen (HeO_2) total saturation equipment is built around the same basic theory, it varies in physical configuration from one company to another. Even the nomenclature varies. For instance, the diving bell itself, which we call a submersible diving chamber (abbreviated SDC), is referred to by many other companies as a personnel transfer capsule (abbreviated PTC). One of the main differences is in the variety of ways the SDC is attached to the on board decompression chamber (DDC). There are various davit-like arrangements for handling the SDC on the surface and mating it to the DDC. Some SDCs referred to as the side-entry type have a transfer door in the side that flanges to a transfer tunnel in the end of the DDC. Most of our saturation equipment is designed in this manner. While others mate to a transfer hatch on top of a DDC and the personnel transfer is made through the hatch in the bottom of the SDC. A structural steel base frame, which extends over the side of the support platform, is fitted with an A-frame on the outboard end. The SDC is lowered and raised from the A-frame. When on the surface in position for transfer, the SDC is held firmly in the guides of the A-frame and locked in a fixed position. The DDC is mounted on skid runners that match channels of the base frame. By means of a hydraulic cylinder, the DDC is slid outboard until the flange of the transfer tunnel matches with the side-entry flange of the SDC. While many of the SDCs are cylindrical in shape with either hemispherical or elliptical heads, others are spherical and built as dual pressure vessels.

Total saturation HeO_2 diving is the ultimate technique in the industry. However, it is seldom used at depths shallower than 150 feet, except in the case of hyperbaric welding. The reason for this is that most people consider saturation diving not economically feasible in shallow water or in deep water where only an occasional dive has to be made. A surface-to-surface compressed air diving system has a value of from approximately $20,000.00 to $35,000.00; surface-to-surface HeO_2 diving systems range from approximately $50,000.00 to $100,000.00; while a complete saturation diving system with all the ancillary equipment would run in the neighborhood of $1,000,000.00. As the depth of water increases, a saturation system becomes more and more economically feasible.

Following is a typical example of the economics of saturation diving at a depth of 300 feet. The 300 ft depth is being used as an example for several reasons, among which are: (1) the majority of hyperbaric welds undertaken by Taylor Diving have been completed in the 200 to 400 ft range with less than 10 percent of all welds completed at depths greater than 400 ft; and (2) Federal regulations dictate that the cutoff depth for surface supplied diving is 300 feet.

The daily cost for surface-to-surface diving using 8 divers rather than 6 saturation divers includes surface-to-surface equipment at 27 percent of the cost of saturation equipment; labor, 75 percent; depth bonus to the divers, 171 percent; total daily cost being 87 percent of the saturation cost. But here is the difference in actual cost per hour of productive work: Six saturated divers can produce 22 hours bottom time per day; eight surface-to-surface divers, 8 hours bottom time per day. The cost per hour of surface-to-surface bottom time is, therefore, 240 percent higher than that for saturation diving. A surface-to-surface diver is between 65 and 70 percent as effective as the saturated diver. One of the reasons for this lack of efficiency in deep water is the encumbrance of the long umbilical and the effects of current against it. When divers are changed every hour or less, much time is lost while the succeeding diver becomes oriented. Sometimes 15 minutes or longer is required to get oriented to where the other diver left off. Taking this into consideration, the surface-to-surface diver is now costing 350 percent more per hour of productive bottom time.

As a final example, if 100 productive hours of work were to be performed in a depth of 300 feet, it would require over 15 days of surface diving, whereas the saturation divers could perform the same task in approximately 5 days. Considering that the diving support platform is usually a construction barge costing over $1,000.00 per hour, to say nothing of support vessels (such as tugboats, crew boats, and supply vessels), and the cost of support from shore, there are tremendous savings to be realized by using the saturated technique. In the deeper depths now being encountered, saturation is the only feasible method.

Along with the virtues of SAT diving, one disadvantage may be found in the cost of mobilizing the equipment, which is greater than for the simpler methods. For instance, it is *double* the cost of mobilizing a surface-to-surface system. Among the topside support personnel, more technically oriented people are required. After a crew has been in saturation for 30 days, they are generally decompressed and a new crew saturated, if the work is to continue. Whether or not the work continues, it requires approximately 24 hours of decompression for each 100 feet of depth pressure. During this time, the equipment remains on rent and the personnel can be reduced. Most of the Taylor systems are built in such a way that one crew can be undergoing decompression while another crew is in saturation continuing on with the work, thereby eliminating job shutdown due to decompression. In many instances, this type of shutdown is a major complaint on the part of the contractor when mixed gas surface diving is being advocated.

Hyperbaric Welding

Before getting into a comparison of deep diving and hyperbaric welding, a brief review is required to acquaint anyone not familiar with how the diving industry and, in particular, Taylor Diving and Salvage Company, Inc. proceeded to get involved in the art of subsea welded connections.

In the early 1960's the founder and president of Taylor Diving saw the future need for industry to have the capabilities of making code-quality welded pipeline connections or structural repairs beneath the sea's surface.

A research and development project was initiated to develop the equipment and procedures required to reach this goal. It soon became apparent that future requirements for the application of hyperbaric welded connections or repairs would most likely be dictated by (1) the type of weld required, (2) the reliability of mechanical connections, (3) environmental conditions, and (4) increased water depth. The types of welds required can be varied and considerable, ranging anywhere from a rather straight forward riser tie-in to that of a complicated structural repair.

The argument over the reliability of mechanical connectors (and Taylor's philosophy) is one of assurance rather than one of justification. In other words, it is possible to justify various other forms of connectors as a substitute for the hyperbaric weld, with emphasis being plainly put on the word *substitute*. Complete assurance, however, can only be provided by a welded joint that has been proven 100 percent reliable.

Although there are several applications for hyperbaric welding (pipeline repairs, riser tie-ins, expansion loops, structural repairs) involving various items of specialized equipment and complexity, this paper will dwell on the pipeline connection simply because more pipeline welds have been completed and at deeper depths than any other type of welded repair. The pipe is welded in place on the seabed with the pipe ends inside a dry environment so that the joint properties will be comparable to those obtained from a conventional surface weld.

This involves the use of an open-bottom enclosure or underwater welding habitat, which is placed over the pipes to be joined. This method of joining pipe together is called "habitat welding," which has come to mean "fusion welding at hyperbaric pressure by diver/welders wholly within an underwater dry environment."

The first habitat welds made by Taylor Diving and Salvage were pipeline repairs in the St. Lawrence River and in the Gulf of Mexico in 1968, made at a water depth of 60 feet.

From this first year's operation, the present hyperbaric welding process was developed and has been used since to weld all the major grades of pipeline steel and many proprietary grades.

This process basically consists of:
1. The procedure qualification
2. The diver/welder qualification
3. The offshore phase

The weld procedure qualification has to be carried out at the same depth or slightly deeper than the depth of the pipeline repair. This is necessary to ensure that the effects on the weld of the ambient gases and gas partial pressures are fully reflected in the finished product. The environmental conditions required to sustain life at a depth of 500 ft would be 3.0 percent oxygen, the remainder being helium, for example. This represents an oxygen partial pressure of 0.5, which compares with 0.2 at the surface in the atmosphere. This increase of partial pressure results in an increase of oxygen absorption in the weld.

At 500 ft, this increase is approximately 100 percent by weight in oxygen content in the weld when compared to the equivalent surface weld.

The helium, while it is an inert gas, has a thermal conductivity six times greater than air. Therefore, to prevent very rapid cooling of the weld and the heat-affected zone, which could lead to thermal stress problems such as cracking and excessive hardness areas, the pipe temperature is maintained throughout the welding process by the use of heating blankets. The entire weld procedure qualification and weld testing are observed and approved by the customer and a representative from a certifying authority, such as Lloyds Register or Det Norske Veritas.

The properties obtained from a hyperbaric weld will meet or exceed the specification requirement expected from an equivalent surface atmospheric weld.

Before a diver/welder is permitted to weld a pipe repair, he has to qualify to that particular pipe weld procedure at the appropriate depth. This qualification is carried out either in the depth chamber or in the habitat at the job site. The qualification and the destructive testing that follows is witnessed and approved by the customer and the certifying authority. This qualification is approved for a set period and is renewed by further experience or a retest.

The diver/welders are also given instruction in the use of radiographic equipment, which eventually leads to the Assistant Radiographic Technician Level 2 qualification.

Training is also available in the use of ultrasonic equipment. Such training is set up to a particular project requirement at the time it is needed.

Offshore Phase

After the procedures are qualified, the submarine pipe alignment rig, the habitat, and other equipment are mobilized for the job, based upon the joining requirement. An adequate work platform facilitates habitat welding. It must have hotel facilities for the personnel involved and a positioning system that will enable it to maintain location in poor weather. It must have a crane or davits, or both, to handle the submarine pipe aligning rig and underwater welding habitat.

When the work platform has been located over the job site, divers go down, survey the pipe, and rough-cut it with an oxyarc torch. The cut is made by first removing the concrete weight coating from the top of the pipe, cutting a hole in the pipe, and then cutting the remainder. The cut sections of pipe are then removed and recovered. Depending on the circumstances, this may involve many hundreds of feet of pipe.

The concrete weight coating, which frequently contains reinforcing rods, is kerfed circumferentially and longitudinally with a diamond-tipped saw blade over the area where the habitat will rest. The saw is driven by an underwater hydraulic pump, which is electrically powered via umbilical from the surface. After the cuts are made, sections of the weight coating are pried off and removed by the diver. Approximately eight feet of each pipe end is bared. Davits are used to place the pipe ends in line with each other.

Next, guide ropes are attached to the pipes a measured distance from the ends to ensure the habitat will land over the joint(s) to be made.

After all systems have been checked out, the submarine pipe alignment rig and underwater welding habitat are lowered to the bottom with the vessel's davits. The guide ropes, having been attached to the pipe ends a distance wider than the guide eyes on the SPAR, restrict movement of the latter, yet allow small longitudinal position corrections to be made immediately before the submarine pipe aligning rig and the underwater welding habitat are placed on the bottom.

The pipe ends are grasped and raised off the bottom with clamps of the submarine pipe aligning rig by divers operating local controls. The pipes are then coarsely aligned horizontally, each end opposite the other. The clamps are moved by hydraulic cylinders in either the vertical or horizontal direction and are powered by underwater hydraulic pumps

The habitat is now lowered down over the pipe ends and seals are established. Plugs are inserted in the pipes and inflated. The bubble of gas in the top of the habitat is increased to below the habitat floor, displacing the sea water that was within. The environmental control system is energized and all systems are checked. Video cameras are activated to monitor the activities in the habitat.

The pipe ends are accurately aligned with the submarine pipe aligning rig clamps through the use of remote controls located within the habitat. The pipe ends are cleaned of the mastic corrosion barrier thereon, then beveled for welding with a hydraulically powered orbital milling machine. Within the habitat, a short piece of pipe called a "pup" has been stowed. This pup has been very carefully selected for circularity, examined ultrasonically, and prebeveled for welding. The dimensions between the cuts of the milling machine on the pipes are made to match the length of the pup, plus allowance for weld shrinkage. The pup is then placed between the pipe ends and held there by line-up clamps, which are used to reform the pipe ends to concentrically match those of the pup. After alignment is obtained, preheating equipment may be installed, depending upon the weld procedure. If used, the root and initial filler passes are deposited while maintaining the preheat and are made without removing the line-up clamps. The remaining fill passes and cap passes are usually applied without the line-up clamps in place. Postheating, when required, is regulated automatically without the presence of divers in the habitat.

The habitat environmental control system is used to maintain safe and comfortable conditions for the diver. The breathable gas environment facilitates fit-up of the pup since the divers need not wear masks. From the onset of welding through to completion, the wearing of masks is required.

After the welding is completed, each joint is radiographed. Three or four overlapping exposures are made circumferentially around the joint using a small, remotely operated exposure device. The exposures are made after the diver/assistant radiographers temporarily leave the habitat and are completed before they return. The exposed film is transported to the surface for developing and interpretation.

After gamma radiography, the pipe is wrapped many times with plastic tape or cloth that has been soaked in catalyzed epoxy. The weight coating is seldom replaced, but if protection is desired, the catalyzed epoxy can be applied in water.

The habitat equipment is stowed away and the end seals cut, flooding the habitat to about half its height. The pipeline is then lowered to the sea bottom and all of the clamps are released. The submarine pipe alignment rig and underwater welding habitat are raised to the surface, placed upon the work platform, and readied for the next job

The greatest economic value of habitat welding occurs with new pipeline construction, because the integrity of a welded joint eliminates potentially high maintenance costs associated with mechanical joints. For the same reasons, habitat welding is advantageous for pipeline repairs and likely the only "universal" joining method able to be used on a large variety of pipe sizes and repair situations. For such repair contingencies, a prequalified weld procedure would significantly reduce the time a flowing pipeline would be out of service or a structural platform would be restricted. As for welder qualification, jurisdictional authorities have permitted qualification of experienced diver/welders on site to facilitate such matters.

To date, Taylor Diving and Salvage has completed approximately 200 hyperbaric welded tie-ins. In service, not one weld has ever leaked or required any subsequent maintenance. Approximately 20 percent of the welded tie-ins have been pipeline repairs. Anchor damage has accounted for 40 percent of repairs; replacement of leaking couplings and mechanical connectors by welded tie-ins for 35 percent; defective material, 15 percent; and pipeline buckles and unknown causes, 10 percent.

The maximum size of pipeline presently being welded is 48 in. in diameter. Fifty-four inch diameter pipe is within the present equipment capability, subject to minor modification. This modification is the increasing in size of certain components that have been purposely kept small to reduce helium gas consumption. The maximum depth proved in open sea tests is 1036 feet. The ultimate depth that hyperbaric welding can be used is limited by the diver's physiological limits. Although a diver's work output at extreme depths is somewhat reduced, this is not considered to be a limiting factor.

Welding at these extreme depths, therefore, will probably be done under atmospheric conditions by working inside a pressure vessel attached to the pipeline.

Most of the atmospheric welding systems so far designed and developed require the permanent installation of a pressure vessel on the pipe. While this is satisfactory for new construction where the location of the weld is previously known, this system is not suitable for the random location of welds such as required for pipeline repairs. The atmospheric welding system being fabricated and developed by Taylor Diving and Salvage has been designed for new construction, and specifically, pipeline repairs. This is achieved by using a split pressure vessel that closes over the weld area.

The vessel is evacuated to atmospheric pressure for the welding process, and then after the weld completion and nondestructive testing, the pressure vessel is flooded to depth pressure, opened, and lifted clear of the pipe.

The system is being designed initially for 1,000 feet with the use of divers for carrying out preparation work such as concrete cutting and equipment setting and will ultimately be capable of diverless operations to 2,000 feet with the use of a special submersible and remote-control equipment.

Conclusion

The challenge to perform coded welds at depths greater than those presently established is one being confronted every day. Continuing research is being undertaken to overcome the various obstacles. The comment could easily be made that man has successfully spent considerable time and performed limited tasks at pressures exceeding that of the deepest laid pipeline. As encouraging as this may sound, it does not present a true perspective of the actual situation. In order to do that, it is necessary to provide certain factual information, which has been acquired through past experience. For example, there have been very few actual offshore working dives at depths greater than 1000 feet. I can cite two with which I am familiar: 1) the setting of Shell Cognac Platform and 2) the hyperbaric weld already referred to. Although both dives were undertaken in relatively the same time frame and by the same company, each required a considerable amount of predive preparation. In the case of the hyperbaric weld, it was four years from concept to actual completion. Therefore, from this example it becomes quite obvious that deep diving is not done on the spur of the moment or on a call-out basis. Then again one might ask the definition of deep diving, and how deep is deep. A hundred years ago, sixty feet was deep. Fifty years ago, one hundred fifty feet was deep. Twenty-five years ago, three hundred feet was deep. As recent as five years ago, who, but a very few, would expect a diver making his first saturation dive offshore to be working at a depth of one thousand feet? Also, who would have thought it routine for divers to spend anywhere from 100 to 200 days a year confined under pressure? Today, this is not the unusual, but the norm. What about tomorrow? Will deep be 3000, 4000, 5000 feet? For today, 2000 feet is deep, and this is where the immediate challenge lies. This challenge is not only being met by such companies as Taylor, but also conquered.

Appendix 4 - A Very Short History of Saturation Diving
by James Vorosmarti, Jr., MD

In 1962 it was my great fortune to apply for and be accepted into the Navy submarine and diving training programme. Unbeknown to me at the time this was the beginning of the recent 'Golden Age' of diving with the advent of saturation diving and extensive activity around the world of diving medical research and advances in diving equipment. This brought me into the United States Navy SEALAB programme. I never realised it until I was preparing my lecture on the history of saturation diving for the HDS Conference last year, that this allowed me to meet and work with the world famous (and infamous) personages of saturation diving and enabled me to count some of the 'greats' of diving research from the 1930s and 1940s as colleagues and friends. The purpose of this article is to publish a short history of saturation diving over the period from the late1950s to the early 1970s.

Saturation diving is defined as the situation where one is at a depth or pressure for a long enough period of time (12 hours or longer) to have the partial pressures of the dissolved gases in the body at equilibrium with the partial pressure of those in the ambient atmosphere.

This concept was not a new one. Haldane, Boycott and Damant in their 1907 report were well aware of the fact that saturation would occur. At pressures up to 45 psi, or four atmospheres of absolute pressure, there appears to be no substantial objection to keeping men for six hours, or even more, continuously under pressure, provided that the mode of decompression is safe.

However, there is no clue in these writings that they ever considered the practice of saturation diving. I think that the most obvious reason is that there was simply no foreseeable need for this technique at the time. Most diving was done at less than 50ft and certainly diving deeper than 100ft was rare. Most jobs did not require long bottom times so decompression was not excessively long. Even in tunnel work, decompression time was not overly long except when working at the highest pressures. Another reason was that Haldane, et al were concentrating on surface supplied diving for the navy. No equipment for this type of saturation diving existed then, although construction of an underwater habitat would have posed little problem with the engineering knowledge of the time. Atmosphere control however, would have posed an almost impossible problem because of the inability to easily and accurately monitor gas composition. Temperature control also would have proved to be a problem. Another clue to their awareness of saturation diving was shown in an exchange between Damant and Haldane in 1935 in a discussion of caisson decompression. Damant commented on Haldane's idea of extending shifts to eight hours. He stated that "a complete table from hour to infinity is the thing (required) - as you have drafted it". Again there was no real need to extend the tables for long bottom times, but the idea was certainly there.

Another close miss with saturation diving is illustrated by the underwater diving station proposed by Davis. Unfortunately, there is no date attached to this idea but it was probably devised in the 1920s or 1930s. It is obvious that Davis was thinking ahead to having divers live, at least for short periods of time, probably days, under the sea. The problem here is that the habitat is maintained at one atmosphere so that the diver still would have required decompression. Why was this not adapted for staying or living at ambient pressure? Again, probably because there was no real need.

FIRST SATURATION DIVE

The first intentional saturation dive (although not called that at the time) was done in December 1938 (1). It was planned by Dr Edgar End with Max Nohl as the diver. The dive was done because of problems with animals not humans. At the time tunnelling operations were underway in Milwaukee and mules and donkeys were used for hauling material. They were kept under pressure for weeks and months at a time. However, whenever decompression of them took place they died. The details of the decompression schedules used are unfortunately not available.

Therefore this dive was planned to demonstrate that animals (and humans) could be decompressed after extended periods of time at pressure. Nohl entered the chamber at 1100 on or around December 19th (the record is not clear on the exact date) and spent 27 hours at a depth of 100ft breathing air. End spent about 11 hours in the chamber doing physiological testing, the results of which are not available as no report was ever published. Decompression took about five hours and resulted in Nohl suffering decompression sickness on reaching the surface. He recovered fully after recompression treatment except for feeling bad for several days afterwards. We now know that this was probably due to a combination of the decompression sickness and pulmonary oxygen toxicity from the long period of breathing a high partial pressure of oxygen. Two conclusions reached by End, at least as reported by Look Magazine, were that 27 hours was the limit for staying under pressure without risking life, and that helium substituted for nitrogen in the breathing mix may reduce diving hazards.

A few years later, in 1942, Dr Al Behnke stated the first clear concept of saturation diving with excursions. In an article published that year in the Medical Clinics of North America (2) discussing working at 50 psi he wrote, "It would appear advisable therefore to keep men at work on a job continually under pressure. Following a work shift at maximum pressure, the pressure could be lowered rapidly to between 20 and 30 pounds and maintained at this level during the rest and sleep period. The final decompression prior to emergence into a normal atmosphere would be uniform over a period of 8 to 24 hours". He also made a statement in this article that prolonged exposure for up to seven days at pressures of 30 psi gauge had been made repeatedly. Presumably he was referring to tunnel or caisson work. Unfortunately he gives no reference for this statement. At the time there had been a fair number of experimental exposures to 90fsw for 9 to 12 hours. However, using the current definition of saturation these are not considered saturation dives.

He was certainly familiar with the exposure of the survivors of the USS Squalus sinking as he was the on-scene medical officer. These sailors were at a pressure of 27fsw for over 24 hours. They were brought directly to the surface without any cases of decompression sickness.

The term 'saturation dive' was used for the first time in 1945 by Dr Otto van der Aue. He was working at the USN Experimental Diving Unit conducting a large series of experimental dives in order to produce acceptable surface decompression schedules. These dives were done to test the still used 2:1 ratio for safe decompression. The decompression schedules were the first in which a tissue half-time of 120 minutes was used in their calculation. Tissue half-time refers to the mathematical concept of dividing the body into a series of hypothetical components called tissue compartments. Tissue half-time refers to the hypothetical time required for a tissue to gain or lose one half of the inert gas dissolved in it, or which could be dissolved into it. It is a concept used for the mathematical construction of decompression schedules not for correlation with any specific anatomic tissue and does not correlate to any body tissue. As part of this series four dives were done which were called, and actually were, saturation dives. All were done in October 1945 with air. The first was to 33ft for 24 hours with direct surfacing. No cases of DCS resulted in the four divers. The next two dives were to 33ft for 36 hours with 4 divers in each exposure. Two of the divers developed bends. The last dive was to 99ft for 12 hours followed by decompression to 33ft for a stay of 24 hours. Both the divers using this schedule suffered DCS. The conclusion was that for decompression from longer dives long half-time tissues needed to be assigned lower ratios than short half-time tissues. In other words, the 2:1 ratio for decompression did not work (as Haldane had already discovered).

No more was heard about saturation diving until 1954 when, for reasons that are obscure, a diver named Ed Fisher stayed underwater at 33ft for 24 hours beginning on August 21st. This event took place in Florida, and he did this without the benefit of anything but his wetsuit, an inflated inner tube anchored to coral and the support of friends who brought him replacement air tanks and food from a support boat nearby. He reportedly also speared a fish and ate it raw for dinner. He decompressed at 10ft for 15 minutes, although he did not think this was necessary, and reached the surface with no problems. In an interview, he said that the only problem he had was the pain when he had to remove his wetsuit. Surprisingly he did not peel off any skin with his wetsuit!

GENESIS
There was no activity in saturation diving until 1957 when Dr George Bond, Dr Walter Mazzone, and Dr Robert Workman began to explore new approaches to inner space exploitation at the Naval Submarine Research Laboratory in New London, Connecticut. They began with a series of animal experiments to ascertain what, if any, were the results of exposures in various animals to normal air and synthetic atmospheres at a pressure of 200fsw. These experiments were called Genesis.

The original material documenting these experiments are not available and most of them were not published in a scientific format. I have relied on the description by Dr J Miller and Ian Koblick as published in their book, Living and Working in the Sea, for the following naming and chronological order of these studies (3). The first study, Genesis A1, exposed rats at 198fsw on air. All died in 35 hours from oxygen toxicity, which although expected, was not a very auspicious beginning. This experiment was a follow-on of some animal saturation experiments done in 1932 by FJC Smith, JW Heim, G Bennett, RM Thompson, and CK Drinker at Harvard who were interested in oxygen toxicity (4).

In those experiments rats were exposed to air at 5atm for up to 72 days. Those rats could be called the first mammalian saturation divers. Bond, et al were familiar with this work which was published in the Journal of Experimental Medicine.

In Genesis A2, rats were exposed to a normoxic nitrogen-oxygen mixture at 198fsw for 14 days. All but one survived, but all showed lesions in the lungs. The cause of these lesions was unknown. Genesis A3 rats were exposed to pure oxygen at 45fsw which provided the same oxygen partial pressure as in the A1 exposure (1.5 atm). As expected, all rats died due to oxygen toxicity, again in 35 hours. The next step was to show that rats could survive in a synthetic atmosphere of heliox with 20% oxygen. This exposure, Genesis B1, took place at 1atm and no adverse effects were found after 16 days. Rats were again exposed in Genesis B2 at 200fsw for 14 days. No adverse effects were seen even on life span or breeding. From 1959 - 1961 four more species, including goats and monkeys were exposed to normoxic gas mixtures at 200fsw with the production of no physiological problems.

Genesis C began in 1962 after the Secretary of the Navy finally gave permission to expose humans to a synthetic atmosphere at pressure. Two Medical Officers, John Bull and Albert Fisher, and Chief Quartermaster Bob Barth spent 6 days in a helium-oxygen atmosphere at one atmosphere absolute. This was done at the Naval Medical Research Institute in Bethesda, MD. The problem of thermal control and comfort in a helium atmosphere was discovered on this exposure. The Medical Officer was Charles Aquadro, who later left the US Navy and worked for years with Cousteau in his endeavours in undersea living. Finally, in April 1963, in the Navy Experimental Diving Unit in Washington, DC, three humans were exposed to prolonged pressure in a helium environment (Genesis D). Barth and Bull were joined by Raymond Lavois, another Navy diver, in a dive to 100fsw for 6 days in an atmosphere of 7% nitrogen, 7% oxygen, balance helium. This was the first helium oxygen exposure to take place which lasted for more than a few hours at pressure. No studies showed any deviations from normal, but the thermal problem was again noted and the problem of communication when breathing helium was exacerbated by the increased pressure.

The final Genesis phase, Genesis E, took place in August and September 1964. Bull, Barth, and Chief Hospital Corpsman Sanders Manning were pressurised to 198 fsw for twelve days in a chamber at the Submarine Medical Research Laboratory in New London. During this dive, in addition to the thermal and communication problem, the divers were made more uncomfortable by the high humidity. Once again, the physiological studies showed no adverse effects as a result of this exposure.

At this juncture, so as not to raise any old stories about individuals stealing from others, I would point out that from 1957 onwards Bond, Mazzone, and Workman had full discussions with Cousteau about the Genesis team's ideas and experimental results, and that Cousteau has always given credit to Bond for the idea of saturation diving. Later, Ed Link was also a party to these discussions and results.

MAN-IN-THE-SEA I
Link was the first actually to organise an 'at sea' saturation dive.

As part of his Man-In-The-Sea programme he devised a chamber which could be used as very cramped living quarters at depth, and could be sealed for retrieval to a ship with subsequent decompression of the diver on board. Robert Stenuit was the diver and he began the dive on September 6, 1962 at 200ft off Villefranche on the French Riviera. Link himself had made several trial dives to check out the equipment but none was longer than 8 hours and the deepest depth was 60fsw. The dive duration was planned to have been 48 hours. Unfortunately, a combination of helium leaks, the sinking of the boat with additional helium supplies and bad weather, caused the experiment to be terminated after only 24 hours. Stenuit required treatment for decompression sickness of his right wrist.

Sometime in the 1920s or 1930s Davis developed the Transfer-Under-Pressure (TUP) system. This allowed the diver to be transported to and from a shipboard chamber to a work site under water and allowed him to be brought to the surface either while beginning decompression or decompressing after the transfer to the shipboard chamber. Anyone familiar with modern saturation systems will recognise that the principles are those used in current saturation diving. Link's Man-In-The-Sea system is certainly very similar in appearance and utilisation to the Davis TUP system. This again points up the fact that saturation diving would have been possible well before it was finally developed into the technique as we know it today.

CONSHELF
Cousteau, on September 14, 1962, began the first of his series of experiments in saturation diving and living in the sea. Conshelf I took place about 100 miles from Link's experiment. The habitat in which Albert Falco and Claude Wesley lived for seven days, was a large cylinder (called Diogenes) anchored in 10 metres of water.

The atmosphere was air in both the habitat and the breathing apparatus. They made frequent dives and made at least one excursion to 180 metres.

Conshelf II followed shortly thereafter in June 1963. This was a much more ambitious operation with two habitats, Starfish House and Deep Cabin. The site was in the Red Sea near Port Sudan. Starfish House was located at a depth of about 11 meters and was again supplied with an atmosphere of air. It was large, and had spacious living and diving quarters. Deep Cabin was a large upright cylinder with three levels, the upper two of which were living quarters and the one below a diving centre. Five divers spent 4 weeks in Starfish House.

Two divers lived in Deep Cabin for 1 week at a depth of about 27 metres. They breathed a mixture of 50% helium and 50% air. During their stay they made several excursions to 110 metres. Deep Cabin had several problems including leaks, breaking cables and, the most serious, a tendency to slide off the ledge on which it was moored. It was finally securely anchored, but not before falling once with the divers in it. These divers can be considered as the first to have truly lived in the undersea environment, as they did all their own cooking and were a part of the underwater world.

MAN-IN-THE-SEA II

Man-In-The-Sea II was planned by Link to extend the depth at which humans could live underwater. This was an experiment at 400fsw, and was based on the results of several US Navy exposures to 400fsw for 24 hours conducted in late 1963.

For this trial Link built a collapsible habitat that could be easily lowered over the side of a ship. The SPID, for Submersible Portable Inflatable Dwelling, was an 8x4ft inflatable bag on a steel frame anchored to a ballast tray. In June 1964 it was lowered to the bottom at 415 feet in the Bahamas. Robert Stenuit and Jon Lindbergh were lowered to the SPID in a Submersible Decompression Chamber (SDC) (shades of the Davis TUP). They spent 49 hours in the helium-oxygen atmosphere before decompression. They also had a range of equipment problems to overcome, but the major difficulty was hypothermia caused by the helium-oxygen atmosphere.

SEALAB I

The first US Navy habitat operation, SEALAB I, began shortly afterwards, in July 1964. This was a scheduled three week stay for four divers, Barth, Manning, Anderson and Thompson, at a depth of 193 feet. The habitat reflected the level of funding for the project, as it was constructed of two salvaged harbour security net floats and ballasted with railroad car axles. It was located about 26 miles off Bermuda near Argus Island, a man-made tower from which the operation was supported. In contrast to the earlier experiments this was planned as a full scale investigation of human physiology underwater. Unfortunately, it had to be terminated after 11 days because of an approaching tropical storm. Decompression was to have been done by raising the habitat with the divers in it.

At a depth of 81 feet they had to leave the habitat because the increasing sea state made it impossible to continue to handle the habitat safely. They swam out to the SDC which was raised to the deck of the tower and completed the remaining 56 hours of decompression in the extremely tight and uncomfortable quarters provided by that equipment. One can only imagine the state of hygiene of the divers and the SDC when the hatch was finally opened!

SEALAB II

This was a much more ambitious programme than any up to this point, involving even more physiological testing and a busy underwater programme testing new methods of salvage, new tools, an electrically heated drysuit, porpoise training and work, and behavioural studies.

A completely new habitat was built with all modern conveniences and an adequate support ship was provided. Beginning on August 28, 1965, three teams of divers spent 10 -16 days each at a depth of 205 feet in the La Jolla canyon off Scripps Institute of Oceanography in California. One of the aquanauts, Scott Carpenter, ex-astronaut, stayed on the bottom through two team shifts. Three unusual events occurred during his stay. A conversation was held between Carpenter and astronaut Gordon Cooper who was circling the globe at the time in the Gemini space capsule. Later aquanauts Griggs and Sheats spoke to oceanauts Cousteau and Lebon in Conshelf II. As part of the public relations effort, it had been arranged that Scott would speak to President Johnson. Dr Bond was speaking to a White House operator setting up the call and explained to her that Scott was in a chamber filled with helium gas, and therefore, his voice would sound very funny.

The operator said that the President did not speak to persons in gas chambers and immediately hung up! Needless to say the connection was finally made, but it was obvious that the President had no idea what Scott was saying in helium speech. However, the PR people were happy!

CONSHELF III

This experiment followed many animal dives and a manned chamber dive by Dr Chouteau and Dr Aquadro to 400 feet, plus a trial dive in Monaco harbour. It began in September 1965 when the habitat reached the bottom off Cap Ferrat at a depth of 328 feet. A six-man team spent 22 days on the bottom although it was planned to be only a 14 day experiment. I suppose that after the previous near disasters things were going so well that a good thing should not be wasted. The habitat was a large two-storey sphere which rested on a barge containing the ballast systems for raising and lowering the whole, along with two three-man hyperbaric lifeboats. These could be entered at pressure and released to the surface in case of emergency. The upper floor was for dining, communications and data gathering. The lower level contained the sleeping, sanitation and diving areas. As with other habitats and saturation experiments there were many equipment problems all of which were overcome by the aquanauts themselves. This experiment was unique in that an oil well Christmas tree was lowered near the habitat so that the divers could test actual practical techniques.

GLAUCUS

In order to relieve readers of any anxiety that the US and France were the only two countries in which active saturation dives were being done, at the same time the above two experiments were taking place, the Bournemouth branch of the British Sub-Aqua Club upheld British honour by conducting a saturation dive in Plymouth Sound at a depth of 38 feet of water. Two divers, Colin Irwin and John Heath, spent one week in Glaucus beginning 16 September 1965. The habitat was a small cylinder mounted on a ballast pan. In fact, it appears to have been a smaller and less luxurious version of the SEALAB I habitat. Food and supplies were provided by team of topside support divers who also had to operate in less than adequate conditions. All survived in spite of a short but severe storm which threatened the experiment on the second day. What was proven was that motivated divers could survive in a habitat that was very cheaply put together, but that it was not a pleasant experience, nor could any real science be undertaken in that type of situation.

CACHALOT

This was the first commercial saturation diving system and was designed by Westinghouse Electric Corporation, Underseas Division (Tom O'Neill and Alan Krassburg) for use in clearing the trash rack of the Smith Mountain Dam in Virginia. The system consisted of a large chamber Deck Decompression Chamber or DDC and a Personnel Transfer Capsule (PTC) which could be mated to the DDC at pressure. The divers lived in the DDC and went back and forth to work in the PTC. The operation was between depths of 159 and 240 feet and lasted for four months beginning in August 1965. To do the job using contemporary conventional techniques would have entailed draining the whole reservoir, a two year job. To do the job using two divers at a time from saturation replaced 32 divers using normal surface diving techniques. This system was the forerunner of the great explosion of commercial diving systems which soon spread across the world. In fact, the first at sea commercial saturation dive was done in 1966 in the Gulf of Mexico using this same system.

SEALAB III

This was the most ambitious of the habitat programmes, with work-up dives and biomedical studies, beginning in 1966. These dives were done at the US Navy Experimental Diving Unit in the Washington DC Navy Yard and ranged in depth from 250 to 1025 feet. Most dives included studies of the divers' medical status. For example, there were respiratory studies using high density gases at pressure to simulate heliox at much higher pressures, exercise studies, behavioural studies and work on overcoming the problem of helium speech. Even the studiers were studied. The habitat used in this experiment was that of SEALAB II, which was refurbished. The support craft was the USS Elk River which carried the new double Mk2 saturation diving system and which had been reconfigured to include a moon pool. This was an opening through the centre of the ship allowing the PTC to enter the water in a protected area and thus cut down on the problems of handling a large pendulum in rough seas. Two vans on the deck were completely outfitted as medical and command vans.

The medical van was in fact an up-to-date medical laboratory in which we did almost every test that a major hospital could do and then some, plus all the atmosphere monitoring for the chambers, PTCs and habitat. Diving sets were semi-closed mixed-gas rigs. Five teams of eight divers were to spend 12 days each on the bottom at a depth of 610 feet doing all sorts of tasks including testing new salvage techniques, oceanographic studies, fishery studies, and so on. This was a joint military and civilian programme and included military divers from the UK, Canada and Australia. Philippe Cousteau was also to have been member of one of the teams.

Because of all the different experiments to be done, a lot of bottom time was needed and an umbilical had been designed which was neutrally buoyant to allow the divers to work up to 600 feet away from the habitat. One problem was that the cold water made these very stiff, so trying to pull one to its full length would have been a tough, if not impossible, job. One of the most experienced aquanauts said that if the people topside thought he was going to ever be more than an arm's length away from the habitat let alone 600 feet, they were crazy! So much for prior planning.

The project was delayed by problems with the complex equipment involved and the habitat did not get lowered to the bottom off San Clemente Island until February 18, 1969. The habitat began to flood through what was later found to be an improperly installed electrical hull penetrator, and on a dive to attempt to get into the habitat to solve the problem one of the aquanauts, Barry Cannon, died of carbon dioxide poisoning. The grand experiment came to a halt. The habitat was salvaged with the help of lots of air from a submarine's high pressure air banks only to be later scrapped. The Navy never again attempted further experiments of this kind, although Navy saturation diving continued until recently. Unfortunately the US Navy, the pioneer in saturation diving, no longer has this capability in the fleet.

TEKTITE
This was a joint effort between NASA, the Department of Interior and the US Navy. Basic studies were designed to study small crew behaviour during isolation over an extended period of time, and the use of nitrogen-oxygen for long exposures. The habitat consisted of two cylinders joined together and placed on end.

These were ballasted to be 10 tons heavy. It began operation on 15 February 1969 in Greater Lameshur Bay at St John, Virgin Islands. Decompression was completed on 15 April 1969. Four divers from the Department of the Interior spent this time at 43 feet doing biological studies on the reef life and being spied upon by the behavioural scientists. After the failure of SEALAB III some of the SEALAB crew were sent to provide support and I ended up being a watch officer for several weeks. Living conditions were primitive and there was little to do because of the isolation of the site. About the only fun was to call an emergency drill in the wee hours of the morning and get the camp commander excited.

About 60 habitats were built world-wide, and although the era of habitat diving has long since finished, the active field of commercial saturation diving has spread throughout the world. One habitat that survives is La Chalupa. This was built in 1972 and used for undersea research until 1974. It now is part of the Marine Resources Development Foundation and is known as the Jules Verne Lodge. It is fitted out as an underwater hotel room where one can spend 23 hours at about 30 feet whether an aquanaut or not. This foundation also uses another old habitat, Aquarius, as an underwater classroom.

The real explosion in saturation diving came with the many different commercial systems, ranging from a small portable system to be used on a ship as required, to the huge system built by Shell for use on a semi-submersible platform.

Because of the limits on space I have not discussed many of the contributions made to saturation diving by the Royal Navy and the French Navy and various diving companies such as Comex. During the late 1960s and during the 1970s these groups made many experimental dives to extend the depth at which working dives can be made. For instance, between September 1972 and November 1974, 28 saturation dives to depths of 250 metres were done at the Admiralty Deep Trials Unit at the Royal Naval Physiological Laboratory for proving decompression tables and doing physiological research. Diving companies, research facilities and universities pioneered the use of trimix and, more recently, the addition of hydrogen to the breathing mix in a continuing (albeit at a much lower level) quest to allow man to spend more time in the oceans.

Reproduced from Historical Diving Times Issue 20 (Winter 1997)

References:
1. Look Magazine, March 28, 1939.
2. Behnke A, Effects of High Pressures: Prevention and Treatment of Compressed Gas Illness, Med Clincs N.A., pp 1212 - 1237, July 1942.
3. Miller, JW and Koblick, IG, Living and Working in the Sea, 1st Edition, Van Nostrand Reinhold Co. New York, 1984.
4. Smith FJC, Bennett, GA, Heim, JW, Thompson, RM, Drinker, CK : Morphological Changes in the Lungs of Rats Living Under Compressed Air Conditions, J.Exp.Med, 56:79-89, 1932.

Appendix 5 – General description of Operation and Purposes of Manned Hyperbaric Research Facility (My 1,200 ft home)

George R Morrisey, Vice President of Operations, Taylor Diving & Salvage Company, Inc.

INTRODUCTION
What follows is a description of the buildings, support groups, equipment, and services which compose the Taylor Diving & Salvage Company Hydro-Space Research Center in Belle Chasse, Louisiana.
This center is located on a 42,000 square yard tract, accessible by highway, railway and waterway. Landing space is also available to either helicopter or float plane.

The Research Building is two-storey structure 100 feet wide by 120 feet long, engineered in such a way that it can be readily enlarged to cope with any future expansion. Offices, laboratories and a diving equipment project room are provided and equipped for research groups such as medical, electronic, mechanical, hydraulic and geophysical. The Engineering Department is provided with adjacent offices and drafting room. Other features of the building include administrative offices, conference room, library, pharmacy, cafeteria and quarters for persons required to remain in the building over night during prolonged diving research and training projects. The company's Safety Director's office is also located in this building.

The hyperbaric research complex is the heart of our Research Center. It consists of three interconnecting hyperbaric chambers, the main vessel being divided into an upper and a lower compartment, giving us a total of four separate locks interconnected by pressure proof doors. The main vessel stands vertically with the overall inside dimensions 12 feet by 22 feet. The lower compartment, or wet pot, is 13 feet 4 inches high and the upper compartment, or igloo, is 8 feet 8 inches high. The annex connected to the igloo is 7 feet in diameter and 11 feet 6 inches long. On the opposite end of the annex is the entry lock, a 7-foot sphere. The depth pressure rating of all compartments is 2200 feet. Volumes: wet pot 1250 cubic feet; igloo 1006 cubic feet; annex 404.2 cubic feet; entry lock 179.6 cubic feet. There are 6 view ports in the wet pot; 6 in the igloo; 2 in the annex and 1 in the entry lock. The doors in the entry lock and the annex are circular allowing a 30-inch clear opening. The opening between the annex and the igloo has double doors so that either section can be pressurized separately. A door with a 42-inch clearance is provided in the igloo 90° from the annex connection. The hatch between the igloo and the wet pot has a 48-inch clearance. Directly above it in the top of the igloo is another 48-inch hatch so that large or long objects can be lowered through the top. The intermediate hatch is operated hydraulically from outside the vessel. The hydraulic fluid employed is a water-glycol solution so that the hyperbaric atmosphere will not be polluted in the event of a leak. All outside door frames are drilled and tapped as flanges.

This allows other compartments to be added to the complex or the components to be rearranged. Additional compartments can be added in between or on to the existing ones.

This feature gives us the flexibility to readily modify for any future hyperbaric research that the present configuration would not efficiently conform to. There is a 10 inch and an 18-inch material transfer lock in the igloo and a 16-inch transfer lock in the annex. Through hull fittings are provided for normal instrumentation and 12-inch instrumentation flanges are provided in the annex, igloo and wet pot so that additional through hull fittings can be installed for special instrumentation readouts. Illumination is provided by special pressure proof safety lamps of our own design. The basis of these lamps are mounted on Schedule 80 stainless steel pipe that extends through the pressure hull. These mounts contain the electric wiring so that no exposed wires are in the atmosphere of the chamber. They are also fitted with vent valves that insure only a single atmosphere inside the lamp. In the event of a leak, the power to that particular lamp can be shut off and the vent valve can be secured.

The main vessel is constructed of ASTM A-212, Grade B firebox quality steel, modified to A-300 for low temperature service, with Charpy impact tests being made to — 60°F. This steel has a long history of successful use and permits minor welding modifications with ease. All other shells and heads used in the Research Tank are ASTM A-212 or A-515, Gr. 70. Door rings and port bosses are forgings with stainless steel overlaid on the facings. 100% radiography and stress relieving were employed in the construction of these vessels. The design criteria used was A.S.M.E. Code, Section VIII Unfired Pressure Vessels. All carbon steel parts were sandblasted and coated with an inorganic zinc silicate, primer, and white semi-gloss vinyl finish coat paint to retard corrosion and reduce maintenance costs. The plastic view port design was based upon data obtained from the Naval Civil Engineering Laboratory.

The Wet Pot shells of both tanks are insulated with 1.5 inches of polyurethane foam with a fiberglass resin protective outer layer and 1 inch foam neoprene insulation on the bottom heads. This type of insulation was chosen because of low maintenance and ease of future vessel inspections. An example of the efficiency of the insulation can be noted by the following: approximately 7000 gallons of salt water in the Wet Pot was cooled to 35°F and allowed to stand for 24 hours with the tank in an ambient temperature of 74°F. The temperature of the saltwater rose one degree.

Through-hull fittings are provided for permanent gas sample lines and permanent environmental instrumentation. Additional research instrumentation, however, is via 12-inch instrumentation flanges which are provided in the Annex, Igloo, and Wet Pot. These flanges are drilled to suit specific research experiments. Additional penetrations can be readily added, or existing ones modified if necessary. This flexibility greatly reduces experimental setup time, provides virtually unlimited penetrations, and eliminates much nuisance gas leakage.

The Wet Pot Cooling Unit can be used with either the Research or the Training Tank. Cooling is provided by injecting liquid carbon dioxide into a secondary solvent which is continuously circulated through the shell side of a heat exchanger while the fluid from the Wet Pot is circulated through the exchanger's tube side. The temperature is controlled from +70°F to +20°F within ±'/2°F. The temperature in the Wet Pot can be maintained with a 10 GPM flow of 110° F fluid to the divers inside.

The filtration system consists of a 250 GPM full flow filter located in the external fluid piping of the Research Tank. The filter can be bypassed out of the fluid loop and the filter elements renewed as required. The filter elements currently used are 100-micron cotton honeycomb throw-away tubes. The above housing permits use of a large variety of filter elements of different media and filtration levels down to 0.5 microns.

In operation, the Wet Pot fluid can be pumped to the cooler, circulated through the filter and/or just through the filter. The fluid enters the Wet Pot through vertical nozzle pipes angled to impart a circulating motion to maintain an even temperature. Warm fluid for diver heating is supplied by a parallel loop to the Wet Pot fluid system. Thus, the fluid level in the Wet Pot remains constant throughout a dive. A portion of Wet Pot fluid which is normally pumped to the cooling unit is split off, sent through a metering valve and divided into two paths. One path goes through the tube side of a hot water heat exchanger, exiting as hot fluid to the 'hot' inlet of a three-way mixing valve. The other path, already cold from the Wet Pot, is directed to the 'cold' inlet of the mixing valve. The mixed millet flow is routed through a high temperature tripped adenoid valve and outlet manifold. The manifold is fitted with 1 low meters, valves, etc. to monitor and control the flow to the divers.

The three-way valve is powered by a motor whose circuitry is such that it continually seeks to stay in a null position, plus null position is set manually and is maintained with a platinum wire sensor. The three-way valve can be operated manually. The solenoid valve is provided to prevent accidental scalding of the divers. The system will provide at least 10 GPM at 110°F to the diver and/or his equipment.

Temperature, humidity, and atmosphere purification are provided by a uniquely designed modular environmental system that will maintain comfort conditions for eight occupants in the chamber complex. Temperature is maintained to ±.5°F within a range of 60°F to 96°F. Humidity can be controlled between 35% to 95% relative humidity. Carbon dioxide concentration of less than 0.5% sea level equivalent is easily maintained, and trace quantities of other gases and organic vapors are also removed. The life-support modules can be interconnected through appropriate valves to allow a single module to condition all or part of the chamber complex. There are four absorbent canisters in a duplex arrangement through which the environmental gases are circulated. Thus, they are available for refilling without interrupting a dive in progress.

Two canned motor blower drive assemblies are employed to circulate the environmental gases. With no electrical connections in contact with the environmental gases, contamination from a motor burn is averted. Valves, canisters, and piping are fabricated from stainless steel.

The system utilizes Freon-12 for both dehumidifying the environmental gases and reheating them to a suitable temperature. Each module contains an evaporator and condensing heat exchanger, with Freon on the shell side and environmental gases on the tube side. Double tube sheets are provided on each exchanger with the space between tube sheets vented to atmosphere through valves. The exchangers stand vertically. The environmental gases come from the Research Tank, through the absorbers, down the evaporator, and then are made to flow up the condenser back to the Research Tank.

Condensate is drained from the bottom of the return bend.

Depending upon the type of dive, energy is either added to or removed from the Freon circuit to obtain the desired thermo-dynamic balance.

The gas console is the central control point for the operation of tin- Research Tank. It serves as a reducing station for high pressure gases used to maintain the chamber atmosphere as the mixed gases used as breathing media with various living apparatus. The electric and electronic switchboard's automatic oxygen induction system and automatic ascent control are also a part of this console.

As low, medium, and high-pressure gas piping is stainless steel. The helium recovery piping is copper since it is maintained at atmospheric pressure. The system was chemically cleaned for the service intended and all lines contain 10 micron absolute filters.

Through suitable instrumentation, the level of oxygen is continuously monitored and if it is slightly deficient, the proper amount is injected automatically through an oxygen induction system into the Environmental Control System piping. This aids mixing of the gases. A completely separate oxygen induction system is installed as a back-up. This is in addition to the manual bypasses on the automatic system. A stainless-steel combination wash basin and toilet is provided in the shower area of the igloo. It is a fold shut design with interlocking valves that prevent flushing except in the closed, in the closed safe condition. External to the igloo are the sanitary receiver and the hot and cold-water tanks.

The gas storage building contains 40 cylinders with combined capacity of 400,000 standard cubic feet stored at 2800 PSI. Stored gases usually consist of pure helium, oxygen, compressed air, nitrogen, and various pre-mixed breathing gases.

The helium recovery unit is designed to compress and purify helium gas which is contaminated with nitrogen, oxygen, water vapor, and carbon dioxide, as well as traces of carbon monoxide, hydrogen sulfide and methane. The unit consists of a chemical carbon dioxide absorber, compressor, cooler, water separator, dual tower desiccant dryer, and vacuum insulated cryostat containing a heat exchanger coil and condensate collection pot. The items in the cryostat are cooled with liquid nitrogen.

The selective condensation process utilized in this unit is similar to that used by the U.S. Bureau of Mines in the purification of crude helium recovered from natural gas. At the liquid nitrogen boiling point of —320° F and 211 atmospheres absolute pressure (3100 PSIA), it is possible to obtain helium of better than 99 mol percent purity. The recovery unit can process 57,000 SCF of helium gas at a rate of 25 SCFM and purify before regeneration of the carbon dioxide absorber is required.

A powerhouse containing two automatic diesel electric generators of 235 KW and 75 KW capacities is always at standby condition to provide emergency power.

Redundant instrumentation is provided to insure safety and accuracy in the monitoring of the hyperbaric atmospheric conditions. Depth pressure, partial pressure of oxygen, and carbon dioxide are recorded by 24-hour circular chart recorders. A record of physiological conditions through an entire dive can be automatically recorded. All compartments are monitored at the Research Tank console by closed circuit television. A list and description of instrumentation is included as Appendix A.

Support groups consist of the following: Engineering Department, consisting of Chief Engineer, Assistant Engineer, five staff engineers, three design draftsmen, and 3 draftsmen; Electronics Department, consisting of an Electronics Supervisor and six technicians; Medical Laboratory, consisting of a staff of six men who work in various capacities under Captain Robert Workman, Submarine Medical Supervisor and Diving Physiologist, United States Navy, Retired; a combination warehouse and shop facility, a separate building with 25,000 square feet of floor space, has a staff of approximately 45 men. While their normal job is to support the offshore operations throughout the world, their various skills and equipment can be called on to assist with research and development projects. Individual shops within this complex consist of the following skills: riggers, steel fabricators, machinists, carpenters, electricians, air conditioning and heating mechanics, engine overhaul and heavy equipment mechanics, and hydraulic technicians. All of the people mentioned in various trades and professions have been carefully selected by consideration of their abilities, training, and background relevant to the diving industry. Our Safety Director, a 23-year veteran Navy Master Diver with a subsequent 10 years' experience in industrial safety engineering, is a good example of our method of selection.

Though various shallower dives have been made in the new research tanks since 1969, the deepest and most spectacular to date was one conducted for the U.S. Navy in November and December of 1970.

Although this was planned as a 1000-foot total saturation dive, all went so well that the decision was made to make an excursion to 1125 feet. A hypothetical 1000-foot dive schedule is included as Appendix B. The Wet Pot was filled with 7000 gallons of water, saturated with 8500 pounds calcium chloride to prevent freezing, at a maintained temperature of 29°F. Atmospheric temperature in the annex and igloo was maintained at 86°F and 75^r; relative humidity. The purpose of this dive was to evaluate a special diving apparatus manufactured for the U.S. Navy by the General Electric Company. It consisted of an electronic controlled breath circulated total rebreather type of scuba. It had previously been tested in warm water to a depth of 1000 feet and in 20°F water at shallower depths. This test was designed to combine both low temperature and deep depth. Hot water was provided to warm the diver's body and breathing media by the system previously described. Practically all of the company's instrumentation and recording apparatus was employed to monitor and record the dive. During the underwater phases, the divers were fitted with electrodes taped to various parts of their bodies. Six areas were measured for skin temperature while other physiological devices measured rectal temperature, heart rate, breathing gas temperature, and breathing gas levels. After very thorough physical examinations, five commercial divers with Navy backgrounds were chosen as the human subjects. Ages were 25, 28, 28, 29, and 33.

All food consumed by the subjects was fresh frozen and prepared in the especially equipped galley of the research center. This was done to reduce the chances of outside contamination. During the early stages of the experiment, pressures were increased by increments of 200 feet and maintained at these levels while the divers working as two-man teams went through special exercises designed to test the equipment at progressively deeper depths.

The complete test consisted of five exercises conducted at 200, 400, 600, 800, and 1000 feet. During each exercise, one diver would swim a trapeze type ergometer designed to impose a workload equivalent to swimming against an 0.8 knot current At the same time, - his teammate was put through weight-lifting exercises.

The entire dive required 18 days of confinement, including over 12 days of decompression. Both the Navy and the company were pleased with the results of the experiment. Currently both depth simulators are employed in the R and D of commercial diving equipment we have currently under development for use in the field to depths of 1000 feet and greater.

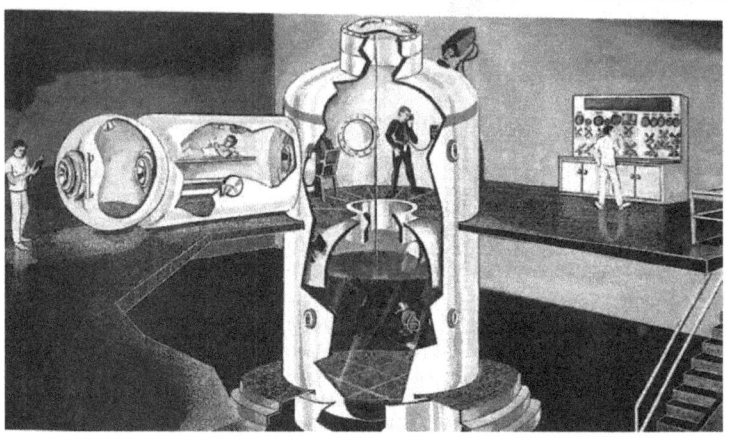

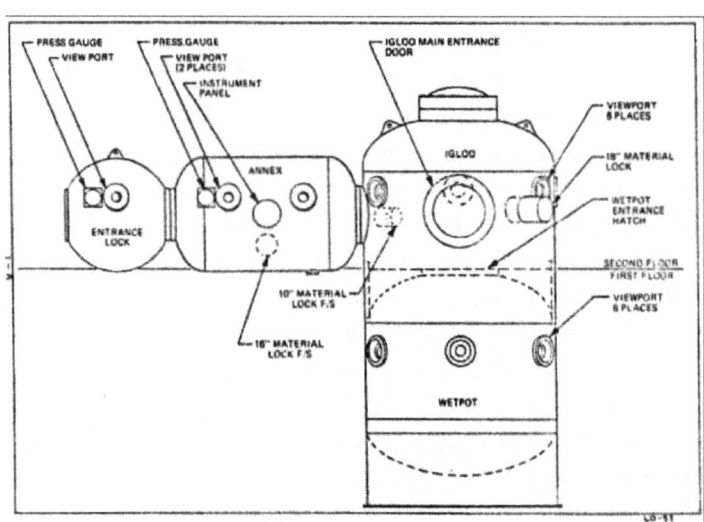

Appendix 6 – Rescue and Recovery of Disabled Bell (SDC) Diver

Mike Cooke, Project Manager, Taylor Diving & Salvage Company, Inc.
Paper presented to the International Diving Symposium February 1980 and referenced in Walker, PA (Ed.) *(1986) Commission of the European Communities: Safety of Diving Operations.* Graham & Trotman Ltd

OFFICE MEMO
TAYLOR DIVING & SALVAGE CO., INC.

TO: Distribution
FROM: Mike Cooke
SUBJECT: Rescue of the Disabled Diver.
DATE: February 12, 1979

A meeting will be held in the Conference Room at 1:30 p.m. on February 13, 1979.

The purpose of this meeting will be:

1. To review and discuss the results of trials conducted January 29 - February 2, 1979. Report attached.

2. Decide what action will be taken to modify existing equipment and procedures to assist in the recovery of the disabled diver.

If you are unable to attend, please send an alternate.

Mike Cooke

MC:pas

Distribution:

**Names
removed**

OFFICE MEMO

TAYLOR DIVING & SALVAGE CO., INC.

TO: Mike Cooke
FROM: Henry L. Hicks
SUBJECT: Rescue of the Disabled Diver, Test and Evaluation Of.
DATE: February 7, 1979

During the week of 22-26 January 1979, we conducted tests and evaluations in the open tank, with SDC 13 on the recovery of a disabled diver.

The purpose of the tests was to evaluate the hot water suit with built in harness; Maasdam rope puller as a lifting device; combination weight belt and come home bottle with quick disconnects for easy disposal, the emergency standby rig located outside of SDC, and the feasibility of administering CPR in the SDC after the recovery of the diver. Also included was to determine the time factor in retrieving the disabled divers slack if not fouled and standby diver's dress out time if fouled.

Thirty four of our most experienced divers were contacted to lend their expertise to this project and twenty participated. Eighteen were made and fourteen written comments were received by the participating divers.

Almost all of the changes and modifications were enthusiastically received, however, this is not to say a few problems did not exist in our evaluations.

A. Hot Water Suit with Built in Harness: The hot water suit with harness worked very well, once the diver's retrieval "D" ring was hooked, head was in tunnel the body remained upright throughout retrieval and required little or no guidance by the standby bell diver. With the diver hanging vertical inside the SDC there was no restriction in blood flow or chest pressure to limit breathing. One problem

Office Memo
February 7, 1979
Page 2

was the flap at the top of the suit covering the zipper tends to choke the diver while hanging vetically out of the water. The solution was to fold flap over and unzip suit three inches. The other problem was the location of the "D" ring for the umbilical attachment. If located at waist level, as is presently done, the disabled diver arrives at the bottom of the hatch in a horizontal position making it very difficult for the SDC standby diver to right him and attach retrieval snap; however, if the umbilical attachment "D" ring is shoulder level the disabled diver arrives in a semi-upright position making it much easier to attach the snap.

B. <u>Maasdam Rope Puller</u>: The rope puller has many advantages over the block and tackle now employed. Some of the advantages are, positive strain on disabled diver once retrieval hook is attached, excess slack can be pulled in by hand until strain is taken, SDC standby diver not exhausted getting disabled diver in SDC due to 10-1 leverage and portability of rope puller allows installation in SDC almost anywhere.

The biggest problem was releasing the rope puller to let down disabled diver, however in an actual emergency the line would be cut. The rope puller was modified for our tests so that it could be located on the side of the SDC. A stainless steel "L" shaped pin was welded to the steel reinforced ratchet guard of the rope puller which fit in the bracket mounted on the railing inside the SDC.

Office Memo
February 7, 1979
Page 3

C. <u>Combination Weight Belt and Come Home Bottle</u>: Both come home bottles and weight belt are attached with quick disconnects. The C.H.B. straps are connected to "D" rings located chest high on the built in harness on the hot water suit. The weight belt comes with six removal weights and hose clamps to attach C.H.B., the belt is equipped to house either the single or double C.H.B.'s. There were no adverse comments on the weight belt-come home bottle combination. The divers reported the weight distribution as excellent.

D. <u>Emergency Standby Rig Located Outside SDC</u>: There were no adverse diver comments on the outside rig. The rig had external connections for gas and hot water, communications was plugged into head set connector, if required, pneumo is not required. The end of the external rig is tied to the bottom of the hatch, as the external pneumo is now done, with valves on the gas and hot water hoses. Non-returns would have to be installed at the gas and hot water external connection points to eliminate gas and hot water loss if umbilical is severed. A hat would be hooked up prior to diving and removed prior to coming up. The advantage of the external rig is the ability of the standby diver to remove all his slack and not have to be concerned with what to do with it when recovery is made. The problems would be the maintenance of the rig and each SDC and "A" frame would have to be investigated to determine saddle location.

Office Memo
February 7, 1979
Page 4

E. <u>Administering CPR in the SDC</u>: SDC 13 is a medium size bell and due to the configuration of the hatch, proved no problem in conducting CPR. Each SDC hatch is different as to latching and locking devices, however the new 36" false decking hatches now being considered eliminate this problem and CPR can easily be administered in this size bell and larger.

F. <u>Time Factor in Retrieving Disabled Divers Slack and Standby Divers Dress Out Time</u>: The retrieving of the unfouled divers slack with 100 to 150' of umbilical out ran from 40 seconds not racking with 150' slack, to 2 mins. racking hose. Standby diver dress out time ran from 55 seconds to 3 minutes depending on the diver and what state of readiness he was in. These times were taken under ideal conditions with the diver expecting the recovery.

There was a slight modification to the SDC to allow the disabled diver to be brought all the way to the bell so that the hatch can be closed. The lights were originally located in the center of the SDC with a bracket surrounding them and a padeye underneath to hook up block and tackle for diver retrieval. This did not provide enough headroom to bring diver all the way into bell. The lights were moved to the side with no lighting loss and the light holder which is screwed into the top of the SDC was removed and a plug with padeye welded on was inserted. This allowed us approximately 13" more headroom and almost any diver can be brought in. The other modification that should be made is a 1" stand pipe approximately 2' high to allow

Office Memo
February 7, 1979
Page 5

the diver to flood the SDC in the event he had to go out and retrieve a fouled diver. This could be incorporated in the bilge drain system and would not require further penetration.

The below is a list, in priority order, of the changes that should be made in our present diver recovery method.

1. Install maasdam rope puller - remove block and tackle.
2. Modify bell lights and install padeye at center apex of SDC.
3. Modify hot water suits with built in harness.
4. Combination weight belt and C.H.B.
5. Install stand pipe for flooding bell by diver.
6. External emergency S. B. umbilical.
7. Provide training in diver recovery and make mandatory for all divers.

HLH:pas

OFFICE MEMO
TAYLOR DIVING & SALVAGE CO., INC.

TO: Distribution
FROM: Mike Cooke
SUBJECT: Minutes of Meeting - Recovery of Disabled Diver
DATE: March 1, 1979

Attendees: **Names removed**

The following items were discussed and decisions were made as to what action will be taken.

1) Cost items:

   a) Modifications to SDC 4, 8, 9, 10, 12, 13 and 14, to include flooding stand pipe, moving lights and manufacture of hardware to accommodate Maasdan puller.

   b) Install shuttle valve in SDC 4, 8, 9, 10, 12, 13, 14, 87 and 89.

   c) Install "A" frame over large training tank to support SDC for instructional purposes.

9) H. Hicks to advise on quick release for Maasdan puller, to eliminate the need for cutting the line to lower the disabled diver.

10) M. Cooke to supply Fred Bigger with complete documentation of equipment and procedure for approval by regulatory agencies in North Sea area.

Information concerning Items 2 - 9 to be turned in to M. Cooke by March 7, 1979.

Mike Cooke

OPS-1
Rev.-1, 3/79

SDC RESCUE OF A DISABLED DIVER PROCEDURE

INTRODUCTION

This procedure is intended for diving Supervisors/Superintendents and divers who may one day be put in the situation of having to deal with a diver becoming disabled outside the SDC.

Past experience has proven that due to various reasons, divers may run into difficulties outside the SDC which could render them disabled. Among the recognized factors which have been identified are the following:

a. Inability to control breathing rate
b. Sugar level in blood
c. Cold (Hypothermia)
d. Overheating (Hyperthermia)
e. Thermal shock
f. Asphyxia
g. CO_2 poisioning
h. O_2 poisoning
i. Electric shock
j. Drowning
k. Vomiting
l. Physical injury

Whatever the reason, a disabled diver is in danger of dying and no time must be wasted in removing him from this situation.

SDC Rescue of a Disabled Diver Procedure
Page 2

As every Superintendent/Supervisor and diver is familiar with basic first aid techniques, only the adaptions to this specific situation are described here.

I. <u>Equipment</u>

   A. <u>Lifting Device</u>: A Maasdam rope puller has been provided as a lifting device to secure the disabled diver in the SDC. The rope puller may either be mounted directly to the padeye at the top of the SDC or side mounted on existing rail, and rope reaved through a block in the overhead. The lifting device permits the SDC tender to secure the disabled diver and free his hands for other tasks. Excess slack may be taken in by simply pulling the free end of the rope. An inch-by-inch lowering device is built in, however, when lowering the disabled diver after hatch is shut, the rope should be cut for expediency. The rope is fitted with a snap shackle allowing a safe and quick connection using only one hand. See Figure 1-1.

   B. <u>Harness/Hot Water Suit</u>: The hot water suit has a built-in harness to eliminate excessive straps. The harness consists of shoulder, leg and waist straps with "D" rings on each side of waist strap and for lifeline attachment, "D" rings on both front chest straps for come-home-bottle quick disconnect attachment and a "D" ring located in the center neck area in the back for lifting device snap shackle connection. See Figure 1-2.

C. <u>Come-Home-Bottle/Weight Belt</u>: The weight belt consists of six adjustable weights and a parachute type quick connect/disconnect for buckling. Two hose clamps are located in the very back for attaching come-home-bottle. The two shoulder straps with quick disconnect buckling devices are attached to the top of the come-home-bottle with an adjustable hose clamp. See Figure 1-3.

D. <u>Medical Kit</u>: An emergency medical kit will be stored in the SDC which will consist of:

1. Knife
2. Blunted end scissors
3. Mouth opener
4. Airway tube
5. C.H.U.T. bandage

This medical kit will be inventoried and accounted for during each bell check. See Figure 1-4.

II. <u>Rescue of an Unfouled Disabled Diver</u>:

A. <u>SDC Standby Diver Action</u>: The SDC standby diver will remain in a state of readiness which will facilitate a speedy departure in the event a casualty occurs; i.e., hot water suit on, standby hat checked out and lifting device line with snap shackle dropped through hatch.

When notified by topside that casualty has occurred, the SDC standby diver will:

SDC Rescue of a Disabled Diver Procedure
Page 4

1. Check divers breathing gas pressure gauge and activate emergency gas if necessary. (If diver's breathing gas has pressure, DO NOT activate emergency gas.
2. Commence taking in disabled diver's slack.

    NOTE

    When taking in disabled diver's umbilical, feed the slack back through hatch tunnel to provide room in SDC for diver retrieval.

3. When diver arrives at bottom of tunnel, attach snap shackle to "D" ring on harness.

    CAUTION

    If diver is unfouled, do not flood SDC as standby diver will have to reach through hatch tunnel to attach snap shackle.

4. Take up slack on lifting device until strain is taken, then commence ratcheting.
5. When diver's head is out of water, remove hat and feel the carotid artery for pulse. This will determine the action to be taken after diver is secured in SDC. Remove weight belt and come-home-bottle.
6. Shut off gas to disabled diver hose. Cut umbilical and drop both hat and hose end through tunnel.

SDC Rescue of a Disabled Diver Procedure
Page 5

    7. Bring disabled diver into the SDC and shut hatch. Inform topside that you are ready for a seal.

    8. Cut the lifting device line and lower disabled diver to the deck. Commence CPR or first aid, whichever is necessary.

NOTE

Only in cases of severe hemorraging will first aid be performed before CPR.

    9. CPR and/or first aid must be continued until the diver recovers or is pronounced dead by appropriate authority.

B. <u>Disabled Diver Action</u>: If capable, the disabled diver must remain calm, activate emergency gas and notify topside of the extent of disability.

III. <u>Rescue of a Fouled Diver</u>

A. <u>Standby Diver Action</u>: The SDC standby diver will remain in a state of readiness which will facilitate a speedy departure in the event a casualty occurs; i.e., hot water suit on, standby hat checked out and lifting device line with snap shackle dropped through hatch.

When notified by topside that a casualty has occurred, the SDC standby diver will:

    1. Check diver's breathing gas pressure gauge and activate emergency gas if necessary.

SDC Recovery of a Disabled Diver Procedure
Page 6

2. Commence taking in disabled diver's slack. When strain is taken and no more umbilical can be recovered, throw off one turn of slack, and prepare to retrieve diver.

   NOTE

   When taking in disabled diver's umbilical, feed the slack back through hatch tunnel to provide room in SDC for diver retrieval.

   Advise topside of situation.

3. Don diving hat, weight belt and insure sufficient umbilical is available to reach disabled diver.
4. Activate flood control system.
5. Follow disabled diver's umbilical to location and upon reaching diver insure free flow supply valve is on and in the case of a severed umbilical, the come-home-bottle is activated.
6. Pull disabled diver back to SDC and attach snap shackle to "D" ring. Disconnect weight belt and come-home-bottle and cut whip between hat and bottle.
7. Enter SDC and remove hat.

   NOTE

   If time does not allow for racking umbilical, cut and drop through tunnel.

SDC Rescue of a Disabled Diver Procedure
Page 7

8. Pull the slack through lifting device until the weight of the diver is felt, then commence ratcheting.
9. Have topside blow down SDC.
10. When diver's head is out of water, remove hat and feel the carotid artery for pulse. This will determine the action to be taken after diver is secured in SDC.
11. Shut off gas to disabled diver's hose. Cut umbilical and drop both hat and hose end through tunnel.
12. Bring disabled diver into the SDC and shut hatch. Inform topside that you are ready for a seal.
13. Cut the lifting device line and lower disabled diver to the deck. Commence CPR or first aid, whichever is necessary.

<u>NOTE</u>

Only in cases of severe hemorraging will first aid be performed before CPR.

14. CPR and/or first aid must be continued until diver recovers or is pronounced dead by appropriate authority.

B. <u>Disabled Diver Action</u>: If capable, the disabled diver must remain calm, activate emergency gas and notify topside of the extent of disability.

Appendix 7 – Taylor Diving Hyperbaric Welding – Brochure

FOREWORD

As early as 1965, Taylor Diving could foresee problems arising from the increasing depths at which marine pipelines were being constructed.

While pipe could be laid successfully in comparatively deep water, the flexibility of longer risers made the latter very difficult to set.

In the process of doing this, laid pipe was often damaged while attempting to bring the ends to the surface for connection. Simultaneously, large diameter pipes — or those lying beneath other pipelines — could not be raised under any circumstances.

Increased depth also impaired the installation of mechanical joints and aggravated their subsequent repair when leaks developed.

Taylor's solution to these problems was to develop a method for welding pipes in place, in a dry environment, so joint properties could be obtained which would be comparable to or exceed surface-welding criteria.

The methods developed originally for pipeline tie-in and repair has since been adapted to riser tie-ins to existing jackets, riser tie-ins on concrete platforms, repair of damaged offshore structures, and the installation of valve assemblies, by-pass assemblies, and tie-in assemblies to existing lines.

The basic technique involves the use of an open-bottom enclosure or Underwater Welding Habitat (UWH) which can be placed over opposing ends of the members to be joined.

After seals are established against the pipe surface and sea water is dispelled with breathing gas, diver/welders

enter the UWH to perform the preparatory work and complete the welds in a completely dry environment.

Thus, the term hyperbaric welding has come to mean fusion welding at hyperbaric pressure by diver/welders working wholly within the protection of a dry underwater environment.

Since the first successful hyperbaric pipeline welding job was performed by Taylor Diving in 1968, techniques and equipment have been refined to the point where Taylor crews are doing hyperbaric welding in more than 500-feet of water on a routine basis. To date, a majority of this work has been done from Brown & Root barges in the Gulf of Mexico and North Sea.

Taylor's newest welding habitats measure approximately 10 feet square and are

READY TO BE LOWERED to the bottom of the North Sea from Brown & Root's derrick barge "Hugh Gordon" is Taylor Diving's Submersible Pipe Alignment Rig. The Underwater Welding Habitat is the gray unit at the center of the SPAR. Although the SPAR is shown being supported by cables from the barge's derrick, it is set in place over the pipeline by chains from the two davits shown at either side of the picture.

designed to handle pipe up to 54 inches in diameter. These advanced units are fitted with sophisticated electrical equipment, hydraulics, environmental controls, and pipe handling machinery. In addition, they are installed as integral parts of the company's patented Submersible Pipe Alignment Rigs (SPARs) from which they can be controlled by hydraulics to a precise degree. In 1975, the company developed an independent Modular Underwater Welding Habitat (MUWH) for special situations where a SPAR cannot be used. Standing on four support columns fitted with hydraulic controls for vertical height adjustment, this type of habitat is employed primarily for cell deck and sea-bed tie-ins and repairing production platforms.

To date, most of Taylor Diving's hyperbaric welding assignments have involved new pipeline tie-ins and the setting of risers to production platforms. Other assignments have included the repair of pipeline buckles, repairs to damaged production platforms, installation of tap valve assemblies, replacement of mechanical pipeline connections, and pipeline connections at SPM bases.

An examination of records of all hyperbaric welding jobs performed by Taylor (see attached addenda) shows that a major portion of time spent on-site is consumed by delays involving bad weather. On two separate occasions during 1969, diver/welder teams were forced to break off operations because of hurricanes. On other occasions, heavy seas have retarded operations for up to 25 days.

At least half of all the company's hyperbaric welding jobs were done in moderate to heavy seas.

It is important to note that Taylor's hyperbaric welding equipment is specifically designed for rapid abandonment in emergencies. On several occasions, diver/welders have left the UWH, been brought to the surface in a Submersible Diving Chamber (SDC), and been locked safely inside a Deck Decompression Chamber (DDC) with the entire exercise taking only 45 minutes.

In perfecting its hyperbaric welding techniques, the company has experimented with and evaluated many types of power supplies, consumable electrodes, and cover gases. The latter are used to flood the area being welded to insure the best possible weld.

All tests are initially performed inside the company's hyperbaric research and training complex which is certified to simulate ocean depths of 2,200-feet. Most recently, successful welding tests have been performed at a simulated depth of 1,200-feet.

In new construction, it is advantageous to customers if Taylor is called in at an early date to counsel on such critical details as proximity of pipelines to be connected to production platforms and other items of similar importance.

PHOTO AT RIGHT: Cutaway model of Taylor Diving's hyperbaric research and training complex shows the "annex" at right where divers live between working assignments in the "igloo" at upper left, and the "wet pot" beneath the "igloo." At far left is the console where breathing gas mixtures are controlled. All hyperbaric welding equipment and procedures are first tested in this unit at Belle Chasse before being used in the open sea.

2

The Pressure Zone by Mike Cooke   316

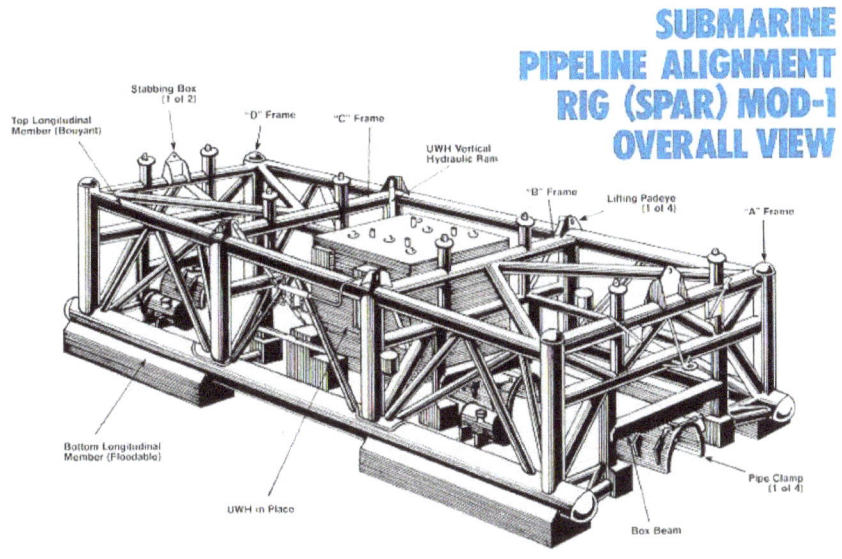
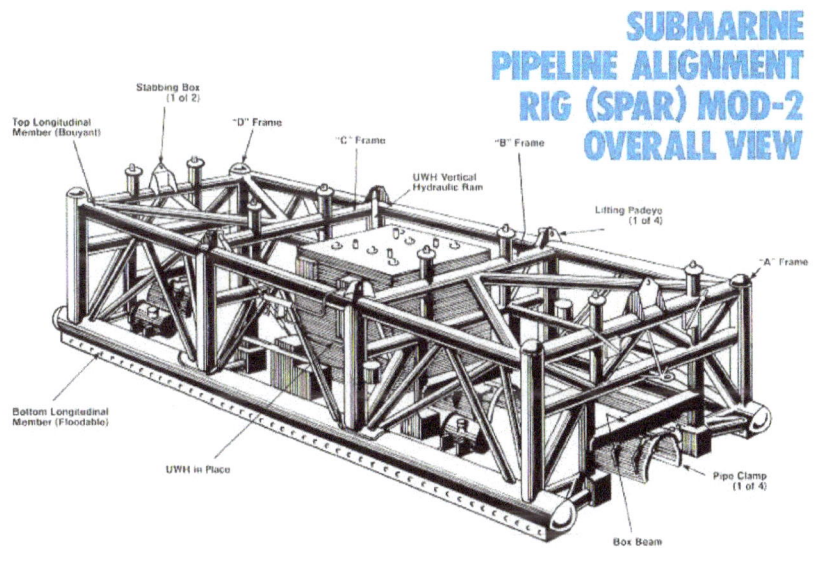

UNDERWATER WELDING HABITAT (U.W.H.) AS USED WITH SPAR

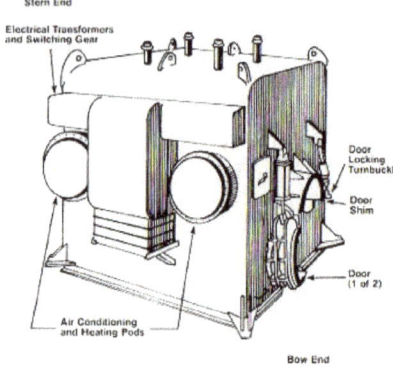

UNDERWATER WELDING HABITAT USED INDEPENDENTLY OF SPAR

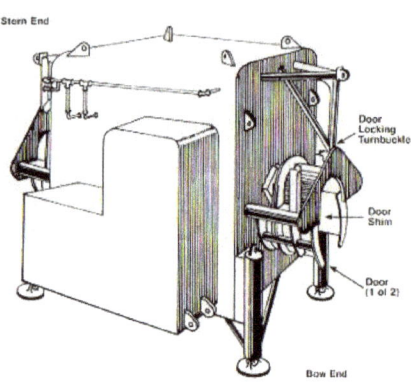

SPAR/U.W.H. DETAILS OF SIZES AND WEIGHTS

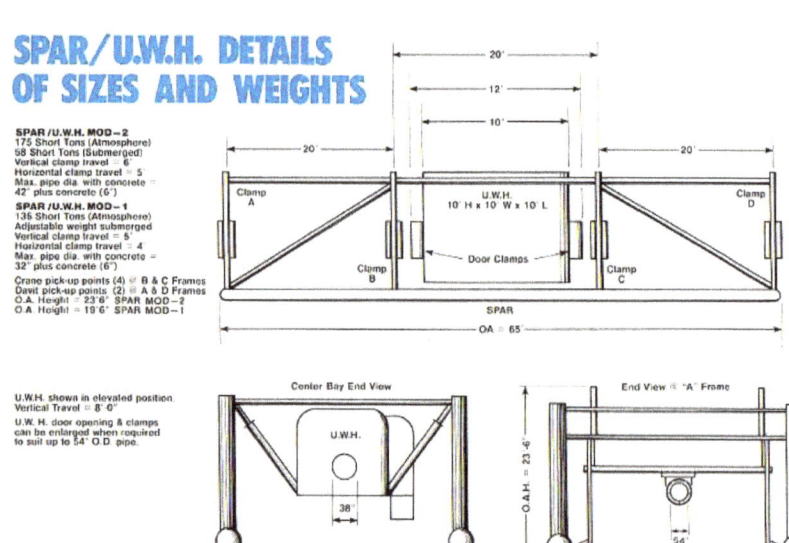

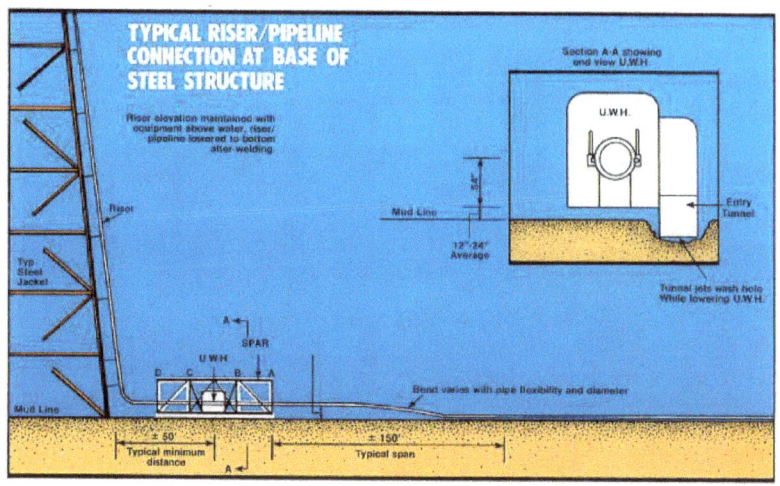

The Pressure Zone by Mike Cooke

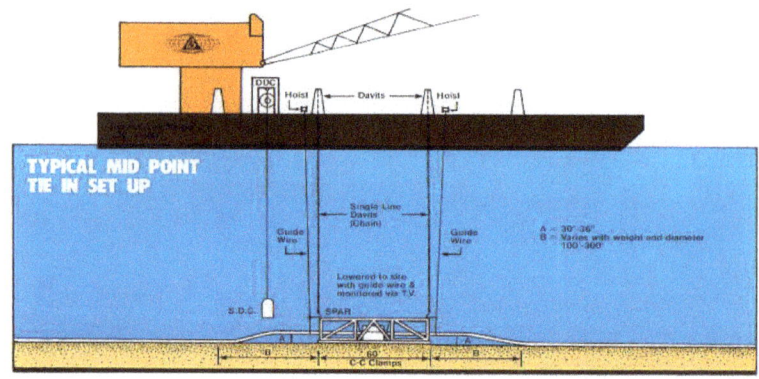

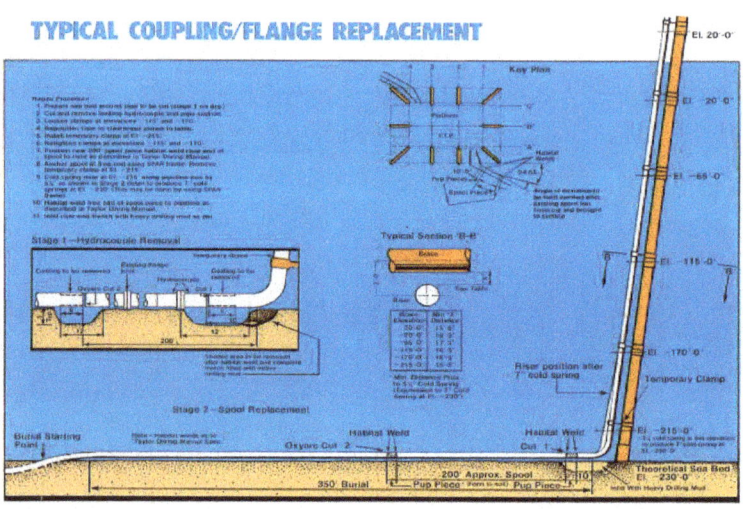

The Pressure Zone by Mike Cooke

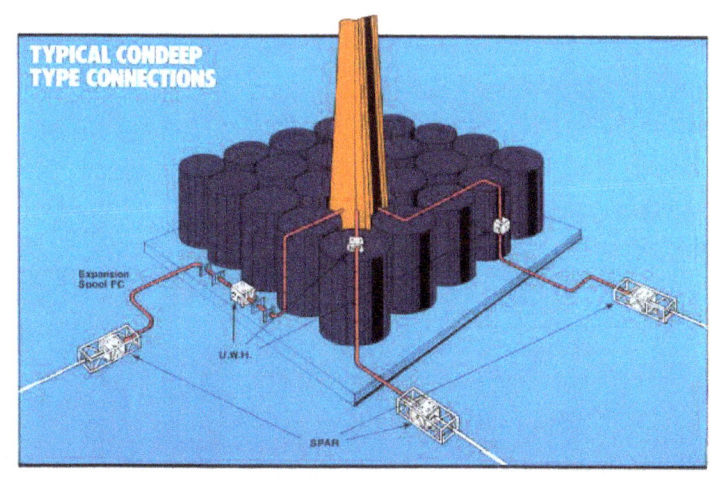

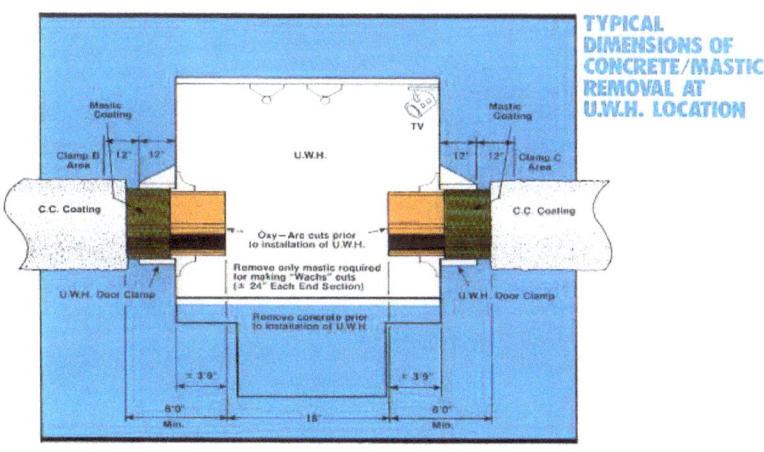

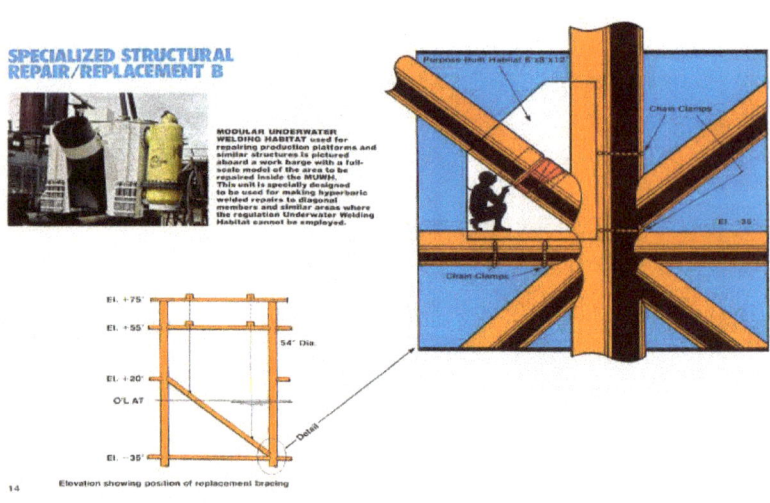

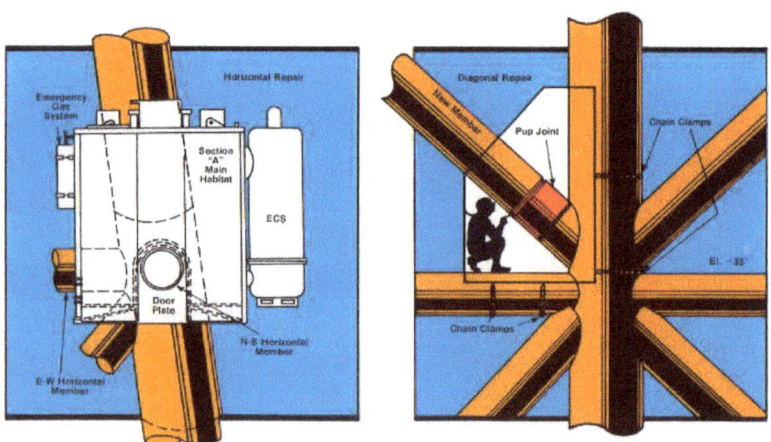

INSTALLATION OF A TYPICAL TAP VALVE ASSEMBLY

The accompanying illustration shows a typical tap valve assembly installation procedure.

Taylor's most acceptable method of installation calls for selecting either an area where the pipe is un-buried or to run a jet barge over the desired location and create a suitably wide ditch.

With the line having been previously flooded, the next step is to cut out approximately 80-feet of pipeline, install the tap valve assembly, and then weld it into the pipeline using pup pieces as required.

The merits of this type of installation are that a pre-tested assembly can be installed into the pipeline using hyperbaric welded connections of a quality comparable to or exceeding surface welding criteria, thereby retaining total integrity throughout the system.

Should customers envision any type of installation differing from that described in this brochure, Taylor Diving will be pleased to review it and offer appropriate suggestions.

However, it should be explained that on at least two recent occasions, Taylor diver/welders have successfully performed assignments similar to that described in preceding paragraphs. In the first instance, approximately 80-feet of buckled 36-inch pipe in 300-feet of water was removed prior to installing a new section. In the second case, the assignment involved removal of a section of 20-inch line containing a proprietary mechanical connection close to a platform.

In the first case, the line was buried. In the second, the line was not buried.

TYPICAL IN-DITCH PIPELINE REPAIR

This project describes and outlines the parameters for an actual repair to a 16-inch pipeline in the North Sea.

The depth of the ditch ranged from 12 to 14-feet while the damaged area (dents and holes) measured 12 to 14-feet in length.

Prior to commencing repairs, the overburden in the area was removed using criteria specified by Taylor Diving following an initial bottom inspection.

In the area under discussion, the bottom soil was very sandy so that it backfilled and solidified shortly after evacuation of the existing soil cover.

The following procedures, which were adhered to in this

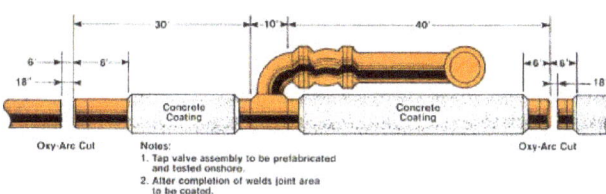

Oxy-Arc Cut

Notes:
1. Tap valve assembly to be prefabricated and tested onshore.
2. After completion of welds joint area to be coated.
3. Drawing N.T.S.

Oxy-Arc Cut

sample exercise, should be applied to all in-ditch pipeline repairs:

I. Evacuation of the pipe cover soil should be accomplished with minimum jet pressure and maximum air lift so existing ditch side wall disturbance will be held to a minimum. This will insure firm footing for the SPAR/UWH. **SEE SKETCH NO. 1.**

II. Evacuation should extend to a minimum of 250-feet to either side of the area to be repaired or replaced with a spool piece. (If the spool piece is 80-feet, then the total length of cleared pipe should be 580-feet). **SEE SKETCH NO. 5.**

III. Using hoist lines from the barge (starting approximately 50-feet from either end of the ditch) and working to the damaged area, the pipeline should be lifted approximately 3-feet and sandbagged to secure this elevation. The hoist lines are then re-located every 50-feet with the pipeline again raised approximately 3-feet (and secured by additional sandbags) until an 80-foot span at the damaged area is approximately at sea bed elevation. This insures that sand drifting back into the ditch will not cause problems when the tie-in is started. **SEE SCHEME A, SKETCH NO. 4.**

IV. If it is impossible to follow the procedure recommended in Item III, then the damaged area should be rough-cut before the remaining instructions in Item III are initiated. It is important to note that nightcaps or stopper pigs should be installed to prevent soil and other foreign objects from entering the pipe.
HYPERBARIC SPREAD ON LOCATION:

Divers inspect the pipeline, ditch, and surrounding area to insure that the preceding criteria has been accomplished. If alignment of the two pipes (or one continuous pipe) is correct, they continue with operations as outlined on Pages 20-28 of Taylor Diving's Hyperbaric Welding Manual. If mis-alignment is encountered, the procedure to be followed is described in the manual's chapter on Typical Pipeline Alignment Procedures.

If a spool is required in excess of 4-feet, then a minimum of 30 to 40 feet is recommended for ease of alignment. **SEE SKETCH NO. 5** (Positions 1 and 2.)

A spool piece in excess of 4-feet should be lowered into position in the ditch prior to lowering the SPAR/UWH to the work site.

In most cases when spool pieces are used, the first weld will be accomplished by a single weld without a pup joint. In all cases, a second weld will require a pup joint with a minimum length of 30-inches of large diameter. Backfill soil which will be sent down with the SPAR/UWH.

Refer to **SKETCH NO. 2** for normal type tie-ins with the pup joint only.

NOTES

SKETCH NO. 3 portrays an alternate scheme that is possible but avoided because of evacuation problems arising in such large areas.

SKETCH NO. 3 is generally required when installing tap valve assemblies in old lines of large diameter. Backfill soil is very sandy or solid and, in most cases, disturbing the pipeline is undesirable.

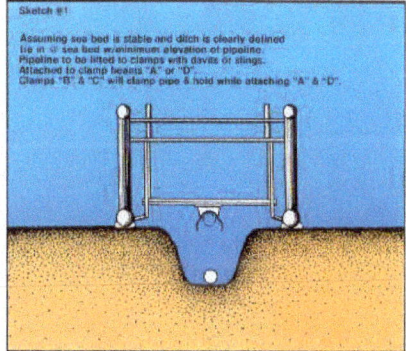

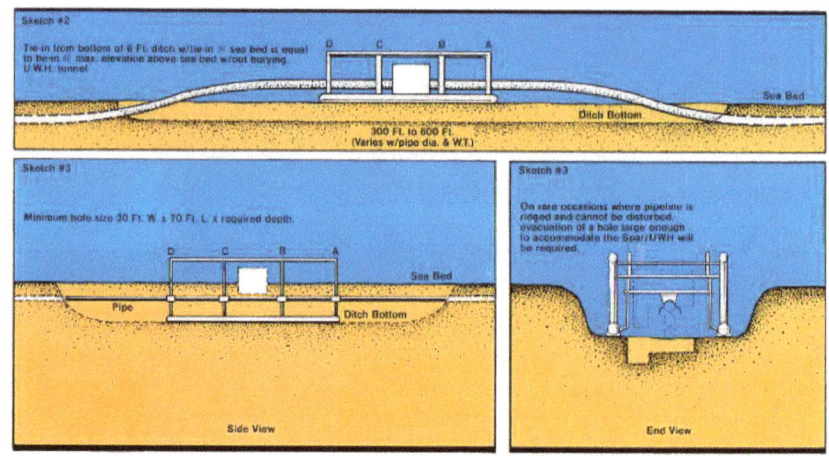

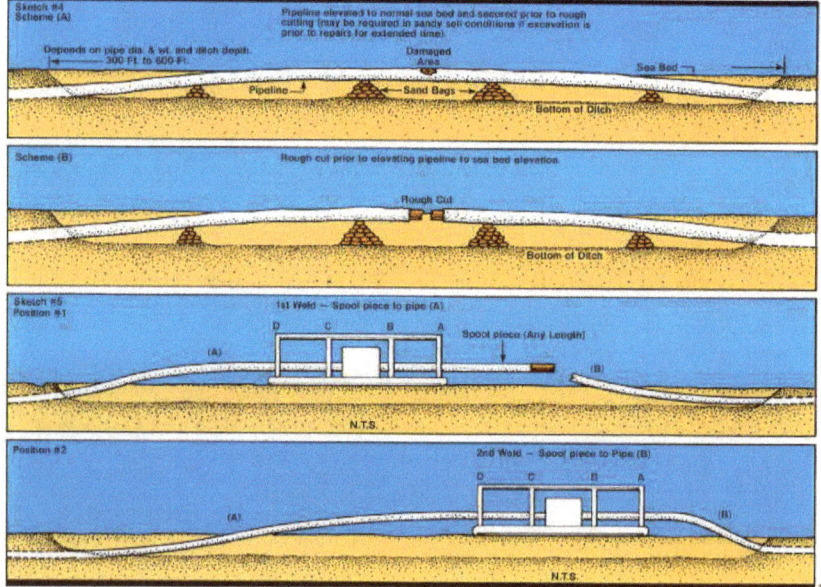

The Pressure Zone by Mike Cooke

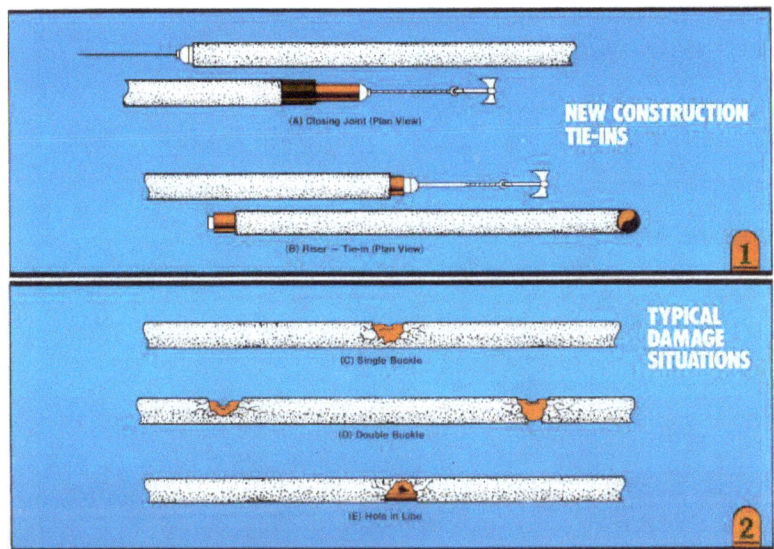

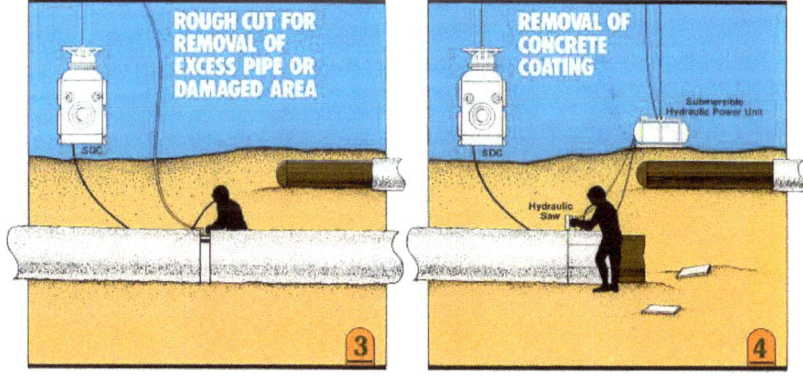

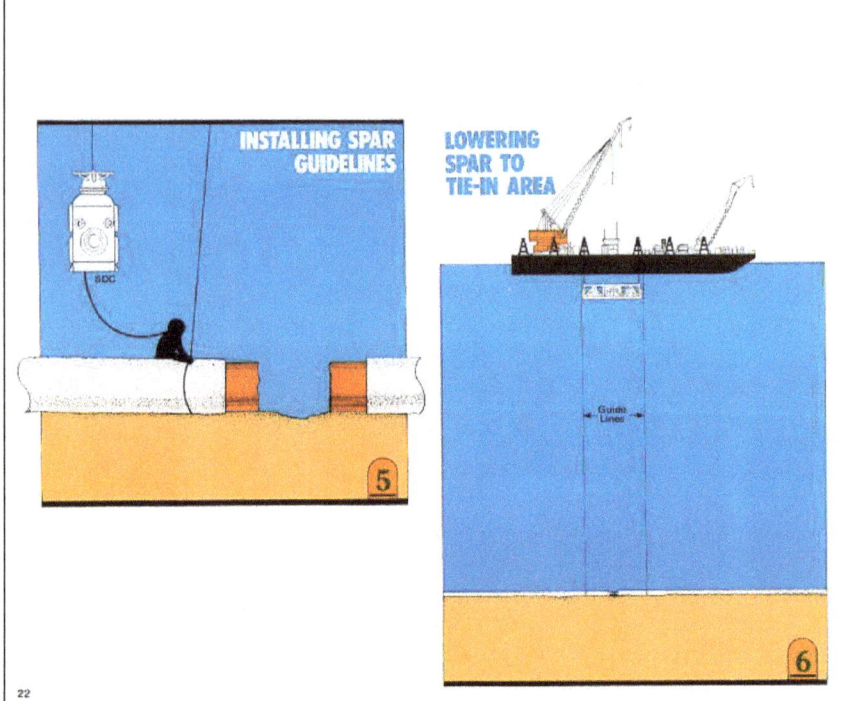

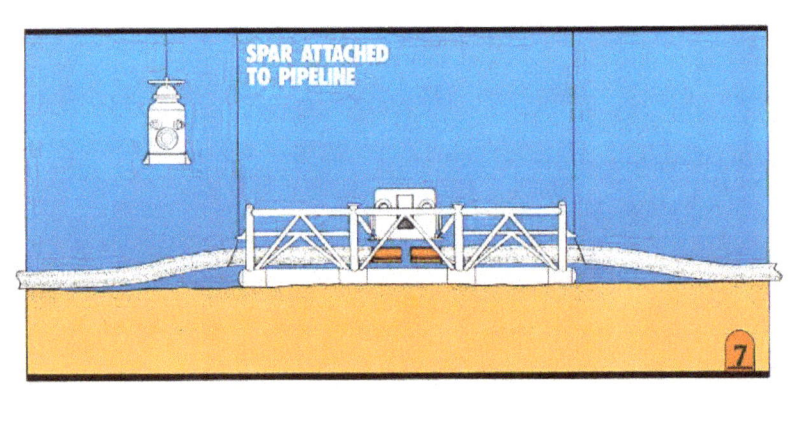

The Pressure Zone by Mike Cooke

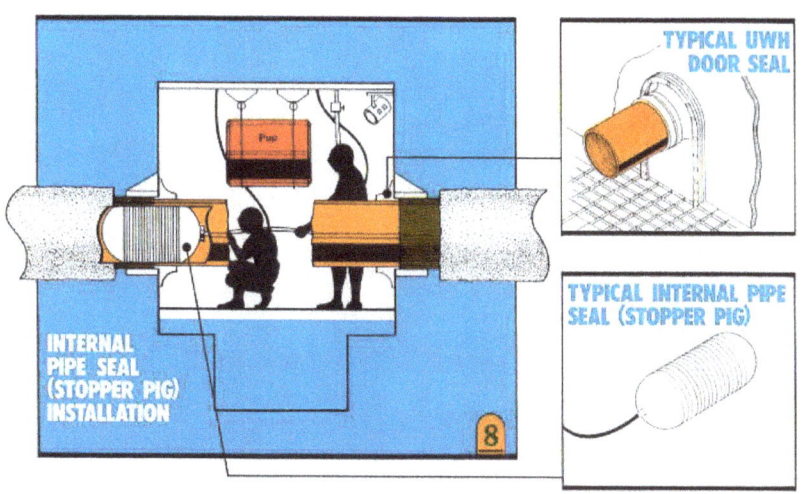

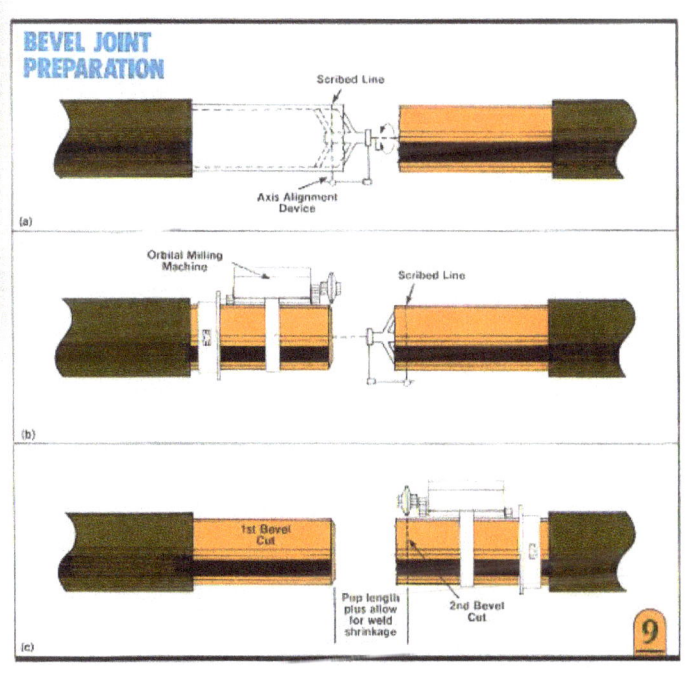

The Pressure Zone by Mike Cooke

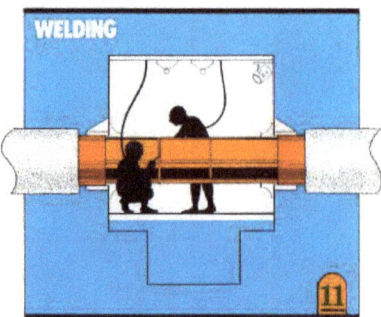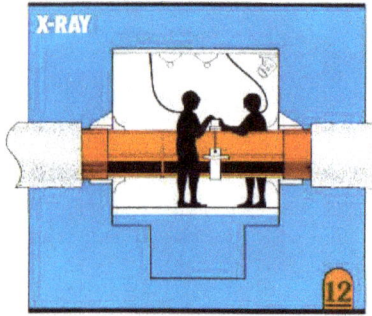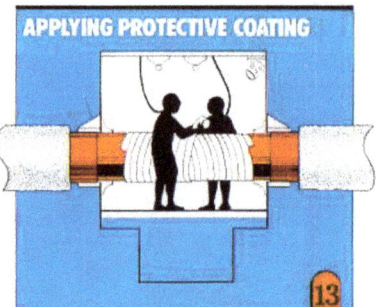

The Pressure Zone by Mike Cooke

Appendix 8 – Taylor Diving Special Edition 'Diver' Magazine 1978

Taylor Diving, Brown & Root Set New Record For Deep Water Hyperbaric Pipeline Welding

A team of diver/welders employed by Taylor Diving & Salvage Co., Inc. has established a new world record by welding two sections of 36-inch diameter pipeline in 1,036-feet (316-meters) of water near the island of Raasay offshore western Scotland.

Final phases of the test program to prove the feasibility of deep water pipeline tie-in and repair by hyperbaric welding were conducted by Taylor in association with Brown & Root, Inc.

Taylor president Ken W. Wallace said the technique and equipment were essentially the same as those used in performing 63 hyperbaric production welds in the North Sea since 1975.

The field test was designed to duplicate conditions encountered in the Norwegian Trench, an extremely deep portion of the North Sea which runs parallel to the Norwegian coast.

Initial stages of the exercise were conducted under the sponsorship of Norsk Hydro, a major Norwegian company, serving as project operator for the Petronord Group and the Statoil/Mobil Group. Statoil represented the Statoil/Mobil Group within the project.

Three years of planning and preparation preceded the field testing, with a majority of the preliminary work conducted in Taylor's hyperbaric research and training complex at Belle Chasse, near New Orleans, La.

SUBMERSIBLE PIPE ALIGNMENT RIG is pictured on the dock at Jobshaven in Rotterdam moments before it was lifted aboard Jackson Marine's cargo vessel "Vagabond" for shipment to Norway. Special mud mats were added to the base of the SPAR to control bottom sinkage. The complete unit weighs 240 tons.

NORSK HYDRO PROJECT ENGINEER Erik Archer, left, listens intently while project coordinator John Harter discusses control console for life support system at Taylor Diving's hyperbaric research and training complex in Belle Chasse, La. near New Orleans.

REVIEWING PROCEDURES FOR THE DIVE aboard Brown & Root's barge 324 are, from left, diving superintendent Rocky Mandible, Norsk Hydro project coordinator Bjorn Weibye, Taylor hyperbaric projects manager Dennis Webb, and Taylor project manager John Harter.

TESTING OF HYDRAULIC CONTROLS for one of the SPAR's four pipe clamps is conducted at Taylor's North Sea headquarters in Rotterdam. In actual operation, these controls are operated by divers before the Underwater Welding Habitat is lowered into position.

By way of background, Norsk Hydro decided in 1974 that hyperbaric welding was the most feasible method for deep water pipeline tie-in and repair compatible with the Norwegian Trench, basing their choice on studies of existing and proposed procedures for accomplishing such objectives.

In May 1975, the first simulated manned hyperbaric welding test at 985-feet (300-meters) was successfully performed in Belle Chasse for Norsk Hydro on behalf of the Petronord Group. This test was followed by further studies of existing equipment and methods.

In March 1976, a second welding test took place at a simulated depth of 1,050-feet (320-meters). This exercise also included concrete removal in a wet chamber.

Simulated dive No. 3 was performed July 1977 to verify the capability of various filler rods and techniques to improve weld quality.

Simulated dive No. 4 was performed in November 1977 to further verify welding procedures to be used at the 320-meter depth and to test the welding power supplies to be used in the field test.

The field operation was staged from Brown & Root's derrick/lay barge 324 which was fitted out at Taylor's North Sea operations base in Rotterdam.

One of Taylor's Submersible Pipe Alignment Rigs (SPAR) and Underwater Welding Habitats (UWH) were specially modified for the test. The need for modification to work at increased depths was verified through nine months of engineering studies and hyperbaric welding tests at Belle Chasse.

These studies included mooring, analysis of bottom soil conditions to project the extent of SPAR sinkage in the bottom, analysis of gas flow rates, electrical power requirements, and a detailed safety study of equipment and procedures.

Mud mats were designed, fabricated and installed on the SPAR. The gas system piping was increased in size, a new environmental control system was designed and installed, and welding power supplies with improved characteristics to maintain welding arc stability were developed.

All the new equipment underwent functional testing during simulated dives at Belle Chasse. The complete systems were also thoroughly tested at dockside in Rotterdam following installation on the barge and prior to departure for the field test location. All phases, i.e. engineering, fabrication, mobilization and functional testing, were managed and documented utilizing a project team consisting of representatives from Taylor, Brown & Root, Norsk Hydro and Statoil.

The first site selected for the test was Skaneviksfjorden, about 50 miles inland from Bergen and Stavanger. Detailed bottom surveys performed both from the surface and by use of a Remote Controlled Vehicle (RCV) carrying a television camera showed the site to be ideal from the standpoint of water

DIVERS AND DIVER/WELDERS assigned to the project receive an advance briefing aboard the barge from Norsk Hydro metallurgist Margun Tystad, standing at right, who discussed welding procedures and other criteria related to the welding operation.

BREATHING GASES used in the project are stowed aboard the barge in clusters. Logistical support for the operation including towing, anchor handling, and transportation of supplies were handled by Jackson Marine Corporation.

The Pressure Zone by Mike Cooke

HYDRAULICALLY ACTIVATED pipe beveling machine is tested by technicians on a sample section of 36-inch pipe from which the protective concrete coating has been removed.

PREPARING TO ENTER saturation chamber are, from top, Freddie Joe Roberts and Brian Pittari as tender Steve Jenkins stands by to assist in dogging down the medical lock.

CLOSE PROXIMITY TO SHORE belies the fact that water beneath Brown & Root's barge 324 is more than 1,000-feet deep. The barge was secured by a nine-point mooring system with two anchors on each wire and positioned by a "Cubic Autotape System."

BECAUSE OF ITS SIZE, the SPAR was transported to the deep water welding test site aboard a supply vessel which is moored here alongside the barge. At right are the umbilicals which carry electric power and breathing gases to the SPAR from the surface. Mud mats here have been marked to accurately measure sinkage.

depth and evenness of the sea floor. The bottom consisted of soft clay covered with silt.

After being towed from Rotterdam, the barge arrived on station in early February and was moored in the fjord using a nine-point moor with two anchors on each wire. Accurate barge positioning was accomplished using the "Cubic Autotape System."

Tugs and the supply vessel "Vagabond" were furnished by Jackson Marine Corporation to provide services for towing, anchor handling, and transporting the SPAR and supplies for the operation.

A pair of 250-foot pipe sections was then lowered to the sea floor, after which divers descended and removed the protective concrete coating from opposing ends of the pipes.

One pipe end was cut off with an oxy-arc torch, leaving a gap between the pipes of approximately 20-inches. The two pipe pieces were then positioned to allow the SPAR to be placed over them.

After pipe positioning was completed, the SPAR was lifted off the supply boat and lowered partially into the water where the weight was transferred to two davit chains and a center wire which lowered it to the bottom.

Four hydraulically actuated pipe clamps on the SPAR were maneuvered to lift the pipe ends off the bottom. The UWH was then lowered over the pipe ends in preparation for sealing and dewatering.

After these complicated tasks were successfully completed, the test was halted due to a diver fatality. Following an investigation, independent technical experts and leading physicians established that it would be safe to proceed with the test. One of several pathologists who are expert in hyperbaric medicine

The Pressure Zone by Mike Cooke   337

UN-MATING of the submersible diving chamber from the Deck Decompression Chamber is controlled by a tender under the watchful eye of diving supervisor Bob Driscoll, right.

SATURATION SYSTEM is pictured in its extended position with the SDC ready for lowering to the ocean floor. The unit is designed to carry three men simultaneously.

indicated that the accident was not depth-related and that findings were similar to at least three other fatalities at shallow depths in the North Sea. Taylor personnel were not involved in these earlier accidents.

Taylor Diving and Brown & Root subsequently decided to move ahead with the program in the open sea offshore Scotland near the island of Raasay to demonstrate the hyperbaric welding phases under actual sea conditions. With the divers still in saturation, the 400-foot barge was towed to the new location and pre-beveled test pipes were set in the UWH.

The welding procedure was then accomplished using tungsten inert gas welding for placing the root and two hot passes. The remainder of the weld was filled using a specially selected stick electrode.

The SPAR and UWH were retrieved and lifted aboard the supply boat, after which the pipe samples were radiographically inspected and sent ashore for detailed laboratory inspection.

Extensive use was made of Taylor's RCV throughout the exercise to assist in placing pipe pieces and the SPAR and to aid divers and supervisors in management of the wet work.

The complete Taylor team of 48 men included diver/welders, tenders, diving superintendents and supervisors, engineers, electronics technicians, hyperbaric specialists, mechanics, and an overall project coordinator. Approximately 140 diver man-hours of time were utilized in-water to accomplish the field test. Twenty-two man-hours of this time were spent in actual welding.

Mr. Wallace said successful completion of the exercise under actual "at sea" conditions in extremely deep water served to verify the effectiveness of hyperbaric welding techniques in support of petroleum developments at depths exceeding 1,000-feet.●

APPROXIMATELY 20-MINUTES were required to lower the SDC to the ocean floor where the diver/welders emerged and went about their duties.

AFTER IT WAS CUT with an oxy/arc torch, this end of one pipe section was brought to the surface for examination by engineers and other personnel.

TECHNICIANS ASSIGNED to operate Taylor's Remote Controlled Vehicle prepare the unit for one of its many excursions during the deep water welding test. Cable on winch in the foreground not only supports the weight of the RCV but carries electric power, television transmission, and control wires.

UNDERWATER WELDING HABITAT is partially visible at the center of the SPAR as it lies alongside the barge being readied for davit attachment.

BREATHING GASES, air conditioning, and other environmental controls are handled from this console housed atop the Deck Decompression Chamber.

SUPPLY VESSEL carrying the SPAR was moved ahead after the derrick aboard the 324 lifted the SPAR and lowered it partially into the water. Cables running from the barge to the pipe sections guided the SPAR into accurate position over the pipes for final alignment by the hydraulic clamps.

Norsk Hydro a.s

Taylor Diving & Salvage Co., Inc.
Route 1, Box 795, Engineers Rd.
Belle Chasse, LOUISIANA 70037
USA

Postadr.: Postboks 2594, Solli
Oslo 2 - Norway
Kontoradr.: Lørenfaret 3, Økern
Telefon: (02) 15 90 10
Telegram: norskhydro
Telex: 16473 hydro n

Deres ref.   Deres brev av   Vår ref.   Dato
                                           Engn-div./   28.3.1978
                                           Offshore
                                           KiB

Att.: Ken Wallace, President

Subject: Deepwater Hyperbaric Welding Test

In connection with the DHWP project, we wish to express our satisfaction with your divers, diver/welders, tenders, rack operators, supervisors, superintendents, and all surface personnel who participated in our 320 m welding test.

They are all hard working people and have served a very important function throughout the program.

We would be most pleased to recommend these individuals for other projects.

Yours faithfully,
For Norsk Hydro a.s

Bjørn Weibye

Taylor Diving & Salvage Company, Inc.
Route 1, Box 795, Engineers Road,
Belle Chasse, Louisiana 70037
Telephone: (504) 394-6000. Telex: 058-4152
Offices in Aberdeen • Bahrain • Peterhead
• Rotterdam • Singapore
A HALLIBURTON Company
An Equal Opportunity Employer

Sources

Books

Barth, B (2000) *Sea Dwellers: The Humor, Drama and Tragedy of the U.S. Navy SEALAB Programs.* Doyle Publishing Company, Inc.

Frank, A (2019) *Anne Frank: The Collected Works.* Bloomsbury Continuum

Gjerde, KO & Ryggvik H (2014) *On the Edge, Under Water Offshore Diving in Norway.* Wigestrand

Harris, GL (2007) *Cast A Deep Shadow.* Legacy Publishing Services, Inc.

Hellwarth, B *(2012) Sealab: America's Forgotten Quest to Live and Work on the Ocean Floor.* Simon & Schuster

Kvendseth, SS (1988) *Giant Discovery: A History of Ekofisk through the first 20 years.* Phillips Company Norway

Pratt, JA, Priest, T, Castaneda, CJ (1997) *Offshore Pioneers: Brown & Root and the History of Offshore Oil and Gas.* Gulf Publishing Company

Siiteri, HA (Ed.) (1993) *Papa Topside: The Sealab Chronicles of Capt. George F. Bond, USN.* Naval Institute Press

Sisman, David (ed) (1982) *The Professional Diver's Handbook.* Submex Limited

Swann, C (2007) *The History of Oilfield Diving: An Industrial Adventure.* Oceanaut Press

Verne, J (1992) *Twenty Thousand Leagues Under The Sea.* Wordsworth Editions Limited

Special Reports, Government Publications and booklets

BRCN 5350 (1953) *RCN Diving Manual.*

NAVSHIPS 0994-001-9010 (1972) *US Navy Diving Manual.* Navy Department Washington DC. Dr Workman's original copy.

Proceedings of the First Annual Scientific Meeting (June 1973) European Undersea Bio-Medical Society Stockholm

OPNAV Report 5750-1 *Harbor Clearance Unit One Log Report for Calendar Year 1971*

Taylor Diving & Salvage Co., Inc (1984) *Diving Manual of Safe Practices & Dive Procedures.* Taylor Diving & Salvage Co., Inc

Newspaper and Magazine Articles

Brochure *Taylor Diving Hyperbaric Welding.*

Magazine *Taylor Diving Diver 1978*

Morrisey, GR *General description of Operation and Purposes of Manned Hyperbaric Research Facility.*

Reporter (circa 1946/47) *Hooded Ghost needs a house to haunt.* Sunday Empire News

The Montreal Gazette (15 October 2006) *First Quebec-born entertainer to sing in Las Vegas*

Vorosmarti Jr, J MD *A Very Short History of Saturation Diving.*

Statutes and Jurisprudence

US Court of Appeals for the Fifth Circuit. *478 F.2d 1171* (5th Cir. 1973) May 15, 1973

341 F.Supp. 628 (1972) *Linwood Hugh CARTER, Plaintiff, v. TAYLOR DIVING & SALVAGE COMPANY and Brown & Root, Inc., Defendants. Civ. A. No. 71-161.* United States District Court, E. D. Louisiana, New Orleans Division. March 29, 1972. ALVIN B. RUBIN, District Judge

World Wide Web

Camp Weredale http://www.batshwcentrehistory.ca/camp_weredale

Canadian Naval Divers Association (FDU (Atlantic) https://navydiver.ca

1959 Frogmen Pickup https://www.britishpathe.com

https://www.nord-stream.com

https://www.wikipedia.org

Miscellaneous

Documentary (2000) *Fire and Ice: The Rocket Richard Riot.* Barna-Alper Productions and Galafilm Productions

Dubuc, P *What is a Matelot*

Pink Floyd (1979) *The Wall.* Harvest & Columbia Records

Toby Keith (2018) *Don't let the old man in.* The Mule, Warner Bros Pictures

Recommended Reading

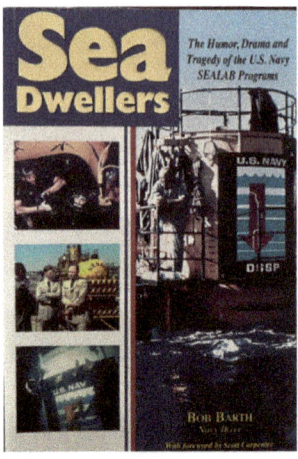

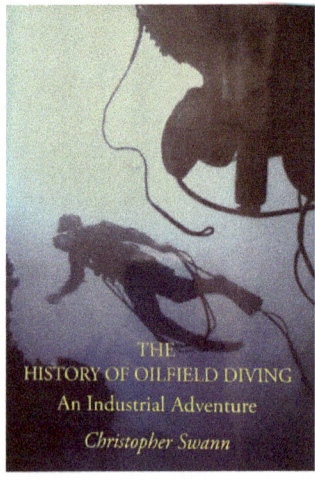
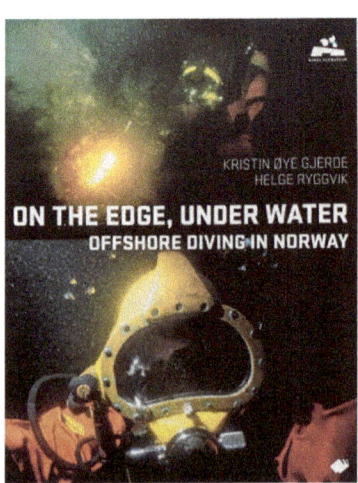

www.ingramcontent.com/pod-product-compliance
Lightning Source LLC
Chambersburg PA
CBHW040902250426
43672CB00034B/2980